Department of the Environment

Training for Tenant Management

London: HMSO

© Crown copyright 1994
Applications for reproduction should be made to HMSO
First published 1994

ISBN 0 11 752889 7

Printed in the United Kingdom for HMSO
Dd297695 1/94 C13 G3397 10170

Acknowledgements

The authors would like to thank all local authorities, training agencies and TMOs who took part in the research. Particular thanks are due to the people involved in the six TMOs who allowed us to use them as case-studies.

The advice and support received from Paul McCafferty, from the Department of the Environment's research division was greatly appreciated.

Finally, we would like to thank Ian Murray from TPAS (Scotland) and Betty Johnstone at the Centre for Housing Research who spent so many hours typing our reports.

Although we have tried to show the views of participants in the research, ultimately the views expressed are those of the research team. These do not necessarily reflect the views of the Department of the Environment.

Contents

Page

ACKNOWLEDGEMENTS iii

1. SUMMARY AND RECOMMENDATIONS 1

BACKGROUND TO THE RESEARCH

2. INTRODUCTION
   - The meaning of participation 13
   - History of participation 14
   - The importance of training 14
   - Aims of the research 16
   - What is training? 16
   - Who is training for? 17
   - How do people learn? 17
   - Evaluation of training 17
   - Research methods 18
   - Other issues 19

3. THE SKILLS, KNOWLEDGE AND ATTITUDES REQUIRED FOR TENANT MANAGEMENT
   - Introduction 21
   - Promotion 21
   - Feasibility 22
   - Development 24
   - On-going tenant management organisations 26
   - Individual office bearers 27
   - Summary 28

4. THE EXTENT OF TENANT PARTICIPATION AND TENANT MANAGEMENT
   - Introduction 31
   - Estate-based initiatives 31
   - Steps towards tenant management 33
   - Established TMOs 35
   - Other tenant participation initiatives 38
   - Tenant training 39
   - Summary 42

TRAINING PROVISION

5. TRAINING FOR TENANT MANAGEMENT
   - Overview 45
   - Training provision at promotion stage 50
   - Provision at feasibility stage 52
   - Provision at development stage 54
   - On-going training 56
   - Views on the role of training 61
   - Summary 62

6. STAFF TRAINING
   - Introduction 63
   - Local authority staff 63
   - Training agency staff 68
   - TMO workers 71
   - Summary 71

THE CASE STUDIES

7. CASE STUDY CONTEXT
   - Background 75
   - Characteristics 75
   - Origins 75
   - Motivation 76
   - Physical and socio-economic factors 78
   - Structure and tasks 81
   - Characteristics of TMO members 83
   - Trainers skills and knowledge 85
   - Summary 87

8. INPUTS AND REACTIONS TO TRAINING
   - Who received training? 89
   - Topics of training 90
   - Methods of training 95
   - Summary 100

9. OUTCOMES OF TRAINING
   - Introduction 101
   - Personal effectiveness 101
   - Group effectiveness 110
   - Organisational outcomes 112
   - Ordinary residents views 114
   - Summary 117

FINANCING

10. COST EFFECTIVENESS AND VALUE FOR MONEY
    National spending 123
    Sources of finance in case studies 124
    Case study cost effectiveness at different stages 125
    Summary 133

11. SELF-FINANCING AND COMMERCIAL DEVELOPMENT
    Self-financing 135
    Commercial development 138
    Summary 141

12. CONCLUSIONS AND RECOMMENDATIONS
    Introduction 143
    Extent of tenant management 143
    Provision of training for tenants 145
    Staff training 146
    Topics of training 147
    Training for ordinary members 150
    Gaps in training 151
    Commercial development 151
    Methods of training 151
    Effectiveness of training on the individual 154
    Organisational effectiveness 155
    Value for money 155
    Self financing 156
    Other issues 157
    Overall 158

APPENDICES

1   RESEARCH METHODS 161

2   TMOs IN ENGLAND 167

3   TRAINING AGENCIES IN ENGLAND 171

4   TMO CASE STUDY HISTORIES 176

5   EXAMPLE OF CASE STUDY TRAINING PROGRAMMES 180

6   KEY TASK ANALYSES OF OFFICE BEARERS 182

7   BIBILIOGRAPHY 187

Chapter 1 Summary and recommendations

SUMMARY OF FINDINGS

1.1 This report sets out the findings of a research project, commissioned by the Department of the Environment on the role of training for tenant management.

Objectives

1.2 The objectives of the research were to:
* Examine the extent of tenant management
* Establish the nature of training
* Identify gaps in provision
* Find out which training is most effective
* Evaluate the impact of other factors
* Assess which training offers best value for money
* Investigate whether training can become self financing
* Identify opportunities for commercial development
* Look at the training needs of staff.

Methods

1.3 The research used a wide variety of methods including postal questionnaires, in-depth interviews, evaluation of training material and attendance at training courses. In addition, we selected six tenant management organisations for more detailed study. A full description of the methods is given in Appendix 1 of the report.

What are tenant management organisations?

1.4 Tenant management organisations (TMOs) are a form of participation in which management of the public sector housing stock is delegated to tenants via a management agreement approved by the Secretary of State. In a tenant management co-operative (TMC), the committee is independent of the council under the terms of its' management agreement. In an Estate Management Board (EMB) the board comprises tenants and local authority representatives who make decisions in partnership. In both cases the houses continue to be owned by the council.

What is the extent of tenant management?

1.5 Chapter 4 describes the extent of tenant management. The research found that 54 local authorities, responding to the postal survey, had 'taken steps' towards the setting up of a tenant management organisation. Although this was only one in five of the respondents, it was a considerable increase on the findings of a survey carried out in 1986/87 by Glasgow University. That survey found that only one in ten councils (21 in all) had considered tenant management.

1.6 In total, the study identified 117 tenant management organisations which were either established or at a late stage of development. Of these:-
- 73 were in London boroughs
- 16 were in the North-West of England
- 13 were in the West Midlands

- 7 were in Yorkshire and Humberside
- 6 were in the North of England.

There was only one TMO in the East Midlands, one at a late stage of development in the South-West and none at an advanced stage in the East or South East of England.

What do TMOS do?

1.7 Typically, established tenant management organisations had responsibility for 11 functions. Almost all had control of a budget and all had responsibility for day-to-day repairs. Other popular functions were dealing with neighbourhood disputes, cyclical maintenance, and letting houses. Fewer TMOS were responsible for enforcing tenancy conditions or dealing with rent arrears.

What training is required for tenant management?

1.8 Chapter 3 outlines the tasks which tenants developing a TMO need to do, from initial consideration of the idea to taking over functions. An analysis of the key tasks then identified the skills and knowledge which were ideally required at each stage of the development process. Chapter 5 examines the provision of training nationally, with reference to the 'ideal' model.

Promotion

1.9 At the promotional stage tenants should gain awareness of tenant participation and the options for control. Ideally, they would form a steering group to identify problems on their estate and assess priorities. The key knowledge needs are:-

- Options available
- Estate issues and priorities
- Tenant participation
- How the council works.

The research found that there were many training events on options for control and tenant participation, but few on estate issues and how the council operates.

1.10 Some steering groups may be formed by tenants who have previously been active in a residents' group or tenants' association. They may already have some knowledge of estate issues, tenant participation and how the council works. However, there were concerns that some TMOs had received information only on one option.

Feasibility

1.11 Groups who decide to proceed further then enter the feasibility stage. This involves 'further in-depth consideration of the options available and the commencement of housing management, equal opportunities and general management skills training'. The key skills and knowledge identified at the feasibility stage were:-

- Overview of housing management
- Responsibilities of TMOs
- Team work skills
- Practical skills.

Almost all TMOs, who had received training, had learnt about housing management policies and the responsibilities of a TMO. However, fewer TMOs had received training on team-work and practical skills, such as public speaking or report-writing.

Development

1.12 In the 'ideal' model, tenants move to the development stage when they have definitely decided to proceed with a particular form of tenant management, although in practice some groups decided this at the outset. Since 1990, tenants have been able to apply for funding themselves at this stage and appoint the trainer of their choice. The key skills and knowledge required are:-

- Management Agreement
- Policies and procedures
- Committee work
- Negotiating skills
- Staff management
- Financial control.

1.13 The Modular Management Agreement was widely used as the basis of training and most TMOs had received training on Committee roles and policies and procedures. However, training on negotiating skills, staff management and financial control was more patchy. Not all TMOs employ staff but the lack of training on negotiating skills and financial control were issues for concern.

What were the gaps in provision of materials?

1.14 The research found that there were particular gaps in the provision of training materials on:

- How the council operates
- Estate problems
- Financial issues
- Negotiating skills
- Practical skills.

Which methods of training are most effective?

1.15 The research in the case-study TMOs assessed tenants' reactions to training and the findings on this are detailed in Chapter 8. All the interviewees stressed that training needed to be locally based and locally relevant, but that meetings with other tenants, at study visits and external events, were important. The most effective training methods were:-

- Small group sessions with role play and games
- Structured practical skills training
- Study visits
- Residential courses
- Local college courses
- Manual and leaflets.

1.16 Although preferred ways of learning varied, few tenants enjoyed lengthy lectures and many found accounts and book-keeping difficult. Learning by observing others had mixed results and learning by doing was sometimes 'learning by bitter experience' which demoralised and dented the confidence of those who tried it.

What impact does training have?

1.17 Chapter 9 assesses whether the training received by the case-study TMOs had been effective. The assessment looked at impact of training on:

* the individual (personal effectiveness)
* the group (group effectiveness)
* the organisation (organisational effectiveness).

Personal effectiveness

1.18   The research concentrated on the Chair, Secretary and Treasurer of the TMOs although additional interviews with one or two other committee members were carried out in each TMO. We found that many of the office-bearers had existing skills from their employment or previous tenants' association experience, but few had the knowledge needed to run a TMO at the outset.

1.19   All the tenants interviewed had gained knowledge from the training and their experience of being involved in the TMO and some had gained skills or had existing skills enhanced. Those with least skills and knowledge appeared to have gained most from training. There was often a gap, however, between the office bearers and other committee members. Knowledge of financial issues and wider tenant participation were thought to be weak areas and training appeared to have little impact on attitudes towards equal opportunities. However, most tenants felt that training was vital and that it had helped them to run the TMO more effectively.

Group effectiveness

1.20   Three of the case-study TMOs appeared to have committees which ran smoothly and effectively. There were signs of conflict in the other three, partly due to the strong personalities involved.

Organisational effectiveness

1.21   The research looked at a number of key indicators of effective performance in the case-study TMOs and obtained the views of ordinary residents. As only three of the case-study TMOs were established it was difficult to draw strong conclusions about performance, but poor condition of the property and the external environment obviously had an impact on performance on repairs and voids and high levels of unemployment had an impact on arrears. Training alone would not overcome these difficulties.

1.22   The views of ordinary residents about services were affected by their surroundings but their views on tenant participation were particularly interesting. In three of the four smaller TMOs residents felt that they were well informed and knew what was going on. However, in the two larger, and one of the smaller TMOs, there were more negative views. It was clearly more difficult to communicate effectively on larger estates and more formal methods, and additional resources, may be required.

What other factors have an impact?

1.23   Training was seen as a very important factor in producing an effective tenant management organisation but other key factors were:

- The existing skills and knowledge of TMO members
- The skills and knowledge of trainers
- The attitude of the local authority
- The physical environment
- High proportions of ethnic minorities.

Is training value for money?

1.24   Chapter 10 analysed the costs of training in the case-study TMOs. This found that total expenditure on training for the promotion, feasibility and development stages varied from £30,405 to £76,100. There were differences in the costs at each stage, depending on the size of the estate and other factors but the analysis suggested that a small TMO, with no problems, should be able to achieve an effective training programme for:

- £2,100 at the promotional stage

- £8,600 at the feasibility stage
- £26,000 at the development stage.

1.25 The analysis of different training methods found that those which were effective were good value for money.

- Study visits cost between £200 and £700 per visit but the cost per tenant was low.
- Residential courses cost around £200 per tenant but were inexpensive on 'cost per hour' basis.
- Role play games and structured practical skills learning were no more expensive than traditional training methods.
- Leaflets and manuals cost little more to produce than forests of handouts.
- Joint sessions involving both local authority and agency staff were more expensive than using a single training agency but provided a broader view.
- Interim committees could be expensive but ensured that tenants were well-prepared.

Is self-financing possible?

1.26 Chapter 3 assesses the needs of established TMOs and Chapter 11 examines how they financed training. Of the 49 established TMOs responding to the postal questionnaire, two-thirds (63%) had received training since becoming established. The research found that the topics required were as wide as those learnt during development. Established TMOs needed:

- Information for new members
- Information for ordinary members
- Training for new Committee members
- Updating knowledge.

1.27 Financing training could be a problem, as Section 16 funding ceases once TMOs are established. Some established TMOs had no training budget and, of those who did, the amounts available ranged from £300 to £3,000. The research found that support by local authorities was varied and, although some TMOs had found effective and inexpensive forms of training, over half the respondents felt that they spent too little on training.

Is there scope for commercial development?

1.28 Chapter 11 also examines the possibilities for development. There was limited scope for true commercial development because there were only a small number of TMOs and training agencies. However, some materials and events could be used by local authority tenant participation officers and tenants' associations. The need for training for tenants involved in Compulsory Competitive Tendering was seen to offer opportunities for the development of materials for a wider market.

1.29 The opportunities for development were:

- Production of materials by groups of training agencies
- Producing materials on word-processor disk
- Videos on skills for tenant management
- Materials produced by TMOs
- Training the trainers courses
- Materials produced by local authorities

- A newsletter for established TMOs
- Use of certificates
- Greater use of local college courses
- More regional networks of TMOs
- Production of a good practice guide.

What are the training needs of staff?

1.30 Chapter 6 describes the findings on staff training. Staff involved in TMOs include:

* Local authority officers
* Training agency staff
* TMO workers.

Local authority officers

1.31 Half of the TMOs responding to the postal questionnaires said that housing department staff were a source of initial information about tenant management. Skills and knowledge about tenant management were found to be needed by:

- Councillors
- Senior staff
- Specialist officers (including solicitors and architects)
- Tenant participation workers
- Generic housing officers
- Front-line staff such as wardens and caretakers.

1.32 It was encouraging that 45% of local authorities said that some staff had received training on tenant participation in the previous 12 months, but this was mainly basic awareness sessions received by senior staff and generic housing officers.

1.33 The key local authority officers involved in support to TMOs were tenant participation officers but most of those interviewed said that they learnt largely 'on the job'. It was clear, from comments made by trainers and tenants, that training for local authority staff was inadequate in many cases. The lack of skills and knowledge about TMOs had, in some cases, led to delays and problems during the development process and recurring problems for established TMOs.

Training agency staff

1.34 Training agency staff needed more in-depth knowledge of TMOs to guide tenants through the development process. Most trainers had backgrounds in community development work or had been active in TMOs or ownership co-operatives. Few had worked in a local authority and their lack of knowledge of council structures was criticised by several local authority officers. Most had learnt 'on the job' and some felt that there was inadequate time available for training.

TMO workers

1.35 Not all TMOs employed staff but the research included interviews with 7 TMO workers. Some had previously worked in local authorities but few had previous experience of TMOs. Training provision varied widely - some TMOs encouraged staff training while others made little provision. In the latter cases workers appeared to be isolated and had little contact with staff in other TMOs.

What did the research conclude?

1.36 The conclusions of the research are set out in Chapter 12. Generally, the research suggests that the Section 16 grant regime has been successful in promoting tenant participation and tenant management. Most training was effective and value for money. However, there were areas which could be improved. The report recommendations for the DoE, local authorities, training agencies and TMOs are listed below.

RECOMMENDATIONS FOR THE DOE

1.37 The DoE should sponsor the production of leaflets on the availability of Section 16 funding and local training agencies and ensure that these are widely distributed to the local authorities and tenants' groups. *(Recommendation 1a)*

1.38 The DoE should seek to monitor the prevalence of tenant participation and tenant management in local authority stock to assess the extent to which tenant involvement increases. *(Recommendation 1b)*

1.39 The DoE should consider the merits of supporting the establishment of additional local and regional training agencies in the North and South-West of England. *(Recommendation 2b)*

1.40 The DoE should ensure that financial arrangements for payment of agencies include provision for staff training. *(Recommendation 6a)*

1.41 Section 16 grants and local authority support for TMOs should take account of the need for provision of materials in ethnic minority languages, use of interpreters and creche provision. *(Recommendation 12b)*

1.42 The DoE should encourage consortia of training agencies and TMOs to produce training packs on estate problems, financial issues, specific housing management functions, practical skills and negotiating skills. *(Recommendation 13a)*

1.43 These training packs should be made available, at low-cost, to local authorities, training agencies and TMOs. Provision of training material on word-processor disk should also be considered. *(Recommendation 13b)*

1.44 The DoE should consider supporting the production of videos on a range of skills needed for tenant management such as negotiation and effective meetings. *(Recommendation 13c)*

1.45 The DoE should ensure that financial arrangements for training agencies include payment for adequate preparation time. *(Recommendation 13h)*

1.46 The DoE should consider the provision of pump-priming support to establish regional networks for TMOs to enable them to meet, exchange views and share training. (Recommendation 19c)

1.47 Established TMOs should be encouraged to raise additional funds by charging for study visits from developing groups and producing materials on their activities. *(Recommendation 19d)*

1.48 The DoE should consider providing support for a regular newsletter for established TMOs which would include details of forthcoming training events. *(Recommendation 19e)*

1.49 The DoE should investigate systems, such as accreditation, which would ensure that trainers have appropriate skills and knowledge. *(Recommendation 20a)*

1.50 The DoE should examine its system of monitoring Section 16 grants with the aim of ensuring that key topics have been covered at each stage of development. *(Recommendation 20b)*

1.51 The DoE should investigate how systems monitoring the quality of training can be implemented. *(Recommendation 20c)*

1.52 The DoE should consider developing a system of quality assurance to monitor the effectiveness of training. *(Recommendation 20d)*

1.53 The DoE should initiate the production of a *Good Practice Guide* which would give guidance on:

- the selection of trainers and agencies
- the key skills and knowledge required to run a TMO
- assessment of training needs
- effective methods of training
- evaluation of training
- value for money in training

The Guide should be made available to local authorities, trainers and tenants considering the development of a TMO. *(Recommendation 21)*

RECOMMENDATIONS FOR LOCAL AUTHORITIES

1.54 Local authorities should provide training for tenants and support tenant attendance at external events. *(Recommendation 2a)*

1.55 Local authority staff should play a more active role in training for tenant management organisations. *(Recommendation 3a)*

1.56 Local authorities and training agencies should work in partnership to support and train TMOs. *(Recommendation 3b)*

1.57 Local authorities should encourage tenants involved in TMOs to attend 'Training for Trainers' courses, to enable them to train tenants in other TMOs and their own new members. *(Recommendation 4a)*

1.58 Local authorities should extend the use of tenants involved in TMOs as trainers. *(Recommendation 4b)*

1.59 Local authorities should ensure that all staff working on housing functions have received training on the implications and benefits of tenant participation. *(Recommendation 5a)*

1.60 The promotional/feasibility stage for TMOs should include training for local authority staff to develop their understanding of tenant management and awareness of the impact of their activities on TMOs. *(Recommendation 5b)*

1.61 Local authorities should ensure that a range of key local authority staff have training at the development stage for TMOs on the management agreement and its implications for the council and the TMO. *(Recommendation 5c)*

1.62 Local authorities should ensure that management allowances for TMOs include adequate financial provision for training TMO staff. *(Recommendation 7b)*

1.63 Local authorities should offer places to TMO workers on appropriate internal staff training courses. *(Recommendation 7c)*

1.64 Local authorities should provide training and information for other tenants, as well as the steering group. *(Recommendation 12a)*

1.65 Local authorities should provide information and training material on 'How the Council Operates'. *(Recommendation 13e)*

1.66 Local authority associations and the Housing Sector Consortium should explore whether National Vocational Qualifications (NVQs) could be extended to tenant managers. *(Recommendation 16b)*

1.67 Local authorities should ensure that TMO management allowances include adequate resources to encourage and support wider participation. *(Recommendation 17b)*

1.68 Local authorities should assess the cost-effectiveness of different training methods and programmes. *(Recommendation 18a)*

1.69 Local authorities should consider whether local colleges can assist in meeting training needs in a cost-effective manner. *(Recommendation 18b)*

1.70 Local authorities should ensure that arrangements for earmarked and adequate training budgets are included in the management agreement and are paid in addition to management and maintenance allowances. *(Recommendation 19a)*

1.71 Local authorities should ensure that they have adequate arrangements to support and monitor TMOs in their stock. *(Recommendation 19b)*

RECOMMENDATIONS FOR TRAINING AGENCIES

1.72 Local authorities and training agencies should work in partnership to support and train TMOs. *(Recommendation 3b)*

1.73 Training agencies should encourage tenants involved in TMOs to attend 'Training for Trainers' courses, to enable them to train tenants in other TMOs and their own new members. *(Recommendation 4a)*

1.74 Training agencies should extend the use of tenants involved in TMOs as trainers. *(Recommendation 4b)*

1.75 Training agencies should ensure that trainers have adequate time for learning new skills and knowledge and for updating. The Audit Commission guide of 10 days training per member of staff per year is recommended. *(Recommendation 6b)*

1.76 Training agencies should provide training and information for other tenants, as well as the steering group. *(Recommendation 12a)*

1.77 Training agencies should ensure that they have quality training materials on all key areas of skills and knowledge as set out in Recommendations 8, 9, 10 and 11. *(Recommendation 13f)*

1.78 Training agencies should invest in desk-top publishing equipment and ensure that trainers have adequate preparation time to produce customised material of quality. *(Recommendation 13a)*

1.79 Trainers should use a wide variety of training methods. *(Recommendation 14a)*

1.80 Training agencies should implement quality control systems to ensure that trainers have skills and knowledge in a wide range of training methods. *(Recommendation 14b)*

1.81 Trainers should carry out a training needs analysis at the beginning of the feasibility and development stages and base training programmes on this. *(Recommendation 15)*

1.82 Training agencies should give certificates to tenants who achieve the key skills and knowledge at each stage of the development process. *(Recommendation 16a)*

1.83 Training agencies should assess the cost-effectiveness of different training methods and programmes. *(Recommendation 18a)*

1.84 Training agencies should consider whether local colleges can assist in meeting training needs in a cost-effective manner. *(Recommendation 18b)*

RECOMMENDATIONS FOR TMOS

1.85 Potential TMOs should extend the use of tenants involved in TMOs as trainers. *(Recommendation 4b)*

1.86 TMOs should ensure that TMO workers are encouraged to plan their training needs and should provide adequate resources so that these needs can be met. *(Recommendation 7a)*

1.87 Potential TMOs should provide training and information for other tenants, as well as the steering group. *(Recommendation 12a)*

1.88 TMOs should be encouraged to produce materials on their development experiences and activities, perhaps in the form of illustrated booklets, which can then be used to generate income. *(Recommendation 13d)*

1.89 Potential TMOs should carry out a training needs analysis at the beginning of the feasibility and development stages and base training programmes on this. *(Recommendation 15)*

1.90 All TMOs should have policies and procedures for wider participation. *(Recommendation 17a)*

1.91 TMOs should assess the cost-effectiveness of different training methods and programmes. *(Recommendation 18a)*

1.92 TMOs should consider whether local colleges can assist in meeting training needs in a cost-effective manner. *(Recommendation 18b)*

Background to the Research

Chapter 2 Introduction

2.1 This introduction sets out the background to the research and the research aims. It then briefly describes what training is, who it is for, how people learn and how training may be evaluated. Finally, the chapter outlines the research methods used for this project.

THE MEANING OF PARTICIPATION

2.2 Tenant participation has been an accepted component of good practice in public sector housing management for over a decade. What is meant by tenant participation can, however, vary. The most general definitions emphasise the sharing of information and the influencing of decisions:

> 'Participation is a two-way process involving sharing of information and ideas, where tenants are able to influence decisions and take part in what is happening.'
>
> Institute of Housing and TPAS, 1989

There are three different aspects or dimensions of participation within which a variety of more specific meanings are possible in practice. These are:

* the structure or methods of participation
* processes in which participation takes place
* the outcomes or achievements from participation.

(IoH/TPAS, 1989)

Structures and methods include newsletters, public meetings and regular meetings between tenant and landlord representatives, including tenant representation on housing committee or estate committees. Processes or forms of participation include:

* providing information to tenants
* consulting tenants on their views
* dialogue, where tenants may influence decisions
* joint-management, sharing decision-making
* control, decision making by tenants.

Outcomes may include tenant satisfaction and better housing management. This research concentrated on forms of participation in which decision-making is devolved to tenant management organisations such as estate management boards (EMBs) and tenant management co-operatives (TMCs). The Department of the Environment definition of these is:

> 'The management by tenants of their own estates, either in partnership with the authority (via estate management boards with tenant voting majorities) or autonomously via a tenant management co-operative. The ownership of the stock remains with the Council.'
>
> (DoE, 1992)

HISTORY OF PARTICIPATION

2.3 Tenants' rights to be consulted on matters which affect them were introduced in the Housing Act 1980 in England, while the Tenant Participation Advisory Service (TPAS) was set up in Scotland. Tenant management organisations (TMOs) were pioneered in the 1970s after powers were given to local authorities to devolve management responsibilities to co-operatives under the Housing Rents and Subsidies Act 1975. The first tenant management co-ops (TMCs) in public sector stock were set up in Glasgow by Glasgow District Council and in London by the Greater London Council and the London Borough of Islington. Joint management of estates was also developed in the 1970s and the idea of partnerships between the council and local tenants was further expanded by the Priority Estates Project to form the model for Estate Management Boards (EMBs). The first EMB was approved in 1990.

THE IMPORTANCE OF TRAINING

2.4 The importance of training for tenant management has emerged gradually over the last decade. Research conducted in 1981 suggested that more training and information was needed if tenant management was to grow (Downey, Matthews and Mason, 1981). The Housing and Planning Act 1986 provided a framework for the promotion of tenant participation and tenant management in England through Section 16 grants. However, there were concerns that arrangements for promoting and supporting co-operatives were inadequate and research carried out in the late 1980s found that few co-op officers had received any formal training (McCafferty and Riley, 1989).

2.5 The Review of Housing Co-operatives was set up in 1988 to examine funding grant arrangements for co-operatives and the Review report *Tenants in the Lead* (DoE, 1989), argued that tenant-controlled organisations would only succeed if tenants were committed and if they had access to appropriate support and training. The report recommended that:

> 'The DoE should continue to develop and co-ordinate the promotion of co-ops and alternatives at both national and local levels by means including support under the Section 16 grant regime; and should consider the case for expanding support for this work in response to increasing demand.'
>
> (Recommendation 5, DoE 1989, p.16)

The Review team argued that it was important that potential tenant management organisations were able to apply for funding themselves and had the ability to shop around for the services needed.

> 'Primary organisations with local authority backing should apply direct to DoE for the support described above. If approved, the support should go direct to the primary organisation to enable it to buy these services from the agent of its choice. Continuing support during the start-up period should be subject to satisfactory progress.'
>
> (Recommendation 7, DoE 1989, p.18)

On-going training was also considered essential, but the Review committee felt that tenant management organisations should make provision for this, with the support of the local authority.

> 'Co-ops and estate management boards should make provision for on-going training from within their budgets ... local authorities are well placed to encourage and monitor co-ops' and management boards' on-going training; and should take responsibility for doing so, as part of the undertakings linked to their management agreement.'
>
> (DoE, 1989, p.17)

The report also recognised that training and support required 'an adequate supply of skilled personnel' and commented on gaps in the network of support agencies. It recommended courses to train the trainers.

> 'During its review of support for training in housing management, the DoE should discuss with appropriate institutions and agencies the provision of new or expanded training courses to create a sufficient pool of people skilled in:
>
> (i) feasibility assessment and development work for co-ops and alternatives;
>
> (ii) training tenants for participation in, and control of, co-ops and alternatives;
>
> (iii) training up of housing workers for co-ops and alternatives.
>
> The DoE should also consider how these courses might be financed.'
>
> (Recommendation 3, DoE 1989, p.13)

2.6 The Review suggested that there were four distinct stages of development for a tenant management organisation. These stages are:

General promotion - the initial awareness of tenant participation and control options.

Feasibility - further in-depth consideration of the options available and the commencement of housing management, equal opportunities and general management skills training, leading to the final choice of option.

Development - concentrates on training for managing a TMO and involves particular emphasis on housing management training and the production of the management agreement.

On-going training - once the organisation has taken over responsibilities there will be on-going training needs for new members and updating skills and knowledge for existing members.

2.7 The DoE accepted the recommendations of the Review report and increased Section 16 grants from £0.9 million in 1988/89 to £4.9 million in 1991/92 (DoE 1992). Grants at the promotion and feasibility stages continued to be paid to training agencies but grants for the development stage were made payable direct to the potential TMO from 1990. The DoE also supported the establishment of an Institute of Housing National Certificate in Tenant Participation to provide training for potential trainers and co-op workers. This was available at 4 educational institutions in England in 1992. The aim of the Section 16 tenant participation grant programme is:

> 'to increase the effectiveness of housing management and to improve the quality of life on public sector estates through local tenant-led management initiatives'

and its operational objective is:

> 'to increase tenant participation in public sector housing management by promoting tenant participation schemes and tenant management organisations.'
>
> DoE, 1992

AIMS OF THE RESEARCH

2.8 The research, on which this report is based, reviewed training received by all local authority sector tenant management co-ops and estate management boards in England but concentrated on more recently established tenant management organisations and those in the late stages of development. The overall aim of the research was to assess the provision of tenant management training, its role, value-for-money and effectiveness. The specific objectives were:

(a) to establish the nature and extent of both formal and informal training for public sector TMOs and identify any gaps which might exist in current provision;

(b) to assess which types of training provide opportunities for commercial promotion and at what stage future training might become self-financing;

(c) to identify how much, and which types of training offer the best value-for-money at each stage in the promotion and development of a public sector tenant management organisation;

(d) to identify how much, and which types of training, are most effective in giving tenants the skills they require at each stage in the promotion and development of public sector tenant management organisations; and

(e) to evaluate the impact of training, amongst other factors, in the promotion and development of public sector tenant management organisations.

WHAT IS TRAINING?

2.9 Before we can begin to discuss methods of evaluation, we must first discuss what training is. The dictionary definitions of training, development and education are given below:

Train: to instruct and discipline in some particular art, profession, occupation or practice, to make proficient by such instruction or practice

Develop: to unfold more fully, bring out all that is potentially contained in

Educate: to bring up so as to form habits, manners, intellectual and physical attributes

(Oxford English Dictionary, 1978)

2.10 Training is seen as a shorter-term process through which an individual masters particular skills and knowledge. Development is intended to assist individual growth to achieve full potential and education. It is not only about skills and knowledge, but is also about character and achievements. We set out to assess the training which tenants receive for tenant management primarily in terms of mastering particular skills and knowledge. However, we also considered whether it develops and educates individuals.

2.11 Training can be formal - given through off-the-job training sessions, or informal - given on-the-job through guidance and instruction. In training for tenant management organisations, tenants are being trained to manage a future organisation. However, there is scope for on-the-job training through working in committees, holding open days and in policy development, where participants can practise and develop skills in team-working, public speaking and mastering concepts. The research aimed to assess both formal and informal training processes. This is not always straightforward, as informal learning through on-the-job training may not be recognised as training by the individuals concerned.

WHO IS TRAINING FOR?

2.12   Within most organisations, individuals have defined roles and tasks, often specified in written job descriptions. Our main interest concerned training for committee or board members of tenant management organisations and, in particular, the office bearers such as the Chairperson, Secretary and Treasurer who have a greater responsibility in ensuring that the organisation meets its goals. However, tenant management organisations require the commitment and participation of a wider group of members who also require information and training. In addition, TMOs must work within a local authority framework and local authority officers and councillors may need training on how to work with them. Finally, the trainers may themselves have training needs to develop their skills and further their knowledge. While concentrating on key committee members, we considered the training needs of this wider group of participants. Harrison (1988) identified key task analysis as a tool for identifying the essential skills, knowledge and attitudes required for a particular post. We drew up a task analysis for each of the stages of development, for key committee members, for participation workers and for trainers. These can be found in Chapters 3 and 6 and Appendix 6 and were used to assess whether training needs were met.

HOW DO PEOPLE LEARN?

2.13   In any consideration of the effectiveness of training, the issue of how people learn needs to be addressed, since inappropriate methods may lead to ineffective results. There are a range of theories addressing this issue, and an extensive literature, which draws on the work of social psychologists and behaviourists. The work of Vroom (1964) has been influential in suggesting that motivation to learn is an important factor and that individuals will be motivated to expend effort if they perceive a useful outcome. The motivations of participants are explored further in Chapter 7.

2.14   Personality theories have also had an influence on views about effective learning. Honey and Mumford (1986) argued that people have different learning styles or preferred ways of learning and they suggested that some people may prefer to learn by active or participative methods while others have a preference for reading or listening. The learning styles of participants are explored in Chapter 8.

2.15   Other writers have suggested that different methods are more suited to different competencies (Gagné, 1977; Harrison, 1988; Smith, 1991). For example, practical skills such as word processing may be best taught by 'hands on' learning, while training aimed at changing attitudes may be most successful in informal small group discussions. Chapter 8 discusses tenants' reactions to different training methods. The research, therefore, aimed to explore motivation and learning styles and assess whether training methods were effective in meeting tenants' needs.

EVALUATION OF TRAINING

2.16   Evaluation of training is a complex activity and there are a wide range of evaluation techniques; most use an evaluation framework involving several stages or levels of evaluation. The most well-known evaluation framework is that developed by Kirkpatrick (1977). He proposed four stages of evaluation. These are:

   Reaction: were the respondents pleased with the programme?
   Learning: what did they learn on the programme?
   Behaviour: did their behaviour change as a result of training?
   Results: did the behaviour have a positive effect on the organisation?

This model was considered too simple for the objectives of our study as it does not examine the nature of training, the types of training or the impact of training in relation to other factors.

2.17 A more holistic approach to evaluation was proposed by Warr, Bird and Rackham (1970). They suggest the need to evaluate the Context of training, the Inputs to training, the Reactions to training and the Outcomes of training. This model of evaluation, known as CIRO, was developed for use in industry and, therefore, required some adaption for use with tenant management organisations. In addition, like most evaluation models, it was developed for use in longitudinal studies, where performance can be measured prior to training and compared with outcomes. We had to adapt evaluation techniques for use in a retrospective study to make an assessment of individual skills, knowledge and attitudes prior to training. The CIRO model is outlined below.

The CIRO Model
Context Evaluation

This considers the context of training and factors which may influence effectiveness. These include the physical and social environment, the motivations and skills of participants, the structure of the organisation and the tasks which are performed.

Input Evaluation

The inputs to training include time, topics, media and training methods.

Reaction Evaluation

This considers the participants' reactions to training, including whether they enjoyed it, what they felt they learnt, whether it kept their attention and whether they thought it was relevant.

Outcome Evaluation

This involves obtaining and using information about the outcomes of training. Three levels of outcome can be identified and assessed. Immediate outcome - have skills, knowledge and attitudes been acquired? Intermediate - has behaviour changed? Ultimate - has organisational performance improved?

(Warr, Bird and Rackham, 1970)

RESEARCH METHODS

2.18 A full outline of the research methods is given in Appendix 1 and is summarised below.

(a) Postal surveys

To establish a national picture of training provision for tenant management organisations, a postal questionnaire was sent to all local authorities in England, all local authority tenant management co-operatives and estate management boards including some at development stage, and a wide range of organisations who provided training for tenants. In total, 257 local authorities (77% response rate), 34 training agencies (76% response rate) and 66 tenant management organisations (60% response rate) replied to the postal survey.

(b) Review of training material

All local authorities and training agencies responding to the postal survey were asked to provide copies of any training programmes or materials they had produced. In addition, material was collected during in-depth interview visits. In total, the review examined 251 examples of material from 66 organisations.

(c) Attendance at training events

In order to gain a flavour of the actual training, 10 training events held by different agencies were attended and evaluated.

(d) In-depth interviews	Qualitative views on training for tenant management were sought via in-depth interviews. Ninety-nine people were interviewed during the course of the research. This total comprised 11 local authority officers, 24 staff in training agencies, 7 co-op workers and 57 tenants involved in TMOs.
(e) Group discussions	To assist in establishing the skills and knowledge required by trainers, group discussions involving 30 trainers were held.
(f) Case studies	To provide a more detailed examination of the role of training and its impact, seen in the context of other factors, and to discover which types of training were most effective, the research identified six case-study tenant management organisations and evaluated them following the CIRO model. Our findings from the case studies are in Chapters 7 to 9.
(g) Cost-effectiveness analysis	In addition to this detailed evaluation of the nature and effectiveness of training, we also carried out a cost-effectiveness analysis. We evaluated the content of each training event in as much detail as possible and costed the inputs including trainers' time, accommodation cost, cost of producing materials and the opportunity cost to residents. Costs were then compared to reactions and outcomes. From this, it was possible to draw some conclusions about value-for-money and the most effective means of achieving training objectives at each stage of development. This discussion can be found in Chapter 10.
OTHER ISSUES	2.19 The objectives outlined by the Department also asked that the research explore opportunities for commercial development and whether future training might become self-financing. The definition of self-financing refers to the ability of tenant management organisations to afford their own training. We explored a range of funding sources, with participants in the research, including government, local authorities and the income of established tenant management organisations. We also discussed commercial development opportunities with trainers, local authorities and tenants to assess whether further materials or training would assist. The findings of this part of the research are in Chapter 11.

Chapter 3

The skills, knowledge and attitudes required for tenant management

INTRODUCTION

3.1   In order to answer the research questions about how much and which types of training are most effective and offer the best value for money, it was necessary to begin by establishing what tenants developing a tenant management organisation through to full maturity ideally need to know and do at each stage of the process. To establish this we used literature on TMOs and sought the views of local authority officers, training officers and tenants via the postal questionnaires and in-depth interviews. Respondents were asked to give their views on the skills and knowledge which were ideally required by all tenants involved in tenant management from initial information to the needs of established TMOs. Tenant interviewees and co-op workers were also asked what additional skills and knowledge key participants, such as office-bearers on TMO committees or boards, were ideally required to have at each stage of development. The research methods are detailed in Appendix 1.

3.2   Using these sources of information, we then carried out a key task analysis for each of the four stages of the development process (defined in Chapter 2). This identified the tasks which members of groups, either collectively or individually, need to do and the skills, knowledge and attitudes required to perform them. A separate key task analysis was also carried out for each of the office-bearers posts. The key task analyses were then used in the research as a framework to evaluate whether committee members and office-bearers had received appropriate training. It should be stressed, however, that these analyses were 'ideal' models. In practice, few of the case-study TMOs followed the four stages of the development process precisely and there was variability in office-bearers' duties and responsibilities. This chapter, therefore, also identifies the most important skills and knowledge required by all members of the group and by office-bearers.

PROMOTION

3.3   The Department of the Environment defined promotion as the 'initial awareness of tenant participation and control options available to tenants.' There was a general consensus from interviewees that this initial awareness was largely about giving basic information to tenants. Trainers also stressed the importance of information-gathering about the problems perceived on estates and about the reasons why there was interest in a TMO.

> 'It's more a general information exchange... we run through with tenants what their major issues are, what improvements they would like to see on the estate... we deal with issues relevant to them first and suggest tenant management if it seems to be an appropriate solution.'
>
> Trainer - Regional Agency

The literature also suggested that understanding the social, economic and political structures and processes in the area were an important pre-requisite to determining priorities and identifying solutions. For example, a major OECD study on local community initiatives said:

> 'Learning the locality is fundamental to an assessment of local resources, physical, economic and human, as well as pinpointing accurately both the major loci of problems and possible solutions'
>
> CERI (1983) pp 35.

3.4 Some trainers said that the skills, knowledge and attitudes required at this stage depended on the group of tenants. Members who had been part of a long established tenants' association might already have some knowledge and would be seeking more detail. In other instances, the initiative may come from the landlord, where there were no existing tenants' groups. Information in this instance would need to be very basic. In some cases, the people on the steering group to develop the TMO may have little experience of committees and few skills. In this situation trainers might therefore wish to begin to develop some team-work and assertiveness skills with a nucleus of interested people.

3.5 Since the stress was laid on identifying problems, as they were perceived by tenants on estates, the range of information given could be very wide. The most commonly mentioned topics in the postal questionnaire were committee skills, raising awareness of tenant participation and how the local authority works, but a wide range of other topics were covered in some instances. Figure 3.1 shows the tasks and the key knowledge, skills and attitudes required at the promotional stage.

Figure 3.1 **Key knowledge, skills and attitude required at the promotion stage**

Task	Knowledge	Skills	Attitudes
* Promote participation * Basic understanding of options * Identifying problems on estate * Deciding priorities * Set up a steering group	* Intro. to tenant participation * Tenants' Associations * What a TMC is * What an EMB is * Other options available * LA Finance * How the council operates * Role of steering group	* Teamwork * Making decisions * Assertiveness	* Interest in participation * Desire to increase knowledge

FEASIBILITY

3.6 The feasibility stage is defined, in Section 16, as 'further in-depth consideration of the options available, and the commencement of housing management, equal opportunities and general management skills training leading to the final choice of option'. The most commonly mentioned topics in the postal questionnaire were committee skills, raising awareness of tenant participation and options for tenant management but a wide variety of other skills and knowledge were mentioned. The interviewees tended to divide into two distinct groups. There were those who stressed the importance of skills and attitudes. They aimed to build an effective group which was open, fair and accountable, which understood the need for wide participation and had an awareness of roles and responsibilities. In some cases, trainers had found tenants who lacked basic literacy and numeracy skills and concentrated on improving these. A few respondents suggested that training should build explicitly on the existing skills and knowledge of participants.

> 'The most important point is to increase "people" skills and confidence. The rest of the training is useless unless they have this first.'
>
> Trainer - Secondary Co-op

> 'If somebody's got some secretarial experience I would try... to get them to do more word-processor training.'
>
> Trainer - Secondary Co-op

However, there was also a diametrically opposite view from some trainers who emphasised housing management knowledge, almost to the exclusion of all else.

> 'I teach along the school-room line - facts, practical exercises... I don't hold with the 'community' fostering idea.'
>
> Trainer - Training Agency

3.7 It may be that those who emphasised knowledge were tenants who already had a range of skills and trainers who had worked mainly with more experienced groups, while those who emphasised skills at the feasibility stage had worked with groups with fewer previous abilities. In our view, a range of skills, knowledge and attitudes are ideally required at the feasibility stage. The extent to which these are taught will depend on the prior skills, knowledge and attitudes of the individuals in the group. Not all participants will need to develop skills and knowledge to the same level, as the secretary would handle letters and the treasurer would deal with the books. However, since committee membership may change, it is useful if a number of individuals have, or develop, specific skills and knowledge so that changes in group personnel do not cause major problems.

3.8 Some trainers noted that changes in the Section 16 funding regime meant that groups have to acquire more skills and knowledge than they previously needed at this stage. During the promotion and feasibility stages the finance for training and support was paid direct to the training organisation. However, following the recommendation in the co-op review report *Tenants in the Lead* (DoE, 1989), groups could apply for funding for the development stage themselves. Trainers said that this change meant that groups needed to acquire knowledge of financial control, budgeting, how to complete forms and their role as an employer. Skills needed for those roles are interviewing, book-keeping and staff management. Tenants also need information on the skills and knowledge needed for development, the ability to assess their own training needs and what to expect from a development agency.

> 'They have to fill regular monitoring forms in, have to send a report in... have to correspond with the housing department, have to meet them round the table... This imposed requirements not only to understand the language but to be able to establish credibility.'
>
> Independent Trainer

3.9 A key task analysis of the activities which may be undertaken at the feasibility stage, and the knowledge, skills and attitudes required to carry these out, is shown in Figure 3.2. Trainers stressed that the extent to which tasks will be carried out depends on the group and that there is an overlap with tasks at development stage. Some groups moreover, may decide, having explored options in greater depth and learnt more about the council and tenant participation, that they do not want to manage their own estate. The basic knowledge and skills programme outlined in the task analysis would provide any tenants' group with a foundation on which to build an effective tenants' association, or take part in other forms of participation, such as estate sub-committees, or tenants' federations, or to deal with Compulsory Competitive Tendering (CCT).

Figure 3.2 **Knowledge, skills and attitudes required at feasibility stage**

Task	Knowledge	Skills	Attitudes
* Develop understanding of options * Identify problems for participation * Attend meetings * Develop the group * Agree a constitution * Decide office bearers * Basic understanding of LA finance * Understand what housing management involves * Appreciate responsibilities of a TMO * Write letters * Hold a public meeting * Send out a newsletter * Deal with issues on the estate * Keep financial control * Apply for funding * Appoint a worker/trainer * Agree future programme of training	* What is a co-op? * What is an EMB? * What tenant participation involves * Other options available * How to work as a team * Constitutions/rules * Roles of office bearers * Basic LA finance * Overview of housing management functions * Holding meetings * Producing newletters * Campaigning * Dogs * Crime * Neighbour disputes * Repairs * Financial control * Role of development agency * How to apply for grants * Role of employer * Recruitment * Skills and knowledge for development	* Chairing skills * Team-working * Letter-writing * Book-keeping * Form-filling * Interviewing * Staff management * Public speaking * Assertiveness * Decision-making * Self-awareness	* Commitment to Tenant Participation * Non-discriminatory * Awareness of accountability * Positive view of equal opportunities * Desire to increase skills and knowledge

DEVELOPMENT

3.10 In the 'model' situation the development stage may be entered when tenants have decided that they wish to pursue a particular form of tenant management. Once that decision has been made, and funding has been received, tenants will develop and negotiate a management agreement with the local authority and prepare to take over responsibility. Section 27A of the Housing Act 1985 (as amended) makes it a duty for councils to consult tenants, and often potential tenant management organisations will assist the council to hold the necessary ballot. The committee need to decide which functions and responsibilities they are going to manage and develop policies and procedures. This means that they need a good grasp of housing management legislation and issues. The group needs to decide whether they will employ staff and if so, how many, and to decide upon their job descriptions. They should be keeping in touch with the wider group of tenants, holding public meetings and sending newsletters. A number of trainers stressed the need to recruit members and hold an AGM. If they have not already done so, they will need to register with the Registrar of Friendly Societies as an Industrial and Provident Society or with the Registrar of Companies as a company limited by guarantee.

3.11 Once the formal agreement to delegate management has been agreed with the local authority, under current arrangements, it needs to be approved by the Secretary of State. When the management agreement is approved, the group and the council need to liaise to set up office systems and transfer files. The management and maintenance allowances also need to be negotiated and a start date agreed. The tenant management organisation may then appoint staff and take over its responsibilities.

3.12 While not everything appears to happen quite as planned in the real world, all groups must complete the core tasks of negotiating a management agreement and taking over responsibilities. The range of skills and knowledge required during the development stage is very wide. The most frequently mentioned skill in the postal questionnaires was committee skills. Local authorities stressed knowledge of local authority structures and awareness of the financial implications of tenant management as equally important. In contrast, training agencies did not mention local authority structures as a major topic but did stress the financial implications of tenant management. Financial matters were most frequently mentioned by respondents to the TMO survey with knowledge of repairs the next most common. Nine organisations, however, said that training was needed on all the skills required to run a TMO.

3.13 The interviews brought out the wider range of skills, knowledge and attitudes needed in more depth. Trainers stressed the need for committees to understand the task of management and be able to manage staff and finance effectively. Maintaining participation was also thought to be important and most agencies stressed the importance of understanding the management agreement.

> 'The skill isn't necessarily about doing the job themselves. It's about how to manage their worker, how to manage their office, how to make decisions.'
>
> Local authority officer

> 'Development is a major participation exercise in itself. Firstly, because the co-op is likely to have its AGM during development, also there is the ballot taking place... they've sold 147 shares by door-knocking... we've established a newsletter.'
>
> Trainer - Secondary Co-op

3.14 Positive attitudes towards equal opportunities was a key area emphasised by many trainers, but changing attitudes amongst tenants was acknowledged to be difficult. Some tenants' reactions to equal opportunities training were very positive about the importance of fair recruitment, equal opportunities in allocations and the opportunities for participation, others, however, thought that this was unimportant as a topic and had been over-emphasised in training.

3.15 We felt that an understanding of management responsibilities and awareness of participation issues are very important at this stage. Necessary skills are committee skills, negotiation skills, financial skills and managing workers. Key knowledge includes an overview of tenant management organisation responsibilities and policies and performance monitoring. All committee/board members need to develop these key skills, knowledge and attitudes to a greater or lesser extent. The development stage, therefore, has a number of clearly defined tasks, as tenants decide on their management agreement and prepare for management, for which a wide range of skills and knowledge are needed. The task analysis is shown in Figure 3.3.

3.16 More detailed knowledge on specific areas, moreover, needs to be developed by particular individuals. For example, the members of a repairs and maintenance sub-committee, not surprisingly, need more detailed knowledge of repair and maintenance responsibilities, and on contracts and tendering procedures if the TMO is going to employ contractors. Some basic building technology knowledge would also be useful. In some cases, committees will also be participating in a capital improvement programme. This obviously requires an extra set of skills and knowledge associated with issues surrounding the development process such as, the role of architects and clerk of works and the ability to read plans.

Figure 3.3 **Skills, knowledge and attitudes required at development stage**

Task	Knowledge	Skills	Attitudes
* Financial control of budget	* Financial control	* Financial skills	* Need for financial control
* Appoint a worker/trainer	* Role as employer	* Managing staff	* Positive view of TMOs
* Set up sub-committees	* Recruitment	* Interviewing	* Positive view of equal opportunities
* Begin work on management agreement	* Committee structures	* Decision-making	
	* Management agreement	* Team-building	* Awareness of accountability
* Decide equal opportunities policy	* Equal opportunities	* Committee skills	* Need for confidentiality
	* Landlord/tenant responsibilities	* Ability to understand reports	* Importance of good performance
* Decide repairs and maintenance responsibilities	* Repair issues	* Report writing	
* Decide rent and areas policy	* CCT/contractors	* Assertiveness	* Importance of value-for-money
	* LA finance	* Self-appraisal	
* Decide tenancy responsibilities	* Rent collection	* Training others	* Desire to increase skills and knowledge
	* Arrears	* Public speaking	
* Decide environmental responsibilities	* Void control	* Negotiating skills	* Commitment to participation
	* Right-to-Buy	* Computer skills	
* Decide allocation policy	* Estate management	* Planning skills	* Confidence
* Decide staff structure	* Neighbour nuisance		
* Decide liaison arrangements with council	* Caretaking and cleansing		
	* Allocation policies		
* Agree allowances	* Confidentiality issues		
* Decide training policy	Homeless law		
* Decide final committee structure	* TMO staff structure		
	* Employment law		
* Draw up budget	* Job descriptions		
* Hold public meetings/AGM	* Performance monitoring		
* Assist in ballot	* TMO finance		
* Send out newsletters	* Training needs assessment		
* Negotiate with council	* Induction - new members		
* Set up office systems	* Budgeting		
* Use of office systems (if no staff)	* Tenant participation		
	* AGMs		
* Recruit staff	* TMO ballots		
* Take over management	* Preparing newsletters		
	* How to negotiate		
	* TMO office systems		
	* Use of computers		

ON-GOING TENANT MANAGEMENT ORGANISATIONS

3.17 The point at which tenants initially take over control and put their skills and knowledge into practice is critical. We found a number of groups for whom this had been a shaky period. This may be particularly so if there is a lengthy delay between the end of training and the date of take-over or where the committee or board, with a number of new members, is elected immediately prior to take-over. Several groups said that they felt the need for a short 'refresher' course over the first few months which would incorporate induction for new members.

3.18 Once the organisations are established, training needs can be identified for four distinct groups. Established committee or board members need 'updating' knowledge on new legislation and policies which will affect them. Tenants also stressed the need for new ideas to prevent staleness. New committee/board members need induction training. This should cover the history of the organisation; responsibilities; policies on all the functions which the organisation manages; the relationship with the council; financial control and committee skills. New office bearers, whether previous committee members or not, need specific skills and knowledge appropriate for the post. And, 'ordinary' members, who are not on the committee or board, need regular information and involvement in decision-making. The task analysis is shown in Figure 3.4.

Figure 3.4 **Skills, knowledge and attitudes required at ongoing stage**

Task	Knowledge	Skills	Attitudes
* Assist TMO to achieve aims * Attend meetings * Take part in decisions * Promote tenant participation * Be accountable * Keep members informed * Represent the TMO * Offer assistance * Carry out delegated tasks * Pass information to rest of committee/board * Ensure confidentiality * Ensure democratic procedures are carried out * Ensure equal opportunities * Monitor finances * Monitor functions * Train/inform new members * Keep skills and knowledge updated	* Aims and objectives of TMO * History of TMO * Legal status of TMO * Management agreement * Tenant participation * Committee member's roles * Effective communication * Effective meetings * Rules/constitution * Tenancy agreement * How council operates * TMO finances * Allocation policy * Repairs policy * Rent arrears policy * Neighbour disputes policy * Equal opportunities policy * Monitoring performance * Induction - new members * Training needs assessment * Where to get help	* Team-working * Decision-making * Assertiveness * Communications * Committee skills * Dealing with difficult situations * Ability to understand tables/graphs * Ability to understand financial reports * Ability to teach others * Self-appraisal * Knowing when to look for help	* Commitment to tenant participation * Positive view of TMOs * Positive view of equal opportunities * Awareness of accountability * Importance of value-for-money * Importance of good performance * Need for financial control * Desire to increase skills/knowledge

3.19   Some tenant management organisations have branched out into other community activities once their organisations are established. Notable examples are Spiers TMC in Glasgow, where committee members were the motivators for the development of a resource centre which provides space for community activities for over 30 local groups, workshop space for community businesses and Employment Training facilities (Yoker Resource Group, 1992). Langridge Crescent TMC in Middlesbrough manages new-build property for a housing association, organises social activities, supports a self-build group and developed an Enterprise Centre from which they intend to run a community business providing training to other tenants (*Inside Housing*, October, 1991). Tenants are using skills, perhaps developed from the tenant management organisation, and building and expanding their knowledge into a variety of areas.

3.20   For those who are less ambitious, there are often other non-housing problems which they may wish to tackle in their areas. PEP suggest a range of community development topics such as employment creation, crime and security, credit unions, special needs and youth groups (Bell, 1991). Some individuals may want to use the skills and knowledge they have developed to enter housing, or training other tenants, as a career.

INDIVIDUAL OFFICE BEARERS

3.21   The task analyses above have identified the skills, knowledge and attitudes which, ideally, all members of the committee or board of a TMO would have. However, reference has been made to the need for specific individuals to have a wider and more fully developed range of abilities. The key posts in TMOs are those of Chairperson, Secretary and Treasurer. Some TMOs also have Repairs and Allocations convenors who chair specialist sub-committees. The skills and knowledge required will vary between organisations. In some TMOs, many secretarial and financial tasks may be carried out by staff. However, in smaller TMOs we found that the Chairperson was also the manager of the organisation, the Treasurer was acting as a finance officer, the Secretary was the administrator and the Repairs convenor was acting as the TMOs maintenance officer. A full task analysis, for each of the common office bearer posts is given in Appendix 6. The key skills and knowledge of the Chairperson, Secretary and Treasurer are given in Figure 3.5 below. This indicates that, in addition to the skills and knowledge required by all committee members, the Chairperson requires chairing, leadership and public speaking skills. Secretaries will need letter-writing skills and an understanding of the legal responsibilities of a TMO and the Treasurer needs to understand accounts and financial control and have some financial skills.

Figure 3.5 **Ideal key skills and knowledge of office-bearers in TMOs**

Chairperson	Treasurer	Secretary
Knowledge	Knowledge	Knowledge
* Aims of TMO * What TP involves * Management agreement * How the council works * Rules/constitution * Finance for TMOs * Tenancy agreement * Staff management	* Aims of TMO * What TP involves * Management agreement * How the council works * Council finance * Finance for TMOs * Accounts * Financial control * Tendering procedures	* Aims of TMO * What TP involves * Management agreement * How the council works * Rules/constitution * Legal responsibilities
Skills	Skills	Skills

* Chairing
* Team-working
* Public speaking
* Assertiveness
* Negotiation
* Planning
* Leadership
* Decision-making
	* Team-work
	* Numeracy
	* Financial skills
	* Planning
	* Negotiation
	* Communication
		* Team-work
		* Literacy
		   Office skills
		   Communication
		   Letter writing
		   Report writing

Attitudes	Attitudes	Attitudes
* Commitment to TP * Positive view of TMOs * Non-discriminatory * Confidence * Desire to increase skills and knowledge * Importance of value-for-money * Importance of good performance	* Commitment to TP * Positive view of TMOs Trustworthy * Importance of value-for-money * Importance of good performance * Need for financial control	* Commitment to TP * Positive view of TMOs * Organised * Importance of providing information

SUMMARY

3.22 Overall, the picture which emerges is that the promotional phase is, for most tenants, a stage of information gathering - gaining basic knowledge of the tenant management options available, tenant participation and how the council works. If a committee does not already exist, then a steering group may be formed to consider the options further and some basic group and committee skills are then required.

3.23 At the feasibility stage, there were two opposite views of what skills and knowledge were required, with one group favouring knowledge and harder 'practical skills' and the other favouring group and individual development and teamwork. We felt that both types of skills would be required, along with some basic knowledge about the roles and responsibilities of tenant management organisations. There would be an overlap, in some groups, with the skills and knowledge that are required for development.

3.24 During the development stage, groups need to carry out a wide range of tasks in preparation for taking control of the housing stock, finance and, in many cases, staff. Potential tenant management organisations need to gain an overview of their responsibilities, with knowledge of policies and procedures. Particular individuals need to develop specific skills and knowledge. Skills in working as a committee, negotiation, staff management and finance are considered to be the most important.

3.25 Once a TMC or EMB is established, individuals have a variety of needs for skills and knowledge. Ordinary members need information about the organisation's activities so that they can be involved in decision-making. New committee members need the basic skills and knowledge acquired by existing members, new office-bearers will need specific skills and knowledge to carry out their role effectively. In some tenant management organisations, skills and knowledge to carry out operational tasks are required. Finally, co-ops or boards who wish to expand into other activities need to acquire knowledge about these options. The most important skills and knowledge for each stage of development are summarised below.

Figure 3.6 **Summary of key skills and knowledge needed**

Promotion

- Options available
- Estate issues and prioirities
- Tenant Participation
- How the Council works

Feasibility

- Overview of housing management
- Responsibilities of TMO
- Team work skills
- Practical skills

Development

- Management Agreement
- Policies and procedures
- Committee work
- Negotiation skills
- Staff management
- Financial control

On-going

- Information for new members
- Information for ordinary members
- Training for new committee members
- Updating knowledge

Chapter 4: The extent of tenant participation and tenant management

INTRODUCTION

4.1 This chapter aims to assess the extent of tenant participation and tenant management in England. It draws on data from the postal questionnaires and in-depth interviews and compares findings from the 1992 survey with earlier surveys where similar questions had been asked. The chapter examines the extent of estate-based initiatives, tenant management initiatives, other tenant management initiatives and support for tenant training.

4.2 Although local authorities have had powers to devolve management responsibilities to tenant management organisations since 1975, and a duty (in England) since 1980 to consult tenants about housing management matters, the growth in tenant participation and tenant management has been uneven. Research carried out in 1986/87, by a Glasgow University team, on the extent of tenant participation, found only 21 authorities in England who had considered tenant management (Cairncross, Clapham and Goodlad, 1990). A DoE study of housing co-operatives of the same period found only 41 tenant management co-operatives, the majority (83%) of which were in London: (McCafferty and Riley 1989). This slow growth was attributed to a lack of enthusiasm by local authorities, apart from a few pioneering exceptions, and the lack of agencies to provide training and advice (McCafferty and Riley, 1989).

4.3 Chapter 2 described developments in the 1980s which have given impetus to tenant participation and tenant management, including the introduction of the Section 16 grant regime and increases in grant levels following the Review of Co-ops (DoE, 1989). Further stimulus was added through government policy to link funds for improvement of run-down estates to tenant participation initiatives in the Estate Action and City Challenge programmes. The 1988 Housing Act, which gave tenants the right to change their landlord through Tenants' Choice was also thought to have had some impact and the proposals to introduce compulsory competitive tendering (CCT) to housing management (DoE, 1992c) have also provided a motivation for increased tenant involvement. Lastly, the introduction of the partnership Estate Management Board model, alongside the autonomous tenant management co-operative increased the range of choice.

4.4 This research aimed partially to update the Glasgow and DoE research to discover the extent of tenant participation and tenant management in 1992. Local authorities responding to the postal questionnaire (see Appendix 1 for details) were asked to answer questions on 'formal' tenant participation structures, including tenant involvement in the form of tenant management organisations, and less formal local estate-based initiatives in which tenants were involved in taking decisions jointly with the landlord.

ESTATE-BASED INITIATIVES
Types of authority with estate initiatives

4.5 Interest in tenant management may come from the landlords or from tenants (McCafferty and Riley, 1989) and in many cases concern about physical conditions on the estate is a motivating factor (Birchall, 1988). The postal survey of local authorities, therefore, aimed to explore whether authorities had set up local estate-based initiatives involving tenants in decision making. Seventy-two councils (28%) said that they had done so. Table 4.1 shows that over half of the London boroughs responding to the questionnaire had set up at least one estate-based initiative. In comparison, 38 per cent of Metropolitan councils and a quarter of district councils had done so. Most district councils had only one estate-based initiative, while Metropolitan and London borough authorities had between two and five such initiatives. In total, 253 estates involving over 100,000 houses were identified.

Table 4.1 **Number of estates involved in local estate-based initiatives by type of authority**

Type of authority	No. of estates				Total no. of estates	Total no. of authority	% of respondents
	1	2-5	6-10	11+			
Metropolitan	2	6	2	1	54	11	38
London borough	5	4	1	2	59	13	52
District Council	24	19	3	2	140	48	24
Total	31	29	6	5	253	72	

n = 257

Source: *Postal survey of local authorities*

Topics of decision making

4.6 Table 4.2 shows that the most common topics for joint decision-making were those concerned with environmental or estate improvements (39 per cent of estates), modernisation or redevelopment (35 per cent of estates). Almost a quarter (23%) of estate initiatives involved joint decisions over an estate budget and fourteen authorities, with 31 estate-based initiatives, claimed that all housing management functions were subject to joint decision-making.

Table 4.2 **Housing management function involved in joint decision-taking in local estate-based initiatives**

Function	No. of mentions	% of estates
Estate/environmental improvements	79	39
Modernisation/redevelopment	71	35
Repairs and maintenance	56	28
Estate budgets	46	23
All housing management functions	31	15

n = 202 estates. Respondents could mention more than one function

Source: *Postal survey of local authorities*

Other factors

4.7 There was some indication, however, that many of these initiatives may be temporary arrangements, perhaps for the duration of improvement works. There were two sources for this view. First, the Glasgow University survey of tenant participation in 1986/87 found 62 authorities with estate-based initiatives (Cairncross, Clapham and Goodlad, 1990a) compared with the 72 identified in this research. However, most (82%) of the estate based initiative in the 1992 survey had begun in 1988 or later. This suggests that those identified in the earlier survey had been dissolved. Second, the fact that the most common topics of joint decision-making were estate improvements and modernisation suggests that the initiatives may cease once work has been carried out.

4.8 Over half (54%) of the local authorities said that their estate-based initiatives had developed from an Estate Action proposal, where commitment to tenant participation was an integral part of the eligibility for funding, but two-thirds of the estate based initiatives mentioned by local authority respondents (64%) were not part of an Estate Action proposal. Estate Action, therefore, appeared to have played a significant role in promoting tenant participation but many authorities had developed joint decision-making on estates without its impetus. Nevertheless, there is clearly scope, based upon this evidence of the number of estates where tenants were involved in joint decision-making, for tenants and authorities to consider tenant management, although not all tenants may wish to progress from more informal structures to take greater responsibilities.

STEPS TOWARDS TENANT MANAGEMENT

Type of local authority with tenant management initiatives

4.9 The local authorities were asked if they had taken any steps towards the setting up of tenant management organisations. Fifty-four of the responding local authorities, had taken such steps, a considerable increase on the number responding to the 1986/87 survey which found only 21 authorities who had considered tenant management (Cairncross, Clapham and Goodlad, 1990a). Table 4.3 shows that most of the growth in interest had taken place in Metropolitan councils; 18 (62%) had taken steps in the 1992 survey compared with 12 (48%) in 1986/87; and in district councils 5 (20%) in 1992 compared with only 7 (4%) in the earlier survey.

Table 4.3 **Authorities who had taken steps to set up TMOs in 1992 compared with 1986/7**

Type of authority	1986/87		1992	
	No.	%	No.	%
Metropolitan council	5	20	18	62
London borough	9	43	12	48
District council	7	4	24	12
All local authorities	21	10	54	21
	n = 210		n = 257	

Sources: *1992 postal survey of local authorities*
1986/87 Cairncross, Clapham and Goodlad (1990)

4.10 It was not clear from the postal survey what steps had been taken to set up a tenant management organisation. However, Department of the Environment statistics for 1991/92 show that promotional grants were paid to 30 advice agencies working with approximately 120 local authorities (DoE, 1992). It may, therefore, be assumed that the 54 authorities who had taken steps to set up a tenant management organisation had considered TMOs beyond merely thinking about it and had taken some practical steps.

Geographical distribution of local authorities

4.11 The geographical distribution of local authorities who had taken steps to set up a TMO was uneven. Table 4.4 shows that 44 local authorities had considered an estate management board, while 33 had considered a tenant management co-operative. Twenty-two authorities had considered both models. Overall, inner London boroughs were most likely to have taken steps to set up a TMO: eight out of ten respondents had considered tenant management. In contrast, only three authorities in the East (4%) and two authorities in the South-East (4%) had taken similar steps.

4.12   While more authorities had taken steps to set up an EMB than a TMC, there were also some geographical differences in preference for the two models. In five regions (Yorkshire and Humberside, East Midlands, South-West, West Midlands and North-West) there appeared to be a preference for EMBs, while in the North and East regions there was a preference for TMCs.

Table 4.4   **The geographical distribution of authorities who had taken steps to set up a TMO**

Region	Respondents	EMB		TMC		TMO	
		No.	%	No.	%	No.	%
North	17	4	24	6	35	6	35
Yorkshire and Humberside	20	4	20	2	10	4	20
East Midlands	27	2	7	1	4	3	11
East	34	1	3	3	9	3	9
Inner London	10	7	70	7	70	8	80
Outer London	15	3	20	3	20	4	33
South East	45	2	4	2	4	2	4
South West	29	5	17	0	0	5	17
West Midlands	27	6	22	4	15	7	26
North-West	33	10	30	5	16	12	36
Total	257	44		33		54	

n = 257

Sources: *Postal survey of local authorities*

Percentages shown are percentage of respondents by region

Size of TMOs under development

4.13   The postal survey of local authorities found 31 EMBs and 32 TMCs under development, though some of these may have been at a fairly early stage, as the DoE funded only 44 TMOs at the development stage in 1991/92 (DoE, 1992). Although the EMB model was originally designed for larger estates, there were indications that it was proving attractive to tenants in estates of all sizes. The TMC model appeared to be most attractive to tenants living in smaller estates (less than 400 properties). Table 4.5 shows the number of properties in TMOs under development.

Table 4.5   **Number of properties in EMBs and TMCs under development**

Number of properties	Potential EMB	Potential TMC
0 - 199	4	25
200 - 399	4	4
400 - 599	6	0
600 - 799	2	0
800 - 999	5	0
Over 1000	5	1
Total	26	29

n = 63: missing = 8

Source: *Postal survey of local authorities*

4.14 The size of EMBs under development varied from 65 properties to 1,800 properties. The mean number of properties involved was 659. In contrast, the size of potential TMCs varied from 18 to 1400 properties. The average size was 160 properties.

ESTABLISHED TMOs

Number of established TMOs

4.15 Desk research for this project, using a variety of data sources including the local authority postal survey and DoE data identified 65 established TMCs, 16 established EMBs and a further 36 at a late stage of development. A list of TMOs, updated to the end of 1992, is given in Appendix 2. These organisations were sent a postal questionnaire of which 66 were returned completed, a response rate of 60 per cent. Data from the survey has been used to give a more detailed picture of TMOs.

4.16 The desk research found that the oldest co-operatives were established in 1976, shortly after local authorities were given powers to devolve management. Of the twelve TMCs established in the 1970s, almost all were in London. After this initial wave of TMCs, only ten were established between 1980 and 1984. Following the introduction of the Section 16 grant regime, a further 23 were set up in the late 1980s. However, since the increase in grants and the development of the EMB model, there has been considerable growth with 36 TMOs established between 1990 and 1992. If all the potential TMOs at a late stage of development complete their training programmes, this number could easily double by 1994 (Table 4.6).

Table 4.6 **Dates of establishment of tenant management organisations**

Date established	TMC No.	EMB No.	Total No.	%
Pre-1980	12	0	12	15
1980 - 1984	10	0	10	12
1985 - 1989	23	0	23	28
1990 - 1992	20	16	36	44
Total	65	16	81	100

Source: *List of established TMOs and those under development (Appendix 2)*

Size

4.17 The organisations varied greatly in size, as Table 4.7 shows. The 41 established tenant management co-operatives responding to the postal survey were smaller on average than the 11 estate management board respondents. Co-operatives varied in size from four to 278 units, and estate management boards from 173 to 1476 units. The average size of tenant management co-operatives was 156 and of estate management boards was 966. This compares with the findings from the local authority questionnaire on the size of potential TMOs (Table 4.5) and confirms the view that EMBs in development, with an average size of 659, units were appealing to a wider range of estates, while the average size of potential TMCs at 160 units, shows a continued appeal to smaller estates.

Table 4.7 **Size of established TMOs by type**

Units of housing	Type and number of TMO		
	TMC	EMB	Total
0 - 100	27	0	27
101 - 200	11	1	12
201 - 500	3	2	5
501 - 700	0	0	0
701 - 900	0	1	1
901 - 1200	0	4	4
1201 - 1500	0	3	3

Source: *Postal Survey of TMOs*

Geographical distribution

4.18 The geographical distribution of tenant management organisations at the end of 1992 was very distinctive. Inner London had the greatest number of tenant management co-operatives and the highest percentage (59%) of TMOs overall. This was not surprising, given the key role played in the development of TMCs by some London boroughs, and the finding by McCafferty and Riley (1989) that 83 per cent of TMCs were in London. However, the concentration of EMBs in the North-West means that this region, though a long way behind London, has the next highest proportion (14%). This appeared to be the result of PEP promotional activity in this region. The third largest number of TMOs was in the West Midlands region. This was due mainly to one local authority, Birmingham, which had a well-developed co-operative and participation support section. The East, South-East and South-West regions had least support: no TMOs were established in these areas at the end of 1992.

Table 4.8 **Geographical distribution of TMOs**

Region	Type of TMO			Total	%
	EMB	TMC	PTMO*		
North	0	2	4	6	5
Yorkshire & Humberside	2	0	5	7	6
East Midlands	0	1	0	1	1
East	0	0	0	0	0
Inner London	3	52	14	69	59
Outer London	0	1	3	4	3
South East	0	0	0	0	0
South West	0	0	1	1	1
West Midlands	2	6	5	13	11
North-West	9	3	4	16	14
Total	16	65	36	117	100

Source: *List of established TMOs and those at a late stage of development (Appendix 2)*
Note: * PTMO = Potential tenant management organisation

Organisation structures

4.19 Most of the established tenant management organisations had a management committee or board. Establishment of such a committee or board seemed to be related to size, as nine TMCs with less than 100 dwellings claimed not to have a management committee. The size of the committee or board varied from 6 to 26 members. On average, the committees of tenant management co-operatives were smaller than those of estate management boards.

Table 4.9 **Size of management committee or board of TMO**

No. on management committee or board	Type and number of TMO		
	TMC	EMB	Total
None	9	0	9
1 - 5	0	0	0
6 - 10	13	0	13
11 - 15	14	4	18
16 - 20	3	6	9
21 - 30	0	1	1
Unknown	1	0	1
Total	40	11	51

n = 54: missing = 12

Source: *Postal survey to TMOs*

4.20 The membership of tenant management co-operative management committees was largely made up of tenants, occasionally of people who hoped to become tenants in the co-operative, and sometimes of other residents in the area. In four co-ops a councillor served on the committee. In comparison, all the established estate management boards included councillors and often council officers. Two EMBs said their own staff were members of the board. Councillor membership of the board varied from two to six places. The larger number of councillors on EMB boards was due to the partnership nature of this type of organisation.

Functions

4.21 The nature of training required for tenant management organisations may be related to the functions and responsibilities carried out. Respondents to the questionnaire were, therefore, asked for details of what they had responsibility for. Table 4.10 shows that almost all said that they had control of a budget with repairs, cyclical maintenance and neighbour disputes being the next most common responsibilities. Co-ops were more likely than EMBs to have responsibility for letting houses but were less likely to be responsible for the allocation policy. Two-thirds of TMCs (66%), and all the EMBs, were responsible for enforcing tenancy conditions but only seven out of ten estate management boards and four out of ten co-ops said that they were involved in drawing up the conditions of tenancy. Typically, established tenant management organisations had responsibility for 11 functions.

Table 4.10 **Functions of TMOs**

Functions of TMO	Type and number of TMO				Total
	TMC		EMB		
	No.	%	No.	%	
Budget control	40	98	10	100	50
Day-to-day repairs	41	100	10	100	51
Neighbour disputes	36	88	9	90	45
Cyclical maintenance	36	88	8	80	44
Letting houses	37	90	7	70	44
Rent collection	30	73	8	80	38
Cleaning	30	73	7	70	37
Improvement/ modernisation	29	71	8	80	37
Maintenance of open space	31	76	6	60	37
Caretaking	26	64	8	80	34
Enforcing tenancy conditions	27	66	10	100	37
Rent arrears	28	68	8	80	36
Staff employment	27	66	6	60	33
Allocations policy	25	61	7	70	32
Drawing up tenancy conditions	18	42	7	70	25
Other	1	2	1	10	2
Base	41	4	10	5	51

n = 51: missing = 15

Source: *Postal survey of TMOs*

OTHER TENANT PARTICIPATION INITIATIVES

4.22 The local authorities were asked whether they had any participation initiatives other than estate-based or tenant management initiatives. This question elicited a variety of responses from 139 local authorities as Table 4.11 shows. Taken together with previous responses 181 authorities (70%) claimed that they had, or had taken steps to develop at least one participation initiative in their area. The most common tenant participation initiative mentioned was the fostering, support or encouragement of tenants' associations (69 authorities, 27%). The next most frequently mentioned initiatives were tenant or 'customer' consultation (50 authorities, 19%) and meetings between the landlord and tenants (45 authorities, 18%). Over three-quarters of Metropolitan councils mentioned tenant participation initiatives and two-thirds of the London boroughs did so. Half the district councils mentioned some form of initiative. It was particularly encouraging to note that one-in-five district councils said that they were trying to promote participation, though one council, which had carried out a survey, said that as only 20 per cent of their tenants were interested they were not proceeding further. A small number of other authorities also felt that there was no interest from tenants.

Table 4.11 **Other tenant participation initiatives by type of authority**

Type of initiative	Type of Authority						Total
	Metropolitan Councils		London Borough		District Councils		
	No.	%	No.	%	No.	%	
Tenants' organisations	13	56	11	44	45	22	69
Consultation	9	39	7	28	34	17	50
Meetings	12	52	9	36	24	12	45
Area forums	15	65	9	36	15	7	39
Trying to promote TP	7	30	5	20	45	22	57
Any TP initiative	23	79	16	64	100	49	139
	n=29		n=25		n=203		

Source: *Postal survey of local authorities*

TENANT TRAINING
Local authority and agency support

4.23 If tenants are to be involved effectively in joint decision making and management of their estates, they need knowledge of how councils operate, to enable them to discuss issues on a more equal basis. Skills in communication, negotiation and committee work are also required. The provision of training is, therefore, an important component of tenant participation. The research, therefore, asked a series of questions in the local authority questionnaire about training for tenants. From these responses, and from other sources, 44 agencies who provided training to tenants were identified. These agencies were by no means the only providers of training for tenants but seemed to represent those which were most interested in providing training for TMOs. These agencies were sent a questionnaire which sought information about the training provided and their views on training generally and 34 agencies replied to this, a response rate of 76 per cent. The agency responses about training were then compared to those of local authorities in their questionnaire.

4.24 In total, 88 councils (34%) said that they had provided or had assisted in the provision of training to tenants, tenants' groups or tenant management organisations. This suggested a considerable recent increase in activity, since the 1986/87 survey found no English authorities involved in the provision of training (Cairncross, Clapham and Goodlad, 1990a). A higher proportion of Metropolitan councils (74%) were involved in training than London boroughs (50%) or district councils (27%). Larger councils were more likely to provide, or assist in providing training to tenants than smaller ones. For example, 81 per cent of local authorities with more than 20,000 houses in management were involved in training whereas only 16 per cent of those with less than 4,000 houses in management provided, or assisted in the provision of, training.

Geographical distribution of support for training

4.25 The training agencies who responded to the questionnaire, and others who took part in in-depth interviews, were asked to describe their geographic area of operation. Agencies which operated in only one local authority district were categorised as local, those which operated in several neighbouring districts were classified as regional, while those which covered a wider area or expressed a willingness to work anywhere were classified as national agencies. On the basis of the replies they were then categorised as national, regional or local organisations. The research identified 12 national agencies and 33 regional or local agencies. These included consultants, educational establishments and secondary housing co-operatives. The geographical distribution of regional and local agencies is compared in Table 4.12, with local authority support.

4.26 There was a greater choice of agencies operating in Inner London, Yorkshire and Humberside and the North-West and these were also the areas where a higher proportion of local authorities supported training. There was only one local agency operating in the South-West, which had a low level of local authority support. There was, therefore, some correlation between the number of agencies operating in the region and the number of local authorities supporting training.

Table 4.12 **Geographic support for training**

Region	LA support (1)	% of respondents	Training agency support (2)
North	6	35	1
Yorks and Humberside	9	45	6
East Midlands	10	37	2
East	7	21	5
Inner London	7	70	13
Outer London	5	33	5
South East	9	20	4
South West	7	24	1
West Midlands	9	33	3
North West	19	58	8
Base	88	257	33

Sources: *Postal survey of local authorities*
Postal survey of training agencies and in-depth interviews.

4.27 However, agencies' areas of operation may be enhanced or limited by local authority willingness to support training. Authorities in the East and South-East were less interested in tenant training, but there were 5 training agencies operating in the East and 4 operating in the South-East. Although there was only one local agency based in the South-West, several national agencies indicated a willingness to work there. In some cases, however, provision by training agencies was encouraged by local authority interest. Banks of the Wear, for example, widened its scope from supporting ownership co-ops because of a partnership with one local authority to support a TMO.

Number of tenants' groups trained

4.28 Both local authorities and training agencies were asked to indicate how many tenants' organisations they had provided, or assisted in the provision of training for in the last 12 months. Table 4.13 shows that the vast majority of support for training by local authorities was directed to tenants' associations (83%). Training agencies appeared more likely to be involved in the provision of training to potential tenant management organisations. It should be noted, however, that several of the larger agencies were unable to estimate how many tenants' organisations attended large regional training events, so training agency contributions to tenants' association training may be underestimated.

Table 4.13 **Number of tenants' groups provided with training**

Type of tenants' group	LA support		Agency provision	
	No.	%	No.	%
Tenant Management Co-operative	36	5	26	7
Potential TMC	18	2	36	9
Estate Management Board	7	1	10	3
Potential EMB	31	4	71	18
Estate Management Sub-Committee	11	1	5	1
Potential Estate Management Sub-committee	16	2	11	3
Tenants' Association	662	83	228	59
Other	15	2	-	-
Total	796	100	387	100
	n=88		n=34	

Source: *Postal survey of LAs and Training Agencies*

4.29 There is likely to be a considerable degree of overlap between the two sets of responses because the 'provision' by local authorities may be to sponsor tenants to attend an external event or engage an outside agency and tenants may receive training from more than one organisation. However, the figures suggested that over 40 established tenant management organisations, and over 100 potential tenant management organisations, received training in 1991/92. This may have included a number of groups at a fairly early stage of the development process.

Training for TMOs

4.30 Both established and potential TMOs responding to the postal questionnaire were asked if they had received training during their development. Seventeen tenant management organisations said that they had received no training during this period. Of these, the vast majority (16) were established tenant management co-operatives and one was a potential estate management board. There are several possible reasons for this response. It may be that the passage of time has eliminated the memory of such training, as longer established organisations were more likely to say that they had not had training. A negative response was also linked to smaller organisations who may feel less need for training. It may be that any training received, moreover, was not perceived as such, as almost all (94%) of TMOs said that they had received advice and support.

Table 4.14 **Whether received training before taking on responsibilities by size of organisation**

	1-200	200-1000	1001+	Total	%
Received training	26	13	7	46	72
Did not receive training	15	2	0	17	27
Didn't know	1	0	0	1	1
Total	42	15	7	64	100

n = 64: missing 2

Source: *Postal survey of TMOs*

SUMMARY

4.31   Overall 181 (70%) local authorities said that they had developed, or taken steps to develop some form of tenant participation initiative in their area. These initiatives ranged from setting up tenant management organisations and joint decision-making with tenants in local estate-based initiatives to meetings between the landlord and tenants.

4.32   Seventy-two authorities had established local estate-based initiatives involving over 250 estates. Support for estate initiatives was strongest in London boroughs, over half having at least one initiative of this type compared with only a quarter of district councils. Half the local authority respondents said that Estate Action bids had influenced the decision to form an estate initiative.

4.33   Metropolitan councils were most likely to have taken steps to develop tenant management organisations and the number of them involved in such initiatives had increased considerably since the 1986/87 survey to 62% of respondents. The number of district councils who had taken any steps had also increased, but from a very low base. Only 24 (12%) had taken steps by 1992. Support for tenant management was strongest in Inner London where 80 per cent of respondents had considered it, and weakest in the east and south-east where only 4 per cent of respondents in each of these regions had taken any steps.

4.34   Fifty-two established TMOs replied to the postal questionnaire. They ranged in size from four to 1,476 units. Estate management boards were larger, on average, than TMCs but spanned a broader range of sizes. There was evidence that the EMBs, as a model for tenant management, were gaining in popularity.

4.35   Eighty-eight councils, a third of respondents, supported tenant training compared with none in 1987/88. Most support was given to tenants' associations rather than TMOs. The research identified 45 training agencies involved in tenant training, who were training or were willing to train TMOs. There was an uneven geographical distribution of regional and local agencies, with only one in the south-west and one in the north. However, 12 agencies expressed a willingness to work anywhere and could be classified as national agencies.

Training Provision

Chapter 5 — Training for tenant management

OVERVIEW

5.1 This section examines the provision of training to groups developing a tenant management organisation. It begins with an overview and then discusses training provision stage by stage, comparing provision with the ideal models developed in Chapter 3. While 88 local authorities and 34 training agencies provided training to tenants' groups, 56 local authorities and 30 training agencies said that they were involved in the provision of training to potential TMOs. Evidence from the postal survey suggested that these organisations assisted more than 100 potential TMOs to receive training in 1991/92. The responses from the survey of TMOs provided a broader picture, since some groups received their development training a number of years ago. It has also been possible, therefore, to make some assessment of how training has changed over time within this Chapter. In addition to the surveys and interviews, information from the review of training material provides contextual background to the findings.

Providers of training

5.2 It is clear from the survey and interviews that local authorities made considerable use of outside agencies for tenant training. PEP and TPAS were the most frequently mentioned agencies, but training was also provided by a wide variety of other agencies. A list of agencies providing training is included in Appendix 3. Table 5.1 shows how often different types of training providers were mentioned. Eighty-two per cent of local authorities who supported promotional training said that they used outside agencies. This may have taken the form of development staff working on an estate or the provision of financial assistance for tenants to attend external training events.

5.3 Over three-quarters of authorities, providing support during the feasibility and development stages, also used outside agencies. In most cases local authorities worked in partnership with an outside agency. Typically, one or two development workers from an outside agency worked closely with the steering group providing training, advice and support throughout the development process. Other trainers, on specialist topics, were brought in as required. Over half the local authorities used their own specialist tenant participation staff usually in conjunction with training by an outside agency. Training by other specialists varied depending on the stage of development. Local authority technical, financial and legal staff were more likely to be involved in the promotional stage (29 per cent of authorities) and at the development stage (26 per cent of authorities) but were less likely to have an input during feasibility work (8%). One-fifth of local authorities said that tenants from other TMOs were providing training during the promotion and feasibility stages.

5.4 In contrast, training agencies were more likely to use their own trainers. Three-quarters of the agencies said that they used their own specialist tenant participation staff at all stages, while technical, legal and financial staff were more likely to be involved at the development stage. The 'other agencies' may be including local authority staff, though involvement appeared to decrease as development progressed. The agencies suggested significantly greater use of tenants from other TMOs as providers of training.

Table 5.1 **Providers of training by stage**

Providers of training	Stage of development					
	Promotion %		Feasibility %		Development %	
	LA	TA	LA	TA	LA	TA
Own specialist tenant participation staff	57	77	52	78	52	76
Own specialist training staff	20	43	12	48	22	57
Own technical, financial and legal staff	29	8	26	52		
Other agencies or freelance consultants	82	40	76	39	78	33
Tenants involved in TMOs	21	30	20	26	13	29
Other	0	0	0	0	0	0
Base	56	30	25	23	23	21

Note: LA = Local Authority: TA = Training Agency
Source: *Postal surveys of LAs and training agencies*
(Organisations could use more than one type of provider)

5.5 The survey of tenant management organisations confirmed that training was received from a wide range of different sources (Table 5.2). The most frequently mentioned sources were local authority housing departments (45% of TMOs) and PEP (45%). While tenant management co-operatives mentioned a wider variety of organisations involved in training, EMB training appeared to have been mainly provided by PEP, sometimes with input from the local authority. It is significant that not all local authorities or tenant management organisations mentioned input by local authority staff, suggesting that in some cases the authority played little active part in the development of tenant management organisations. It should be noted that the important role played by secondary co-operatives is understated in this table because tenants included organisations such as Banks of the Wear, CDS and Solon in the 'other' training agency category.

Table 5.2 **Training provision to TMOs during development**

Training provider	Type and number of TMOs						
	TMC	PTMC*	EMB	PEMB*	Other	Total	%
Housing Department	8	3	6	4	0	21	45
PEP	0	3	11	6	1	21	45
Other training agency	12	4	1	0	1	18	38
Other LA department	3	1	3	2	0	9	30
Other TMOs	0	1	3	1	0	5	10
Housing Association/ Co-operative (incl. secondaries)	3	2	0	0	0	5	10
NFHC	3	1	0	0	1	5	10
Own worker	2	0	2	0	0	4	9
TPAS	2	0	1	0	0	3	6
NFHA	2	0	1	0	0	3	6
Voluntary organisations	0	1	1	0	0	2	4
Other	5	0	0	0	0	5	10
Base	22	6	11	6	1	47	

Note: * PTMC = Potential TMC: PEMB = Potential EMB
Source: *Postal survey of TMOs*

Topics of training

5.6 The postal questionnaire to TMOs asked for details of training topics received during development. Table 5.3 summarises the results. This table must be interpreted with some caution because the case-studies found that individuals did not necessarily remember all the topics which had been covered and the table only shows what the respondent **recollected**. Of the 66 TMO respondents, only 46 completed this question. To enable comparison with the 'ideal' model the topics have been divided into promotion, feasibility and development stages. However, the postal survey did not ask this level of detail so we cannot be absolutely certain that topics were covered at the stages identified.

Table 5.3 **Summary of key topics covered during development**

Topic	Potential			Total	%
	TMC	EMB	TMO		
Promotion					
What a TMC is	19	4	12	35	76
What an EMB is	4	11	8	23	50
Consulting members	9	6	8	23	50
How the Council works	7	6	8	21	46
Feasibility					
Rules/Constitution	17	11	13	41	89
Effective meetings	11	10	13	34	74
Working as a team	11	10	11	32	70
Public speaking	3	7	9	19	41
Writing letters/reports	8	5	4	17	37
Development					
Roles of committee members	18	9	13	40	87
Management agreement	18	10	12	40	87
Equal opportunities	16	8	13	37	80
Repairs	18	11	12	41	89
Rent collection/arrears	17	10	12	39	85
Letting houses	14	10	12	36	78
Tenancy agreement	15	11	9	35	76
Budgets	17	9	11	37	84
Finance for TMOs	14	6	10	30	65
How to negotiate	8	8	7	23	50
Employment law and procedures	7	3	10	20	43
Base	22	11	13	46	

Source: *Postal survey of TMOs*

5.7 Table 5.3 shows that, of the respondents who said they had received training, three-quarters (76%) had received training on 'what a TMC is' but only half had learnt what an EMB was. This suggests that groups may not have received training on all the options available. In the case of some of the older tenant management co-operatives this is not surprising as the EMB model was not developed until the late 1980s. However, only four of the 11 established estate management boards said that they received training on TMCs. The in-depth interviews also suggested that some of the older EMBs were not told about other options. Some of the potential TMOs respondents also indicated that they had only received training on one option. This is an issue for concern because tenants considering tenant management should be made aware of the advantages and disadvantages of all the different models, in order to make an informed choice.

5.8 Only half the respondents said that they had received training on 'consulting members'. This may not be of such great concern because tenants considering a TMO may have had previous experience in tenants' associations and may not need training on this issue. Similarly, previous experience in tenants' groups may have included learning how the council works.

5.9 Nine out of ten respondents said that they had received training on 'rules and constitutions', making this the most popular topic of training. Three-quarters had received training on effective meetings and 70 per cent had covered 'working as a team'. These topics can, therefore, be considered to be well covered. However, turning to practical skills, such as public speaking and writing letters and reports, it can be seen that less than half the TMOs remembered training on these topics. It may be that these practical skills were already developed or that tenants learnt by doing, rather than formal training.

5.10 Once tenants reach the stage of learning detailed policies and procedures, both the management agreement and housing management functions appeared to be covered in the training programmes of most TMOs. Over 80 per cent of TMO respondents had received training on repairs and rents. Slightly fewer (78%) had learnt about lettings but this may be because some TMOs did not manage this function. Most (87%) had received training on the roles of committee members and a high proportion (84%) had received training on budgets, though less (65%) said that they had learnt about 'finance for TMOs'.

5.11 The areas of concern in relation to the ideal model were, therefore, that only half said that they had received training on 'how to negotiate' and less than half (43%) had learnt about employment law or employment procedures. As many of the respondents were very small TMOs it may be that they did not employ staff. However, all TMOs have to negotiate their management agreement and allowances so negotiating skills were considered very important in the ideal model.

Table 5.4 **Forms of training received by TMOs**

Forms of training	Areas of training					
	Options	Skills	Housing Management	Finance	Running a TMO	Total mentions
Single sessions	29	25	31	32	31	148
Series of sessions	24	22	23	18	22	109
Training course	12	16	18	9	13	68
Residential meeting	16	17	18	12	14	77
Study visits	25	21	22	9	18	95
Videos	16	14	11	5	5	52
Reading training material	25	21	19	20	22	107

n = 47: missing = 1

Source: *Postal survey of TMOs*

Forms of training

5.12 Single sessions were the most commonly reported form for all areas of training, with a short series of sessions the next most numerous. Study visits were used frequently for all topics, except finance where single sessions were the predominant form of training. Training courses and residential meetings were most common for housing management but were less used than other forms. Reading training material was the third most frequently mentioned way of receiving information. Many tenants we interviewed had kept the training materials they had received on formal courses for later reference and use by other committee members. Videos tended to be used as part of a training event and were largely restricted to training on options for control, skills and housing management functions.

Who received training

5.13 So far training for tenants preparing for tenant management has been discussed without consideration of who exactly was in receipt of it. The evidence from the postal survey of TMOs and the interviews suggested that in most cases training was concentrated on the steering group or committee, rather than 'ordinary' members. Established TMCs were less likely to report any sort of training (Table 5.5). More recent groups, however, said that their steering groups had received some training on all of the five broad topic areas identified in Table 5.5. Ordinary residents of the estate were more likely to receive training on options and skills, than finance or running a TMO. There was some evidence, from both trainers and tenants in the in-depth interviews, that a wider range of people may be involved in the early stages of training, through small group meetings and surveys, for example.

Table 5.5 **Who received training**

Recipients and subject matter of training	Numbers and types of TMOs reporting training received at development stage						
	TMC	PTMC	EMB	PEMB	Other	Total	%
Options							
- Steering group	14	6	11	6	1	38	81
- Other residents	7	1	7	3	1	19	40
(- both	3	1	7	3	1	15)*	32
Skills							
- Steering group	14	6	10	6	1	36	77
- Other residents	5	1	5	2	1	14	30
(- both	3	1	5	2	1	12)*	26
Housing management							
- Steering group	20	6	11	6	1	44	94
- Other residents	3	1	5	2	1	12	26
(- both	2	1	5	2	1	11)*	23
Finance							
- Steering group	20	5	11	6	1	43	91
- Other residents	4	1	3	1	0	9	19
(- both	3	0	3	1	0	7)*	15
Running a TMO							
- Steering group	19	6	11	6	1	43	91
- Other residents	4	1	3	1	0	9	19
(- both	3	1	3	1	0	8)*	17
Base	23	6	11	6	1	47	

* figures included also under 'steering group' and 'other residents'
Source: *Postal survey of TMOs*
PTMC = Potential TMC
PEMB = Potential EMB

Review of materials

5.14 All the previous sections have been based on the postal surveys and in-depth interviews. Subsequent sections draw on the review of materials which might be used for training. This included books and reports which might be used as source material, as well as materials used on training courses. The review included both published and unpublished written material, in a wide variety of forms from leaflets to training manuals, and visual material including photographic slides, overhead acetates and videos. Materials used as the basis of exercises, games and role-play were also examined. In total, 251 examples of materials produced by 66 organisations were reviewed. The largest producers of relevant information were PEP and TPAS. However, a wide range of other agencies such as CATCH, CHISEL and Banks of the Wear also produced training materials, mainly unpublished. Material was also received from 15 local authorities, three tenants' federations and six tenant management organisations. Many of the materials were suitable for more than one stage in the development process but are discussed below under the most relevant stage. The material covered a wide range of topics, the most popular of which were participation (19%) and committee skills (11%). Table 5.6 shows the breakdown of materials by topic and producer. The major gaps, where few materials were found, were information on how councils operate, financial issues, specific housing management functions and negotiating skills.

Table 5.6 **Training materials by topic and producer**

Topic	TPAS England	PEP	CDS London	CATCH	Hexagon	CHISEL HA	Tenant Action	Solon Wandsworth	Other	Total
Committee skills	3	6	0	1	0	1	0	2	15	28
Consultants services	3	0	0	0	0	1	0	1	9	14
Equal opportunities	1	1	0	1	0	0	1	3	8	15
Estate-based management	0	7	0	1	0	0	0	0	1	9
EMBs	0	3	0	1	0	0	1	0	2	7
Finance	2	0	1	0	1	0	0	0	6	10
Options for change	3	2	4	2	0	1	0	1	5	18
Participation	13	4	1	0	1	0	0	0	28	47
Repairs and maintenance	1	2	2	1	0	0	0	0	3	9
TMCs	2	1	2	0	1	2	2	0	15	23
Tenants' choice	5	0	0	1	0	0	0	0	2	8
Other	6	8	4	5	5	2	3	0	29	63
Total	39	34	14	13	8	7	7	7	123	251

TRAINING PROVISION AT PROMOTION STAGE

Introduction

5.15 The previous sections have given an overview of training for tenant management and the remainder of this Chapter now looks at training provision, in more detail, at each stage of the development process. For each of the stages, the research focuses on the providers of training; topics of training; forms of provision and training materials. Other issues are also discussed where appropriate.

Providers and topics

5.16 Fifty-six local authorities and thirty training agencies responding to the postal questionnaire said that they were involved in providing training at the promotional stage. The topics mentioned by these providers at the promotion stage are shown in Table 5.7. The three most popular topics for training by both local authorities and training agencies were awareness of tenant participation, options for control and committee skills. This list was slightly different to our ideal model, which suggested that options for control, tenant participation and how the council works were the most important topics. There is an indication from the table that local authorities and training agencies had different interests. Training agencies were more likely to mention training on options for control, but some local authorities seemed interested only in training on EMBs. Although the in-depth interviews stressed the importance of training on how the council works, this topic was mentioned by less than one-third of postal questionnaire respondents, indicating that many tenants may not be learning about this at an early stage.

Table 5.7 **Comparison of most frequently mentioned training topics at promotion stage**

Topic	Mentions by LA		Mentions by Agency	
	number	%	number	%
Raise awareness of TP	24	46	15	50
Committee skills	24	46	17	57
Options for control	21	40	16	53
Local authority structure	16	31	8	27
Financial implications of TMO	8	15	6	20
Forming a tenants' association	7	13	4	13
Producing newsletters/leaflets	6	12	4	13
Developing an EMB	6	12	-	-
Assertiveness	5	10	6	20
Other	29	56	19	63
Base	52		30	

Source: *Postal survey of LAs and training agencies*

Forms of training

5.17 The predominant form of provision at the promotional stage was single training sessions, mentioned by 86 per cent of local authorities and 80 per cent of training agencies. Just over half the agencies provided a series of training sessions compared with 43 per cent of local authorities. Training agencies were also more likely than local authorities to mention training courses and study visits. This difference in emphasis may be because most local authorities were using outside agencies to provide the training. The questionnaire also asked local authorities whether they recommended any courses to tenants. The most commonly mentioned topics were 'Options for Control' and 'Tenant Participation', both of which were most relevant to the promotional stage and the most frequently recommended training providers were PEP (46% of mentions) and TPAS (28% of mentions). Both these organisations ran regular promotional events around the country on the options for control and tenant participation.

5.18 The in-depth interviews suggested that the style of training at this stage varied from lectures, mainly at the large external events, to more informal question and answer sessions in small groups. Most training agencies favoured local informal sessions such as small group meetings on the estate. In some cases the information exchange would take place through a door-to-door survey. A typical format for promotion is described below.

> 'We want to provide a wide spread of information... we distribute (leaflets) and then run a series of small meetings to follow up... if it is a small estate... we will do a door-to-door approach and survey.'
>
> Trainer - Secondary Co-op

Table 5.8 Comparison of forms of provision at promotional stage

Form of training	Mentions by LA		Mentions by Agency	
	Number	%	Number	%
Single training sessions	48	86	24	80
A series of training sessions	24	43	16	53
Training course	9	16	14	46
Residential meetings	10	18	5	16
Study visits	21	38	15	50
Other	5	9	3	10
Base	56		30	

Source: *Postal survey of LAs and training agencies*

Training materials

5.19 The most popular topic, amongst the materials which might be used for training at the promotion stage, was tenant participation. The review assessed 47 examples of materials on this topic and found a number which were of a high quality. The largest producer of materials on tenant participation was TPAS but a wide range of other organisations, including six local authorities, also produced training on this topic. There were 18 examples of materials on 'Options for Change' and again many of these were of a high standard. Videos were also seen to be useful by trainers and there were several available on tenant participation or 'Options for Control' topics, although some were out-of-date. There were very few materials available on 'how the council works' which tended to confirm the impression that, although this topic was considered important, it was not well covered in training. There was also little material on problems on estates such as dogs, crime or neighbour disputes.

Other issues

5.20 Few TMOs, or training agencies, produced leaflets or materials in other languages. The research found no external training courses offered in other languages or with interpretation services available, although some training agencies had included interpretation costs in Section 16 grant applications for a few multi-racial estates.

5.21 Creche facilities were sometimes offered at external events and TPAS, for example, always sought to ensure that venues could provide access for people with disabilities. However, creche facilities on estates appeared to be provided much less frequently. Some TMOs had included bids for funding for child-care arrangements in their grant applications but these had not always been successful.

PROVISION AT FEASIBILITY STAGE
Providers and topics

5.22 Twenty-five local authorities and twenty-three training agencies responding to the postal survey said that they were involved in the provision of training at the feasibility stage. As at the promotion stage, the most popular topics mentioned in the postal questionnaires at this stage were awareness of tenant participation, options for control and committee skills (Table 5.9). The similarity in the popularity of topics indicates that there may be a degree of overlap between the promotion and feasibility stages. The 'ideal' model suggested that the most important topics were responsibilities of TMOs, teamwork and practical skills. This difference may be one of terminology rather than of real difference since tenants need to consider options in more depth to learn about responsibilities, and committee skills training may include teamwork and practical skills. The differences in emphasis by providers of training are also interesting. One fifth of the local authority providers specifically mentioned training on estate management boards, while none of the agencies mentioned this. Agencies in contrast emphasised equal opportunities, assertiveness and communication. They were also more likely to stress financial implications and local authority structures.

Table 5.9 **Comparison of most frequently mentioned training topics at feasibility stage**

Topic	Mentions by LA		Mentions by Agency	
	Number	%	Number	%
Awareness of participation	9	39	12	52
Options for control	9	39	11	47
Committee skills	9	39	7	30
Development of EMBs	5	22	-	-
Financial implications of TMOs	5	22	7	30
Local authority structure	4	17	5	22
All aspects of housing	4	17	-	-
Equal opportunities	-	-	7	30
Assertiveness and communications	1	4	5	22
Base	23		23	

Source: *Postal surveys of LAs and training agencies*

Forms of training

5.23 Training agencies responding to the postal questionnaire were more likely than local authorities to mention each form of training (see Table 5.10). Other forms of training mentioned in the in-depth interviews were visits to the local housing office, so that tenants could see functions such as repairs and allocations in operation. In some cases, individual tenants had spent half a day 'shadowing' a local authority officer. External conferences and study visits were stressed as important but most training took place on the estate. Role-play and participative exercises were also mentioned by a number of trainers and most stressed the relevance of practical skills which people could use immediately such as writing letters, producing newsletters, and completing forms. Training agencies seemed to make greater use of overhead projectors than local authorities and ten had produced overhead acetates.

> 'We use overheads as no-one will sit for hours being talked at, you must have changing images, examples, discussion.'
>
> Trainer - Secondary Co-op

Table 5.10 **Comparison of forms of provision at feasibility stage**

	Mentions by LA		Mentions by Agency	
	Number	%	Number	%
Single training sessions	17	68	20	87
A series of training sessions	13	52	19	83
Training course	5	20	11	48
Residential meeting	2	8	4	17
Study visits	11	44	16	70
Other	0	0	0	0
Base	25		23	

Source: *Postal survey of LAs and training agencies. (Respondents could mention more than one form of training.)*

Training materials

5.24 Much of the material suitable for promotion would also be useful for feasibility. There were a number of training materials which gave more detailed information at the feasibility stage on co-operatives (28 examples), but surprisingly few on EMBs (7 examples). There was also a wide range of examples of materials on committee skills. In the in-depth interviews a number of trainers suggested that they would like a greater range of materials for role-play and participative exercises and we felt that more was also needed on specific skills such as giving a presentation, holding a public meeting and campaigning. Lastly, trainers also suggested that there was a need for more videos on skills topics, such as effective meetings and negotiation, which featured tenants.

PROVISION AT DEVELOPMENT STAGE
Providers

5.25 Twenty-three local authorities, responding to the postal questionnaire, said they were involved in providing training at the development stage, compared to 25 local authorities who said that they undertook training at the feasibility stage. Similarly, a slightly smaller number of training agencies were providing training at the development stage (21) compared with the feasibility stage (23). This nevertheless suggests that most authorities and agencies who did feasibility work also did training at the development stage. Half the local authorities said that their own specialist tenant participation staff provided training, a similar level to that at feasibility stage, though a higher level of training and specialist function staff were used. This may be because they were involved in topics such as committee skills and repairs and maintenance training which required specialist knowledge. A higher proportion of outside agencies continued to be used (78%). Training agencies also appeared to increase the use of training and specialist function staff, although they continued to be more likely to use tenants as trainers. Local college courses had been used by some tenants but this appeared to be an under-used resource.

Topics

5.26 The postal survey found a very wide range of topics being covered at development stage. Table 5.11 shows those which were mentioned most frequently. While both local authorities and training agencies stressed committee skills and financial implications at this stage, councils appeared to lay more importance on local authority structures and awareness of tenant participation, than trainers who were more likely to mention assertiveness/communication skills and equal opportunities.

Table 5.11 **Comparison of the most frequently mentioned topics at development stage**

Topic	Mentions by LA		Mentions by Agency	
	Number	%	Number	%
Committee skills	11	52	9	43
Local authority structure	7	33	-	-
Financial implications	7	33	8	38
Development of EMBs	6	28	6	29
Repairs and Maintenance	5	24	5	24
All aspects of housing	5	24	7	33
Awareness of TP	4	19	-	-
Developing TMCs	3	14	6	29
Assertiveness/ communication skills	3	14	5	24
Equal opportunities	1	5	5	24
Base	21		21	

Source: *Postal questionnaires. (Respondents could mention more than one topic.)*

5.27   The most important skills and knowledge at the development stage in the 'ideal' model were policies and procedures, committee work, negotiation skills, staff management and finance. While committee skills, financial implications and various policies and procedures were mentioned in the postal questionnaires, negotiation skills and staff management were not. A quarter of the training agencies mentioned assertiveness/communication skills which could be considered important pre-requisite skills for negotiation and management but the responses from the training providers tend to confirm the impression created by the TMO respondents that these two areas were not given emphasis in training.

Forms of training

5.28   By the development stage local authorities were more likely to mention a series of training sessions and residential meetings as a form of training than previously. Single training sessions, however, remained the most frequently mentioned form of training by local authorities. In contrast, almost all the training agencies saw the predominant form of provision at this stage as a series of training sessions. Training agencies also remained more likely to mention study visits (Table 5.12). Trainers interviewed said that they particularly encouraged tenant contact with other groups through external conferences, study visits and residential weekends during the development stage.

Table 5.12 **Comparison of forms of training at development stage**

Form of training	Mentions by LAs		Mentions by Agency	
	Number	%	Number	%
Single training sessions	17	74	17	81
A series of training sessions	14	61	19	90
Training course	5	22	13	62
Residential meetings	6	26	5	24
Study visits	10	43	14	67
Other	0	0	0	0
Base	23		21	

Source: *Postal surveys of LAs and training agencies. (Respondents could mention more than one form of training.)*

5.29   In the in-depth interviews trainers stressed the need to gear styles and methods to the particular group they were facing. Some participants were willing to do a lot of reading on their own, while others needed someone to go through the material with them. One trainer suggested that formal training sessions might be more suitable where the group was strong and informal sessions were preferred where the group's organisational abilities were weak. Many trainers used flip-charts as their major visual aid and a number gave handouts which could be built up to form a manual.

5.30   Role-play was widely used and most tenants who had experienced this style of learning appeared to enjoy it and find it useful. Trainers have devised a number of impromptu imaginative games and exercises such as using fake money to explain housing finance. 'Learning by doing' was also stressed. Many trainers encouraged tenants to learn the practice of holding meetings, public speaking, producing newsletters and using computers at this stage. Some aimed to have the group operating as a 'shadow' board in the run up to handover, perhaps taking responsibility for some functions and becoming involved in decisions about the estate.

Training materials

5.31 Many trainers used the *Modular Management Agreement* for TMCs (NFHC, 1990) as a basis for training. This was a comprehensive document which sets out optional clauses. It is necessarily legalistic but written in plain English. We felt, however, that this needed to be supplemented by other materials. The TMC development handbook, developed by Hexagon and Chisel training agencies along with Lewisham London Borough (Williams and Swailes, 1991), appeared to be the most comprehensive for TMCs while the book *Joining Forces* produced by PEP (Bell, 1991) was the best material available for potential EMBs.

5.32 Financial skills and knowledge were stressed as important for all committee members and most of the TMOs (78%) responding to the postal survey said that training had been received on budgets, though only half mentioned training on local authority finance. A few individuals had attended local college courses on accounting. Financial control, however, did not appear to be given the prominence that its crucial role would suggest and, although there were some materials, none were considered excellent.

5.33 There was surprisingly little material on specific management functions such as allocations, employment and rent arrears for TMOs. Two examples, produced by CATCH (undated), illustrate what could be done. These were training packs on repairs and caretaking which covered policies, procedures and responsibilities in a very practical way. Negotiation skills were also considered to be important. Half the TMOs responding to this question in the postal survey claimed to have had training on how to negotiate but this was not evident from training programmes and there were very few materials on this topic.

ON-GOING TRAINING
Training needs

5.34 Once a TMO has become established, there may be on-going training needs. There were 49 respondents from the postal questionnaire to TMOs, who had signed a management agreement or taken on management responsibilities. Thirty-one (63%) said that they had received training since becoming established, compared to thirty-three (67%) who had identified training needs. Estate management boards were more likely both to have identified and received training. There was no clear correlation between the age of the TMO and whether training had been received.

Table 5.13 **Comparison of identified training needs and training received by TMOs since becoming established**

	Type and number of TMO			
	TMC	EMB	Total	%
Identified training need	24	9	33	67
No training need	14	2	16	33
Received training	22	9	31	63
No training	16	2	18	37
Base	38	11	49	

Source: *Postal questionnaire to TMOs*

Providers

5.35 Thirteen local authorities and fourteen training agencies responding to the postal questionnaires said that they were involved in the provision of training to established TMOs. This was much smaller than the number of agencies providing training to developing groups, but provision was more likely to be given by specialist local authority tenant participation, technical, financial or legal staff. These types of trainers were mentioned by 69 per cent of authorities, compared to only 46 per cent who mentioned outside agencies. The survey of tenant management organisations also reflected this change in emphasis with 50 per cent mentioning training provision by local authority housing staff compared with 45 per cent who mentioned the housing department as providers during development. However, as Table 5.14 shows, established TMOs had some capacity to provide training themselves: one-in-five had used their own members or their own workers as trainers. It is possible that the postal survey under-represents the training which TMOs provide themselves, since many of the tenants in the in-depth interviews said that they had tried to pass on their skills and knowledge to new committee members. The table also shows that established EMBs were likely to maintain their links with PEP and were less likely to use other training providers.

Table 5.14 **Providers of training for established TMOs**

Training agency	Number of TMOs for whom training provided			
	TMC	EMB	Total	%
Housing department	11	7	18	58
Other LA department	6	1	7	22
PEP	3	7	10	32
TPAS	1	0	1	3
NFHA	2	0	2	6
NFHC	5	0	5	16
Other TMO	1	2	3	10
Own worker	6	1	7	22
Own member	4	3	7	22
Housing Association or Co-operative	2	0	2	6
Other training agency	9	2	11	35
Other	2	0	2	6
Base	22	9	31	

Source: *Postal survey of TMOs*

Topics

5.36 The range of topics covered by established TMOs was as broad as the range during all stages of development as Table 5.15 shows. For most topics the proportion of TMOs receiving training was smaller than those who received training in that topic prior to taking on management responsibilities. However, this may reflect the relative youth of the TMO, or the effectiveness of previous training or experience. The most common topics for tenant management co-ops, in order, were repairs, lettings, book-keeping and the management agreement. The topics most frequently mentioned by estate management boards was the management agreement with negotiating, working as a team, arrears, repairs and budgets ranking equal second place. This different emphasis was likely to be due to more recently established organisations completing negotiations on their agreement and 'settling in' to management.

Table 5.15 **Most frequently mentioned training topics covered by established TMOs**

Topic	Type and number of TMO			
	TMC	EMB	Total	%
Options				
- What a TMC is	6	2	8	26
- How the Council works	2	3	6	19
Skills				
- Effective meetings	6	4	11	35
- Public speaking	3	5	8	26
- Taking minutes	5	5	11	35
- How to negotiate	3	7	10	32
- Identifying training needs	6	0	11	35
- Making decisions	4	5	9	29
- Working as a team	5	7	12	39
- Using a computer	5	4	9	29
Information on housing management				
- Rent collection/arrears	9	0	16	52
- Homelessness	6	4	10	32
- Letting houses	10	6	17	55
- Tenancy agreement	8	6	14	45
- Neighbour disputes	6	5	11	35
- Day to day repairs	14	7	21	68
- Cyclical maintenance	9	4	14	45
- Equal opportunities	8	5	14	45
- Caretaking and cleaning	5	0	10	
- Modernisation/improvement	6	1	13	42
Finance				
- Basic book-keeping	10	3	13	42
- Budgets	6	7	13	42
- Financial control	5	4	9	29
- Finance for TMOs	4	5	10	32
Running a TMO				
- Rules/constitutions	7	5	12	39
- Management agreement	9	8	18	58
- Consulting members	3	5	8	26
- Roles of committee members	7	5	12	58
Base	22	8	31	

Source: *Postal survey of TMOs (respondents could mention multiple topics)*

Forms of training

5.38 The most common forms of training were again single sessions or a series of sessions, with training courses least used. However, from the in-depth interviews it became clear that single sessions were more dominant at this stage. The use of study visits appeared to be considerably less common, although the in-depth interviews revealed that many TMOs had had visits from other groups. More detailed examination of the data revealed that residential meetings and study visits continued to be well used by EMBs, but only one TMC mentioned these forms of training. Video and training materials were also less used, though this may reflect suitability for experienced committee members (Table 5.16).

Table 5.16 **Forms of training received by established TMOs**

Forms of training	Options	Skills	Housing Management	Finance	Running a TMO	Total mentions
Single sessions	12	15	20	18	15	80
Series of sessions	6	7	9	7	8	37
Training course	1	3	6	1	4	15
Residential meeting	3	6	6	3	3	21
Study visit	3	4	3	3	3	16
Video	2	2	3	1	2	10
Reading training material	3	6	5	5	6	25
Other	0	2	1	1	1	5

n = 31

Source: *Postal survey of TMOs*

5.39 Unlike the other stages, local authorities were more likely to mention a series of training sessions as a form of provision at the on-going stage while training agencies were more likely to mention single training sessions. This is likely to reflect the fact that funding for training agency involvement ceases at the end of development and that local authorities with tenant management organisations were taking more responsibility for on-going training. Budgets for training may be included in the management agreement and some councils had co-op sections to provide long-term support and training to TMOs.

5.40 The very different roles of training agencies, once tenant management organisations are established, was also apparent from the in-depth interviews. A number of London-based secondary housing co-ops ran training sessions aimed at both ownership and tenant management co-operatives. The programmes were wide and covered both skills and housing management knowledge. However, knowledge sessions were biased towards the needs of ownership co-ops. A finance course, for example, while covering useful ground for any co-op treasurer, concentrated on Housing Association Grant (HAG) funding and the Housing Corporation's requirements. The agencies reported low attendance from tenant management organisations for any sessions. They tended to see their main role as advisors.

5.41 The Priority Estates Project (PEP) had begun to offer seminars of both one-day and residential courses aimed at groups in development and on-going tenant management organisations. These were held around the country. In 1991 the programme included repairs and capital works, financial control and caretaking. Some colleges also offer tenant training and Northern college, in South Yorkshire, had hosted a number of events for TMOs.

Training materials

5.42 Many of the materials suitable for earlier stages could be used by on-going organisations. New members need basic information about TMOs, new committee members may need committee skills training while more experienced members may wish to explore wider community development options or take on new functions. Four local authorities had produced manuals for use by TMOs. These provided a guide to policies and procedures.

5.43 More information was also needed on monitoring performance. PEP had produced a booklet for staff and board members of EMBs (Chandler, 1991) which aimed to give guidance on the production of useful monitoring information. CDS Liverpool (undated) had produced a workbook for self-monitoring in ownership co-ops and small housing associations which could be adapted for tenant management organisations. There were no training courses or materials on Compulsory Competitive Tendering (CCT) at the time of the research, although several trainers said that they were preparing training on this topic.

5.44   A number of interviewees mentioned that keeping up-to-date with new legislation and policy changes which might affect them was important. Some said that the National Federation of Housing Co-operatives, now defunct, had been a useful source of information on new legislation and sources of training. The National Federation of Housing Associations had no plans to fill this gap. The Department of the Environment had launched a newsletter, produced by CHISEL, which was aimed at potential TMOs and trainers but the gap in provision of information for established TMOs remained.

5.45   Some TMOs may wish to branch into wider areas such as employment initiatives; crime and security; meeting special needs and youth groups. We found little information on these, although some were mentioned in training programmes. However, the in-depth interviews revealed that resourceful committees had found information through such sources as Communities in Business, Community Development Foundation and Community Enterprise units useful in this context.

Table 5.17 **Who received training in established TMOs**

Recipients and subject matter of training	Numbers and Types of TMOs reporting training received		
	TMC	EMB	Total
Options			
- Committee/board members	5	5	10
- Ordinary members	3	2	5
- New members	4	5	9
Skills			
- Committee/board members	9	7	16
- Ordinary members	6	2	8
- New members	3	4	8
Housing Management			
- Committee/board members	11	8	19
- Ordinary members	7	3	10
- New members	3	4	7
Finance			
- Committee/board members	12	7	19
- Ordinary members	7	0	7
- New members	2	1	3
Running a TMO			
- Committee/board members	12	7	19
- Ordinary members	7	1	8
- New members	4	4	8
Base	22	9	31

Source: *Postal survey of TMOs*

Other issues

5.46 Training for established TMOs was also concentrated on committee or board members with housing management, finance and running a TMO the most likely topics (Table 5.17). Training for new members was most commonly given for control options (e.g. what a TMC is, what an EMB is) while ordinary members were most likely to receive training on housing management topics. Co-ops were more likely to provide training for ordinary members while EMBs were more likely to provide training for new members. The in-depth interviews found that some TMOs held sessions for prospective members and several had prepared leaflets, booklets or videos. Lastly, one tenant management co-op insisted that all new members attended a training course.

VIEWS ON THE ROLE OF TRAINING

5.47 Finally, TMOs were asked for their views on the importance training played in their organisation, and on the value for money represented by the training they had experienced. The results are given in Table 5.18. The TMOs are almost unanimous in their positive view about their training experiences. All who expressed a view said that the time spent on training was well spent; only two organisations said money spent offered poor value for money; three organisations said that training was not essential to operating successfully; and five TMOs said that they could have done without training, whereas at least forty had positive views on each question.

Table 5.18 **Tenants' views on training**

View	Numbers and types of TMOs expressing views					
	TMC	PTMC*	EMB	PEMB*	Total	%
Could have done without it	3	1	1	0	5	10
Couldn't have done without it	28	5	10	3	46	90
Total	31	6	11	3	51	100
Essential to operating successfully	30	5	11	3	49	94
Not essential to operating successfully	3	0	0	0	3	6
Total	33	5	11	3	52	100
A waste of time	0	0	0	0	0	0
Time well spent	27	5	11	3	46	100
Total	27	5	11	3	46	100
Good value for money	23	4	10	3	40	95
Poor value for money	1	1	0	0	2	5
Total	24	5	10	3	42	100

n = 52: missing = 14

Note: * PTMC = Potential TMC: PEMB = Potential EMB

Source: *Postal survey of TMOs*

5.48 Local authorities were also asked for their views on the training available. Twenty-seven per cent said it was satisfactory, 26 per cent neither satisfactory nor unsatisfactory and only eight per cent unsatisfactory. Some thought that local authorities themselves should play a greater part in training provision. Other comments were that there needed to be more resources for training (12%) and that training should be more accessible and geared to local needs.

SUMMARY

5.49 It was clear from the postal surveys and interviews that most training for TMOs during development was provided by training agencies, although half the local authority respondents used their own specialist tenant participation staff, often in conjunction with an outside agency. There was also significant use of tenants involved in TMOs as trainers. Tenant management co-operatives had used a wide variety of training providers but estate management boards were closely associated with one national agency (PEP).

5.50 Training during the development process covered a wide variety of topics. At the promotional stage the most frequently mentioned topics were tenant participation, committee skills and options for control. There was good provision of both training courses and training materials on these topics. It was of some concern that some of the earlier EMBs did not appear to have received training on other control options. The major gaps in provision were information on how councils operate, problems on estates and training provision in other languages. Bids in grant applications to the DOE for funding creche provision moreover were not always successful.

5.51 At the feasibility stage the most frequently mentioned topics remained tenant participation, committee skills and options for control. A wider range of forms of provision were used, though single sessions remained the most popular. Trainers suggested that they would like more skills videos featuring tenants. There were few materials on local authority finance and this area appeared to be a major gap in provision.

5.52 The range of topics mentioned at the development stage was very wide. Most trainers appeared to use the Modular Management Agreement as a basis for training but some supplemented this with training on more diverse skills and knowledge. Most TMOs said that they had received training on budgets and finance but this area did not appear to be given prominence in training programmes or materials. Only half the TMOs said they had received training on negotiation skills and less than half had received training on employment law and procedures. Learning by doing and contact with other tenants were stressed as important at this stage.

5.53 Six out of ten fully mature TMOs said that they had received training since becoming established. EMBs were more likely to have received training than TMCs. Provision was more likely to be made by local authority staff and some TMOs used their own staff or members as trainers. The range of topics covered was as broad as during development and many of the training materials used for earlier stages could be used for new members and new committee members. Some training agencies provided training geared towards the needs of established groups.

5.54 Interviewees said that they needed to keep up-to-date with legislation and policy changes and some TMOs wished to expand into wider activities. There appeared to be a shortage of training provision and materials on these issues. A number of interviewees were concerned about Compulsory Competitive Tendering. There was no training or materials on this at the time of the research though a number of trainers said that they were preparing training on this topic.

5.55 Finally, training for TMOs, both before and after establishment, was concentrated on steering group or committee members. Training for new members was most common on 'Options for Control' topics. Some TMOs had produced their own booklets and videos but more could do likewise.

Chapter 6   Staff training

INTRODUCTION

6.1 The skills, knowledge and attitudes of both local authority staff and trainers from outside agencies were found to be an important factor in the development of TMOs. This chapter considers the skills and knowledge needed by local authority staff trainers and TMO workers and examines whether their training needs were being met. The chapter draws on information from the postal surveys, in-depth interviews and a group discussion with local authority participation officers.

6.2 The idea of forming a tenant management organisation may come from a wide range of sources. Half the tenant management organisations responding to the questionnaire said that the first mention of tenant management had come from housing department staff and a further 12 said that another council department or a councillor had first suggested the idea. One quarter specifically mentioned PEP as a source of initial information and a quarter mentioned other training or advice agencies (Table 6.1). However, even where the first suggestion comes from a training agency, this may be because the local authority has taken a strategic decision to develop participation and promote tenant management. Housing staff were also important sources of initial information, advice and support, and were mentioned in this regard by two-thirds of the tenant management organisations, while one-third said that housing staff had provided training during development.

Table 6.1 **Number of TMOs reporting sources of first mention of tenant management**

Source	Type and number of TMO						
	TMC	PTMC	EMB	PEMB	Other	Total	%
Housing Department	19	3	8	2	0	32	52
PEP	2	0	9	5	0	16	26
Other training/advice agency	10	2	0	2	0	14	23
Other TMO	6	1	1	0	0	8	13
Own worker	4	1	2	0	0	7	11
Other LA department	3	0	3	0	0	6	10
Councillors	3	1	2	0	0	6	10
DoE	1	2	1	0	0	4	6
NFHC	3	1	0	0	0	4	6
Voluntary/Charitable Organisation	3	0	0	0	0	3	5
Other	12	1	0	0	0	13	21

n = 62: missing = 4

Source: *Postal survey of TMOs*

LOCAL AUTHORITY STAFF

Skills and knowledge required

6.3 Before staff can provide information support or training they must, themselves, have the relevant skills and knowledge. We identified different skills and knowledge for different levels of staff. Training agencies suggested that senior staff needed to develop a strategic view of tenant participation and understand the implications for the local authority as a whole. A number of agencies also felt that councillors needed knowledge about tenant participation. Some thought that councillors may feel threatened by the development of tenants' groups and tenant management and need training to see such initiatives as an opportunity to be more effective. Throughout the interviews, respondents stressed that the attitude of senior officers and councillors was crucial to the success of tenant management.

> 'The people at the centre... the senior managers (need to) really understand what tenant participation means in terms of staff having to attend meetings.'
>
> Trainer - National Organisation

> 'That's one of the bonuses for (the estate), because ... the council, and the housing department especially, were with us 100 per cent ... We never had no problems at all ... some councils seem to think ... "we're it and you're not" ... that's the impression I get from other people talking, but we've never had that problem.'
>
> Committee member - TMO

6.4 Failure to ensure that staff have training could cause problems. One tenant participation worker felt that despite political commitment by councillors for the development of tenant management, senior officers had been actively obstructive, stalling progress on negotiations for some months. Delays in other authorities were reported by a number of training agencies and tenants simply because key decisions or pieces of information were not given sufficient priority for action.

6.5 Below senior managers it was clear that a wide range of staff may come into contact with a tenant management organisation in their district and that the existence of a TMO will affect a range of housing management functions. Special procedures may need to be developed to cater for a group which is carrying out its own repairs, allocating property, collecting rents and pursuing arrears.

> 'The staff who are going to work with tenants... need training during the process... to help them understand what is happening.'
>
> Trainer - National Agency

> 'Key things for staff are negotiation skills... communications... they need to understand the boundaries between tenants as customers and tenants as representatives. In terms of attitude... it could make their jobs more satisfying.'
>
> Trainer - National Agency

6.6 Knowledge is also needed by non-housing staff. Solicitors will be involved in approving the management agreement and direct service organisations for maintenance and cleansing may be affected. If improvement or environmental work is planned, architects and planners will need skills and knowledge, which they do not always have:

> 'The architects and planners were raw themselves... They were used to having to do a job and going in and doing it... They weren't used to outsiders coming in and saying "hang on, we don't want it like that"... It started to rub a bit.'
>
> Committee member - TMO

6.7   Some staff, such as caretakers, cleaners and wardens were felt to be particularly neglected in terms of developing skills and knowledge about participation. One trainer pointed out that these are front-line staff who are meeting tenants on a daily basis, as the council's representative, and might well be asked questions about plans for tenant management.

6.8   However, in most cases, the key staff involved were tenant participation officers. This was the most common job title, cited by tenant management organisations and local authorities, as the person who had provided information, advice and support. The in-depth interviews and group discussions found that tenant participation workers in local authorities came from a range of different backgrounds. Usually, they had either a community development background and had moved into housing or they started as housing managers and moved into participation work. During the course of the research, however, we did speak to participation workers who had been architects, teachers, councillors, counsellors and tenant activists. From whatever the background, a wide range of knowledge, skills and attitudes were required. As part of the research, we asked a group of thirty tenant participation workers to draw up an ideal key task analysis for someone working with tenants' groups. The results are shown in Figure 6.2. The backgrounds of tenant participation staff often gave them many of the skills and knowledge required. However, few felt that they had begun with all the expertise necessary. Staff with a housing management background felt that they needed to learn community and group development skills while those who had moved from community work needed to learn about housing legislation, policies and practices.

Figure 6.2 **Tenant participation worker - key task analysis**

Duties and responsibilities	Knowledge	Skills	Attitude
* Promote tenant participation	* What tenant participation involves	* Team working	* Commitment to tenant participation
* Ensure equal opportunities	* What tenant management involves	* Communications	* Non-discriminatory
* Promote and support tenant management organisations	* Options for participation and control	* Public speaking	* Non-judgemental
* Promote and support tenants associations	* How the council works	* Assertiveness	* Honesty
* Provide training/support to tenants	* Housing legislation	* Negotiation	* Flexibility
* Provide training support to staff	* Housing finance	* Motivating	* Determined
* Develop tenant participation policies	* Tenancy agreement	* Facilitating	* Optimistic
* Produce newsletters/ reports/tenants handbooks	* Repairs and maintenance	* Listening	* Open to criticism
* Wider community development	* Technical issues	* Counselling	* Self-motivated
* Negotiate tenants demands	* Allocations	* Planning	* Confident
* Involve tenants in capital programme	* Housing benefit	* Time management	* Desire to increase skills/ knowledge
* Carry out administrative work	* Police	* Self-awareness	
* Monitor performance	* Social security	* Administrative skills	
	* Sources of funding	* Dealing with difficult situations	
	* Housing Corp./DoE policies		
	* LA/ HA policies		
	* Equal opportunities		
	* Monitoring performance		
	* Community work		
	* Group work		
	* Counselling		
	* Negotiation		

Provision of training for local authority staff

6.9   The 257 local authority respondents to the postal survey said that they had 32,885 staff employed on housing functions. Forty-five per cent of councils had arranged training on tenant participation, for their staff, in the last twelve months. In total, 3,077 staff (9 per cent) had received some training on tenant participation. In addition, five more local authorities claimed their staff had had training but could not say how many. In most cases, the number of staff in an authority receiving training was small. Half the authorities providing tenant participation training had five staff or less trained in the last twelve months. However, seven authorities claimed that over 100 staff had received training and one metropolitan district said that all 431 staff had received training, on tenant participation though it was not clear whether this had taken place in the last year.

Who received training?

6.10 Staff in metropolitan districts were more likely to have received participation training. Two-thirds of the metropolitan district respondents said that they had provided training compared to half the London boroughs and 41 per cent of district councils. The pattern of staff training, therefore, was similar to that of tenant management initiatives (Table 4.3.), Although district councils appeared more likely to have trained staff than taken steps to develop a TMO. Despite this interest in staff training, interviewees stressed that considerably more training was required.

> 'Ordinary... housing management staff are not going to know anything about co-ops at all unless the council does something. If the council doesn't do anything... the lack of training is a big disadvantage.'
>
> Trainer - National Agency

6.11 Table 6.3 suggests that where training on participation had taken place, the majority of authorities had provided training for senior housing officers and generic housing staff. Fewer councils had provided training for junior housing staff such as clerical staff and receptionists (23%). Where this training had been provided the average number of staff trained was high. Only 19 (16%) authorities provided training for specialist housing staff and only a third (38 authorities) provided training for specialist tenant participation officers. However, not all authorities had specialist participation staff so the low total does not necessarily mean that many tenant participation officers were not receiving training.

Table 6.3 **Type of staff receiving tenant participation training in past year**

Type of staff	Local Authorities providing training		Mean number of staff trained
	No.	%	
Senior Housing Officials	75	65	6.1
Specialist Tenant Participation Staff	38	32	2.2
Specialist Technical/Financial/Legal Staff	19	16	9.9
Generic Housing Officers	74	64	14.9
Junior Housing Staff	26	23	16.6
Other Staff	17	15	7.0

n = 115

Source: *Postal survey of LAs*

Providers

6.12 The most common providers of tenant participation training to local authority staff were the national agencies, TPAS and PEP, who between them provided half the training events as Table 6.4 shows. Twenty-one per cent of events were organised by local authorities' own staff and the remainders of the events (29%) were organised by a wide range of bodies from national agencies such as the Institute of Housing or the NFHA, to polytechnics and colleges or secondary agencies, such as Banks of the Wear Housing Association or CHS (North West), which operated on a regional basis.

Table 6.4 **Providers of training to staff by main topic**

Topic	PEP	TPAS	Own staff	IoH	ACTAC	BOW	Other	Total
Tenant participation	8	35	11	6	3	3	11	77
Options for control	20	7	5	1	-	1	9	43
EMBs	10	1	4	1	-	-	1	17
Tenants' Associations	-	5	5	-	2	-	4	16
Customer care	-	1	6	2	-	-	6	15
General conferences	1	5	-	2	-	-	1	9
Other	9	17	18	1	3	5	6	59
Total	48	71	49	13	8	9	38	236

n = 115

Source: *Postal survey of LAs*

Topics

6.13 The most common topic for training was general tenant participation, with TPAS providing almost half the training on this topic. Options for control and training on Estate Management Boards, in particular, were the next most popular topics with half of these provided by PEP. Most of the training on promoting tenants' associations was provided by TPAS or local authorities' own staff, while customer care courses were run by local authority staff and a range of other organisations. There was a very wide range of other topics, often on very narrowly focused issues such as grants for tenant participation and Estate Action. Much of the provision of staff training on participation was of a general and introductory nature. Staff may have attended national or regional external events on tenant participation, options for control or EMBs. Some training was also provided in-house by agencies as part of a consultancy.

> 'They (local authority) have asked us to train all their front-line staff in tenant participation. We see officer training as an integral part of any of the services we offer.'
>
> Trainer - Secondary Co-op

6.14 However, detailed training, providing the skills and knowledge to help staff work with tenant management organisations, appeared to be rare. Most staff we spoke to, as part of the research, appeared to learn 'on the job' through trial and error rather than through formal training events. The resultant lack of skills and knowledge can cause problems for tenant management organisations both during development and after they have become established. Staff turnover and re-organisations could also cause problems. One long-established co-op had 'suffered' four re-organisations and found teething problems each time. Typical comments were:

> 'What good is training tenants, who then have to go and talk to staff, if the staff don't have a clue... it then takes months... while it goes in and out of the machinery. The tenants get fed-up.'
>
> Trainer - National Agency

> 'They decided to re-roof the properties but did not consult with tenants... when legal action is taken for rent arrears they need to call the co-op to give proofs, it doesn't always happen... they ignore the management agreement.'
>
> Committee Member - TMC

Specialist tenant participation workers

6.15 Specialist tenant participation workers met their training needs in a variety of ways. Educational courses such as a Diploma in Housing and Certificate in Community Work were mentioned in the group discussion and by individual interviewees but neither were thought to provide all the skills and knowledge required, since both types of course aimed to provide a broad background rather than specialist training. The new National Certificate in Tenant Participation was mentioned by several tenant participation staff as a possibly useful course - but this only began in January 1992 and no-one we interviewed had experience of it. One-day seminars run by TPAS, PEP and the Institute of Housing on a range of topics were thought to be useful. However, some staff commented that those on participation and options for control were too basic for their particular needs.

6.16 In fact, overall, skills and knowledge were generally learned on the job, or through reading. New ideas were keenly sought through informal networks and study visits. TPAS held Tenant Participation Workers' Groups regionally on a quarterly basis, and these seemed to be well-attended. The content of sessions was planned by the participants at the previous meeting. One such event, attended during the course of the research, covered training needs, Housing Corporation tenant participation strategies and 'Independence' clauses for TP workers' contracts. Participants appeared to value the exchange of ideas and the opportunity to 'stand back and think', as well as meeting new contacts.

TRAINING AGENCY STAFF
Skills and knowledge

6.17 The skills and knowledge required by workers supporting tenants developing tenant management organisations are similar to those required by local authority tenant participation workers but trainers felt that they needed more in-depth knowledge about TMOs. Ideally, the trainer would have all the skills and knowledge which tenants would require to develop a TMO. A summary of the tasks is given in Figure 6.5.

> 'You have to know what you're talking about... the differences between TMCs and EMBs and get that information over... You have to have enough skill to build up the tenants' confidence... to empower them... There also needs to be an overview of local authorities... to help them enter this world... There's a legal side too.'
>
> Trainer - National Agency

> 'Skills as a trainer... good administrative skills... tact and diplomacy... finance skills are important.'
>
> Trainer - Secondary Co-op

Figure 6.5 **Trainer of Co-op/EMB - key tasks analysis**

Duties and responsibilities	Knowledge	Skills	Attitudes
* Promote tenant participation * Promote tenant management * Identify tenants' priorities * Develop training programmes to suit tenants' needs * Work in partnership with the local authority * Identify other trainers and courses required and co-ordinate programme * Help tenants to develop practical skills * Work with office bearers to develop specific skills and knowledge * Work with tenants' group to develop team and committee skills * Provide training on: TMO responsibilities, * TMO policies, rules and constitutions, * Section 16 grant regime, * TMO finance * Financial control * Employment of staff, * Office procedures, * Housing management, * Housing legislation, * Repairs and maintenance * Negotiation skills, * Equal opportunities	* What TP involves * What TMOs involve * How the council works * Housing legislation * Housing finance * Housing management * How to identify training * Training methods * Organising meetings * Producing newsletters * Public speaking * Rules and constitution * Committee work * Management agreement * TMO policies * Section 16 grants * TMO finance * Financial control * Recruitment * Employment law * Staff management * Office procedures * Repairs and maintenance * Caretaking * Evaluating training * Performance monitoring	* Communication * Public speaking * Team building * Assertiveness * Negotiation * Motivating * Facilitating * Listening * Counselling * Planning * Time-management * Self-awareness * Administrative skills * Dealing with difficult situations * Financial skills * Interviewing * Computer skills	* Commitment to tenant participation * Positive view of TMOs * Non-discriminatory * Non-judgemental * Honesty * Flexibility * Self-motivated * Determined * Confident * Desire to increase skills and knowledge * Importance of good performance * Importance of independent viewpoint

6.18 Many felt that it was not possible for one person to be expert in all the skills and knowledge required to develop a TMO. A number of trainers said that they would carry out the core of the work but would bring other people in to deal with specific parts of the training such as repairs and technical issues. It was thought useful for an organisation to have people from different backgrounds, to provide complementary skills and knowledge.

> 'There are a lot of people coming from estate-based tenant support work... they have promotional and development skills... People coming from the co-op background have management committee, organisational skills.'
>
> Trainer - Secondary Co-op

6.19 Most of the trainers interviewed had backgrounds in community projects, including welfare rights and legal advice, and many also had been involved in ownership co-ops. Some had come from an education or training background. Few had worked in local authorities. A criticism made by several local authority officers was that many agency trainers lacked an understanding of how councils work. There was a further criticism that some trainers were inexperienced and unable to answer tenants' questions. In some cases, this was due to the development of new models but in a number of cases, trainers were working with their first TMO. One of the difficulties was that, until recently, few councils had developed tenant management organisations and the pool of experienced workers was small. Most workers had learnt on the job, a process that was resented by tenants who felt frustrated that there was no-one to answer their queries. A number of trainers admitted that this had caused problems. This problem was decreasing as the 'pool' of experienced trainers grew but training needs remained.

> 'They are not very good at working with the local authority because they don't know how (it) works... they also lack any management experience.'
>
> Local Authority Officer

> 'I think we met their training needs up to the end of year one but then... they knew as much as I knew. They needed an advanced level... the expertise wasn't there.'
>
> Trainer - National Agency

Provision of training for trainers

6.20 Some trainers felt that the pressure of work, and the need to earn income, meant that there was inadequate time available for developing skills and knowledge 'off the job'. A few trainers said that they had never had training on areas such as skills development and felt unable to teach skills. Most of the agencies were small, half employed less than 20 staff and four-fifths had seven staff or fewer, involved in providing training. It may, therefore, be difficult for staff to spend time on training, unless adequate provision for this is made in funding.

6.21 A number of agencies supported the Tenant Management Training Group, paying a fee for each individual member of staff per year. This operated in a similar way to the Tenant Participation Workers' Groups and was serviced by PEP. Meetings took place bi-monthly and were a combination of committee meetings, to discuss items of common interest and training sessions with invited speakers. However, some trainers told us that, in the past, established agencies had been much more willing to share information and materials with new organisations, but that the competitive nature of the Section 16 regime which encouraged tenants to shop around meant that there was less 'co-operative spirit'. Agencies were said to be unwilling to share their 'bread and butter' work. There was direct evidence of this in the research as several agencies refused to provide examples of materials for the research evaluation.

6.22 A few trainers felt that their organisations were good at organising in-house training to meet specific needs and felt that this was a cost-effective way of providing training.

> 'I want to be better-informed about how Estate Action works, so we would employ somebody to come in and do an afternoon session for us, which only cost £232 for three staff members.'
>
> Trainer - Secondary co-op

6.23 There were criticisms, however, that the hourly rates which agencies negotiated with the Department of the Environment did not make sufficient allowance, either in time or in finance, for training for staff. Several trainers said that they were studying for qualifications, such as the Institute of Housing professional qualification, in their own (limited) spare time. The National Certificate in Tenant Participation was seen as a good base for new trainers, particularly tenants who wished to enter training as a career, but the need for on-going training, keeping up to date with knowledge and enhancing skills was stressed.

TMO WORKERS
Skills and knowledge

6.24 A final important group of staff who need skills and knowledge are the people who work for TMOs. Some tenant management organisations employed a worker during their development process to act as an administrator. Others employed staff to carry out functions once the TMO became established. In Estate Management Boards the staff were often seconded from the local authority to work with the TMO. The detailed job descriptions of such staff were found to vary widely and depended on the number of staff employed, the functions the TMO was responsible for and the split between office bearers and staff responsibilities. In some TMOs the staff carried out many office-bearers' delegated responsibilities and took minutes at committee meetings, managed the finances, produced newsletters and arranged meetings. It was not possible, as a result to draw up a job description which would fit all staff. Some workers felt that they had a responsibility to provide training for TMO members, such as giving new members information about the TMO, helping new office bearers to learn the skills and knowledge they needed and ensuring that existing committee members were kept up-to-date. Others felt that they attempted to teach their employers. One did not think that training the committee members was necessary and suggested that running the TMO was all common sense! Six of the seven TMO workers had local authority backgrounds, one as a Councillor and five as staff. They had gained relevant skills and knowledge of housing management as a result of this. The seventh worker had a background as an administrator in a private sector small business and brought accounting, secretarial and administrative skills to the post.

Provision of training

6.25 Provision of training for TMO workers varied. Some TMOs positively encouraged staff training and the worker regularly attended training courses. However, in two TMOs, the workers had never visited another TMO or met other TMO workers. Attitudes towards training by the workers also varied. One worker, someone who did not think that the TMO committee needed any training, did not think that workers with previous housing experience needed any training either, while another felt considerable need for training but felt unable to spare the time to attend courses.

6.26 Experience from Glasgow tenant management organisations indicates that there may be considerable demand from TMO staff for training provision. A survey carried out in Scotland on training needs (Scott, 1993) found that TMO staff had identified a wide range of needs for both skills and knowledge and often felt isolated. The survey also found that most TMOs had small or no budgets for staff training.

SUMMARY

6.27 The research found that half the TMOs responding to the questionnaire said that the first mention of tenant management had come from their local authority housing department. Housing staff were also an important source of initial information and support, mentioned by two-thirds of TMOs. It is, therefore, important that housing staff have the relevant skills and knowledge to provide support to TMOs.

6.28 Skills and knowledge are required by a wide range of people in a local authority. The research identified training needs for senior staff, councillors, specialist function staff, including architects and solicitors, and front-line staff such as caretakers and wardens. However, in most cases the key staff involved were tenant participation officers.

6.29 Forty-five per cent of local authorities responding to the postal questionnaire said that some staff had received training on tenant participation in the previous twelve months. In total, 9 per cent of staff employed on housing functions had received training in the previous year. The staff most likely to receive training were senior housing officers and generic housing staff. Only 19 authorities (16%) provided training for specialist technical, financial or legal staff.

6.30   It was clear, from the in-depth interviews, that much of this training was of a general and introductory nature. Most specialist tenant participation staff appeared to learn 'on the job'. Networks, such as the Tenant Participation Workers' Groups organised by TPAS, were valued and many learnt by reading. Educational courses such as a Diploma in Housing or a Certificate in Community Work were felt to be useful in providing basic skills and knowledge. The new National Certificate in Tenant Participation was mentioned by several officers as a potentially useful course, but no-one had experienced it.

6.31   Comments made by trainers and tenants, indicated that training for local authority staff was inadequate in many cases. The lack of skills and knowledge had, in some cases, resulted in delays and problems during the development process and frustration and difficulties for established TMOs. Some interviewees suggested that staff training should be an integral part of the development process and sessions for staff should proceed in parallel with tenant training.

6.32   The skills and knowledge required by trainers in training agencies were found to be similar to those required by local authority staff but trainers needed an in-depth knowledge of TMOs. Like tenant participation officers, most had learnt 'on the job', and many felt that the pressure of work left inadequate time for training. Networks such as the Tenant Management Training Group, serviced by PEP were favoured forms of learning new ideas though some agencies ran in-house training sessions for their staff.

6.33   A final group of staff were the workers employed by TMOs. Several of these had previously worked in local authorities, but others had no previous experience of council or TMO work. Training provision also varied. Some TMOs encouraged staff training while others made little provision. Some workers appeared to be very isolated, with little contact with workers in other TMOs.

The Case Studies

Chapter 7 Case study contexts

BACKGROUND

7.1 In order to evaluate the role of training, and the impact of other factors, six tenant management organisations were selected for more detailed study. This chapter outlines the characteristics of the sample and identifies a range of factors in the case studies which may influence the effectiveness of training. These factors include the origins of the TMOs, the motivations of participants and the physical and socio-economic characteristics of the area. The skills and knowledge which tenants will require may vary, depending on the functions which the TMO intends to manage and whether the tenants aim to carry out operational tasks themselves, or employ staff. Finally, the training can be affected by the skills and knowledge of trainers who work with the TMO, local authority officers and the existing skills and knowledge of the TMO members. These factors are explored in turn, while a more detailed description of the history of the case study organisations is given in Appendix 4.

CHARACTERISTICS

7.2 The case studies were chosen to represent a range of different factors - including type of TMO; number of dwellings; type and age of property; different local authorities and trainers. In this way we hoped to cover a range of structures, tasks, people and environments. Due to the difficulties of evaluating training retrospectively, the research concentrated on tenant management organisations which had been developed over the previous four years. However, we included one co-operative which had been established for a several years, to provide an assessment of the long-term effects of training and an indication of on-going training needs. Table 7.1 shows the key characteristics of the case study organisations.

7.3 The case studies included four tenant management co-operatives and two estate management boards. Three of the co-operatives were close to the average size of 156 dwellings found in the postal survey and one was substantially smaller. The established EMB was smaller than the average size of 966 dwellings while the EMB still in the development stage was substantially larger. The property types ranged from a tower-block to pre-fabricated bungalows and ranged in age from dwellings built in the 1930s to those completed at the end of the 1970s. Three were in London while the remainder were in other regions of England. Each case-study was assisted and supported by a different training agency. In order to protect anonymity these case studies have been given alternative names in this report.

ORIGINS

7.4 Previous studies (Birchall, 1988; McCafferty and Riley, 1989) have suggested that TMOs may be formed by the landlord as a 'shell' TMO in empty property or formed from the 'grassroots' as a result of tenant pressure. In practice, these are not necessarily mutually exclusive categories. 'Tower' TMO, the smallest and longest-established of the case studies, was a classic shell co-operative which originated when the landlord decided to promote a TMC while a tower block was being refurbished. At the other extreme 'Bungalow' TMO was the closest to a grassroots co-operative. In this TMO tenant activists had heard about tenant management and took the initiative to survey residents and approach the council. 'Hilltop' TMO was also close to the grassroots' model, although the suggestion that tenants consider tenant management originally came from a local authority officer. After visiting several established co-operatives, the tenants felt that they could take over management.

> 'I think it was the turning point when we saw what they were doing ... they were no different from us and if they could do it, we felt we could do it.'
>
> Committee member - TMO

7.5 The other three organisations lay somewhere on the continuum between a shell TMO and a grass-roots TMO. In 'World' TMO, the local authority already had well-developed tenant participation structures and the estate had an advisory management board. Both the council and tenants became interested in tenant management after attending a seminar on the then new idea of estate management boards. In 'Family' TMO the impetus seemed to have come from several quarters with both the council and residents looking for ways to improve the estate. In this case a national agency provided the catalyst by inviting authorities to participate in pilot projects to develop EMBs. An external agency also played a major role in 'Five Streets' TMO. The area had been a pilot project for a neighbourhood initiative and a consultant had been working with a group of residents. In the course of this the tenants visited a TMC and expressed an interest in pursuing this option. The consultant helped the group to apply for funding.

7.6 This outline of the origins of the case study organisations shows that, in practice, the idea to consider tenant management may come from a variety of sources. In each case study there was a small group of people, including tenants, local authority officers or councillors who had heard about tenant management and decided to pursue this option. Visits to established TMOs played an important part in the process and attending external seminars helped some. Lastly, external agencies also provided a catalyst for the decision.

Table 7.1 **Characteristics of the case study TMOs**

Characteristics	Tower	Hilltop	Five Streets	Bungalow	Family	World
Type of TMO	TMC	TMC	TMC	TMC	EMB	EMB
Stage of development	Ongoing	Development	Development	Ongoing	Ongoing	Development
Date training began	1984	1988	1988	1988	1988	1989
No. of dwellings	78	152	179	186	810	1685
Type of property	Flats	Maisonettes	Mixed	Bungalows	Houses	Flats
Age of property	1960s	1950s	1930s	1940s	1950s	1970s
Type of agency	Regional Secondary	Regional Secondary	Mixed Independent	Local Secondary	National Agency	Local Authority

MOTIVATION

7.7 The discussion above explains **how** the case-study TMOs began but not **why**. The *Review of Co-ops* report (DoE, 1989) suggested that a key factor in the success of a TMO was that tenants were committed. The development of a TMO requires considerable time and effort by both tenants and the local authority. There are a variety of reasons for forming a TMO and motivations may vary between participants. Government policy had clearly played a part in the decision making process. Chapter 4 indicated that there was a considerable increase in interest in TMOs in the late 1980s and four of the case studies began considering tenant management in 1988, the last began in 1989. In four of these cases the 1988 Housing Act, which gave tenants the right to change their landlord and enabled government to consider transferring ownership to a Housing Action Trust, was a significant factor for some tenants. In each case study, some tenants mentioned their fears of being taken over by a private landlord and their desire to remain as public sector tenants.

7.8 The government's Estate Action programme also played a part, particularly in giving motivations to local authority officers to pursue tenant management. Under the Estate Action programme, which was set up in 1986, local authorities could bid for supplementary credit approvals, in other words permission to borrow funds for improvements on specific estates. However, it was a condition of funding that the local authority involved tenants in this process and set up local offices. In three of the six case studies the councils' decision to support the development of a TMO was explicitly linked to a bid for Estate Action loan approval. The desire to improve their estate was also a key factor for many tenants. All six case study areas were in need of major repair and maintenance works. In Tower TMO, the council carried out refurbishment prior to letting the properties. In four of the other areas, modernisation and environmental improvements were carried out in parallel with the development of a TMO and the TMO steering groups participated in decisions about the modernisation as well as training to take over management responsibilities.

> 'Seeing the houses being improved ... wouldn't have happened if we hadn't got involved, because you need the tenant participation to get the allocation money from the government and I think it gave us a lift from the start to know it was going to happen.'
>
> Board member - TMO

7.9 A motivating factor, mentioned by some tenants, was the desire for better services and greater control over the estate in the long-term. This may be important because many estates, as Chapter 4 has shown, enjoy a great deal of tenant participation in modernisation but tenants' involvement may decline once the work is completed. In several of the case study TMOs, the tenants felt that they had received poor services, particularly for repairs, and that they could do better themselves.

> 'We figure that no matter how badly we do, we can do better than the council.'
>
> Board member - TMO

7.10 A final factor, for both landlords and tenants, was a general desire to increase participation. Three of the six councils had long-standing and well-developed tenant participation structures, with regular meetings between tenants' associations and the council. In a fourth area, although tenant participation was not well-developed, the estate had had a neighbourhood project for several years. All the case study areas except Tower TMO, had existing tenants' associations and, in four, the committee members of the tenants' association became office bearers in the steering groups of the TMO.

7.11 However, there was evidence of conflicting views about the value of tenant management. In three of the case studies there were some participants who had negative views of tenant management, which was seen as a form of privatisation. General commitment to high levels of tenant participation did not ensure that the council would be highly supportive of tenant management, which was seen as a loss of council control by some councillors and officers. Access to Estate Action was also a source of conflict in three areas, where some interviewees stated that there was resentment of the funding and support for particular estates from tenants in other parts of the district.

Delays and problems

7.12 Conflicting views could cause delays and problems and there was evidence of this in the case study TMOs. In one case study, there appeared to be delays because local authority officers had not provided vital information, despite a council wish to develop tenant management. In contrast, in another area some interviewees felt that staff were not committed because the council had an ambivalent attitude.

> 'If an important officer thinks it is a good idea and it will do their career a bit of good, things will move quickly. But, if no-one feels they will get any Brownie points out of the idea then it dies a death.'
>
> Trainer - Secondary Co-op

7.13 The development time, from the decision to consider tenant management to approval of the management agreement ranged from under two years to over four years. All of the six TMOs were the first tenant management organisations to be developed in their local authority area and, to some extent, the slow progress of some was due to lack of knowledge on the part of their council about what would be required and how to deal with it. This lack of knowledge could persist even after the TMO became established and both trainers and co-op officers stressed the need for wider officer training.

> 'The housing officers ... even the neighbourhood managers don't really know what the co-op's about. They don't really know the ideals behind (it) and what its function is, and a lot more emphasis could have been given in staff training ... I could ring up a new department within the council and they wouldn't be aware that we even existed or what the idea of a co-op is.'
>
> Estate manager - TMO

7.14 Both World TMO and Hilltop TMO felt that they had suffered from changes in key local authority support personnel. Clearly, it is not possible to guarantee that key staff will not be promoted or change employment but lack of wider training may mean that replacements are not found quickly. Wider training, to provide knowledge about TMOs, may also reduce the conflicting motivations of councillors and local authority staff by overcoming fears about the role of TMOs. There was no doubt that delays caused frustration, loss of morale and a decline in motivation to steering groups affected. The low morale had caused World TMO in particular, to experience high turnover in steering group members, which meant that training for new members had to take place during the development process and, in Bungalow TMO, two of the key office bearers resigned towards the end of the development stage and the replacements did not, therefore, benefit from the training.

PHYSICAL AND SOCIO-ECONOMIC FACTORS

7.15 The purpose of training for tenant management is to enable tenants to run organisations which carry out a range of housing functions. One view of the ultimate outcome and success of training can be measured by examining the performance of the organisation as a manager of housing. There are a range of key indicators of performance such as rent arrears levels, repairs targets, controlling voids and tenant satisfaction (Centre for Housing Research, 1989). However, measures of performance must take the context in which the organisation operates into account. If there is high unemployment, it will be more difficult to keep arrears low and if the properties are in poor condition, it will be more difficult to deliver an effective maintenance service. Research also suggests that tenant satisfaction with services is influenced by their views about their economic and physical environments (Scott and Kintrea, 1991).

These factors also interact and there is evidence from studies of how allocation policies operate that poorer households tend to live in less popular estates (Clapham and Kintrea, 1985).

7.16 The environmental survey described in Appendix 1, assessed observable external repair and neighbourhood problems such as litter, graffiti, dogs and parking difficulties. Each factor was assessed at three points on each estate and 'pointed' on a scale from 0 to 10 with 10 indicating the worst problems, to provide a ranking out of 30 for each element. These were then totalled to provide an overall ranking of the environments in our case studies. The results are shown in Table 7.2. The percentage of tenants on Housing Benefit was taken as a proxy for socio-economic problems and tenancy records were used, where possible, to assess social the types of household and ethnic mix in the area.

Table 7.2 Assessment of environmental and socio-economic problems on case studies estates

	Tower	Hilltop	Five Streets	Bungalow	Family	World
Roof	0	0	2	7	5	0
Gutters	0	0	2	7	5	0
Wall finish	0	0	2	4	5	16
External windows	0	0	12	12	5	14
Paintwork	0	0	9	10	5	17
Fences	0	0	7	9	5	5
Paths	0	0	15	12	20	25
Traffic management	0	10	0	5	10	15
Parking	0	5	0	10	0	10
Vacant sites	0	5	20	0	5	0
Public open spaces	0	5	20	0	0	10
Street improvements	0	0	30	5	20	20
Play areas	0	5	20	0	10	0
Litter	0	2	15	2	2	12
Graffiti	0	0	12	0	2	15
Vandalism	0	2	15	0	2	15
Unkempt gardens	0	5	9	7	4	0
Vacant properties	0	0	20	0	5	10
Loose dogs	0	0	12	2	2	10
Total	0	39	207	100	112	194
% of Tenants on Housing Benefit	43	M	c75	60	74	c75

Notes: Each factor may score 0-30 with 0 = no problems and 30 = worst problems

M = Missing
c = estimate by local authority

Tower TMO environment

7.17 The study found that the environment in which the TMOs were operating varied considerably. 'Tower' TMO had no physical problems and the only complaint was about young couples courting on a public bench. The tenants were largely mature households and either working or retired. The properties had been fully modernised in the mid-1980s and further upgrading had been carried out since. There was an appearance of prosperity far removed from run-down council estates and less than half the households (43%) were receiving Housing Benefit.

> 'We are not on a council estate. We are amongst private property and in our own grounds ... A lot of people don't recognise this as council.'
>
> Co-op worker - TMO

Hilltop TMO environment

7.18 The properties in Hilltop TMO had recently been extensively modernised and considerable environmental improvements had been carried out, but some problems remained. There appeared to be a wide variety of age groups and the estate included a small number of ethnic minority households. The impression was of a poor community with a high proportion of Housing Benefit recipients and a small proportion of wage earners. Residents were concerned about vandalism, unruly children and car-parking. There were complaints about the amount of natural light in some properties which were described as being 'like dungeons'. Generally, tenants were happy with the external work but there were a number of unkempt gardens, where elderly tenants could not cope.

> 'It's like a rain forest now.'
>
> Ordinary tenant - TMO

Bungalow TMO environment

7.19 The general area in Bungalow TMO was pleasant, with well-kept gardens. Many of the tenants were elderly and there were few children. There were parking problems but the major environmental blight was the external appearance of some of the properties. An external painting programme had improved some properties but a considerable number were still to be done and had peeling paintwork. Some roofs and gutters also required attention as did fences and gates. The properties had not been modernised and most had only a single coal fire and original kitchen and bathroom fittings although some residents had carried out their own improvements. New lets tended to be made to families from the 'homeless' list. This had introduced a few ethnic minority households but there were some conflicts between older established residents and younger households with children.

Family TMO environment

7.20 Family TMO had also had major modernisation work which was in its final stages at the time of the research. Environmental work in the first phase of the programme however, was considerably more extensive than later phases, and this was a matter of some resentment to the residents of those areas where the project was being completed. The condition of the estate was generally good but there was still evidence of litter and unkempt gardens. Residents were particularly concerned about traffic management in the area as several children had died due to accidents caused by speeding cars. The estate was populated predominantly by families. One-third of residents were aged under 18, over half were aged between 18 and 65 and the remaining 10 per cent were pensioners. The number of ethnic minority households was very small and unemployment on the estate was high (77%) as was the number of households (74%) receiving Housing Benefit.

World TMO environment

7.21 World TMO was a large estate, consisting mainly of blocks of flats and maisonettes with deck access and linkways. The linkways were being demolished and replaced with concierge entrances and glazed emergency stairwells. The blocks were built in hexagons, overlooking grassed areas with childrens play spaces and pedestrian routes. An estate road ran round the outside of the estate and there was a multi-storey car park. Externally the environment was reasonably attractive. There was little graffiti, although several of the blocks had street-art murals. Inside unimproved blocks, however, the common areas were dark, rubbish strewn, heavily covered in graffiti and the results of many fires were still evident. Residents said that the modernised blocks were considerably better and that security had improved. Crime levels were also said to have reduced following the establishment of a small police station on the estate. Turnover of tenants was high and, although the number of void properties had been reduced, vacant properties were noticeable. The area was racially mixed with a wide range of ethnic backgrounds represented. There was a wide range of households, from young single people to very elderly households and a large number of children. It was estimated that 75 per cent of households received housing benefit, and rent arrears were very high. The views of ordinary residents also reflected concerns about socio-economic problems.

> 'There are psychiatric problems, alcohol problems which are not dealt with. There are people picking through dustbins.'
>
> Ordinary Resident - TMO

Five Streets TMO environment

7.22   The worst environment, however, was found in Five Streets TMO. This estate consisted mainly of a mixture of houses and flats which were partially-modernised in the mid-1970s with central heating being installed in the 1980s. Whilst externally, properties appeared to be in reasonable condition, apart from some attention needed to windows and external paintwork, internally, tenants complained of bulging walls and dampness. Gardens on the estate had been fenced recently but there was still a large area of wasteland which had problems with unauthorised tipping and fires. There were also a number of voids, which gave some streets an abandoned look. The area was severely economically deprived and between 70 and 80 per cent of households were on Housing Benefit. The majority of families and young people were unemployed or on employment training schemes. It was obviously a close-knit community with several generations of some families living there. A few years ago there were riots on the estate which caused considerable damage and this was still evident at the time of the research. Crime was said to be a major problem but the police have recently established a local office on the estate and carried out foot patrols.

> 'Everyone is on the dole, nothing to occupy them'
>
> 'Kids running about in cars'
>
> 'No play scheme, no park'
>
> 'They call us scum'
>
> Ordinary residents - TMO Group interview

STRUCTURE AND TASKS
Functions

7.23   The skills and knowledge needed by TMO committee members may be influenced by the structure of the organisation and the functions it carries out. Three of the case studies were not fully established at the time of the study, although two had completed their development and were awaiting approval of their management agreement. Both these TMOs had taken over responsibility for repairs reporting and one was interviewing applicants. The third organisation still had some way to go in drawing up policies and negotiating the management agreement. As a result, it was not possible to obtain complete information for all six case studies and the analysis of the structure and tasks is based on both the existing situation and the TMOs' plans for the future (Table 7.3).

Table 7.3 **Comparison of functions managed (or planned to manage) in TMO case studies**

Function	Tower	Hilltop	Five Streets	Bungalow	Family	World
Allocations policy	TMO	LA	TMO	LA	LA	LA
Letting houses	TMO	Mix	TMO	TMO	TMO	TMO
Day-to-day repairs	TMO	TMO	TMO	TMO	TMO	TMO
Cyclical repairs	TMO	TMO	TMO	TMO	TMO	TMO
Improvement/modernisation	TMO	LA	LA	Mix	TMO	TMO
Caretaking	TMO	TMO	LA	LA	TMO	TMO
Cleansing	TMO	TMO	LA	LA	TMO	TMO
Open space maintenance	TMO	TMO	LA	LA	TMO	TMO
Rent collection	TMO	LA	LA	TMO	TMO	TMO
Rent arrears recovery	TMO	LA	LA	TMO	TMO	LA
Neighbour disputes	TMO	TMO	Mix	TMO	TMO	TMO
Drawing up tenancy conditions	LA	LA	LA	LA	LA	LA
Enforcing tenancy conditions	TMO	Mix	LA	TMO	TMO	TMO
Employment of staff	TMO	TMO	LA	TMO	TMO	TMO
Control of budget	TMO	TMO	TMO	TMO	TMO	TMO
Other						

Tasks

7.24 Although the list of functions was broadly similar, there was considerable variation between the case studies in how these were carried out. Each organisation had negotiated policies and practice with its own council and whilst some had considerable autonomy, others were required to operate within more narrowly defined limits. For example, in one TMO, allocations were made by staff according to the council's allocation policy and the TMO committee play no role in this. However, in most of the TMOs, the council nominated three or four applicants when a property became vacant and prospective tenants were interviewed by a sub-committee. Even here there were variations in policy and practice. One TMO had become involved in a dispute with the council over its rejection of a disabled applicant, on the grounds that the vacant property was unsuitable for them, while in another two the allocation criteria explicitly set out housing need, suitability of property and commitment to co-operative principles as factors to be taken into account.

Staff structure

7.25 The skills and knowledge required within the TMO may also depend on whether the TMO has staff. Family TMO, the largest established case study, was responsible for the activities of ten local office staff and board members did not carry out any operational tasks themselves. In fact, the board only made decisions on action to be taken on tenants in arrears, tenancy matters as well as agreeing the approved list of contractors for repairs. The degree of operational involvement did not, however, appear to be dependent on size. The smallest case study, Tower TMO, employed a part-time estate manager and a caretaker to carry out most of their operational tasks. Committee members did however carry out some tasks themselves. Completed repairs, for example, might be inspected by the estate manager or by a sub-committee member, and applicants for housing would be interviewed by a sub-committee. Two other case studies (Hilltop and Bungalow) also employed, or intended to employ, an estate manager, but in Five Streets, which was of a similar size, the committee had decided to carry out the functions themselves. In the run-up to taking over responsibility the TMO had begun to take over functions, and committee members had begun to carry out home visits to prospective applicants and process repair requests.

Committee structures

7.26 McCafferty and Riley (1989) found that most co-operatives had committees and office bearers, typically a Chairperson, Secretary and Treasurer. Some co-ops were also found to have separate convenors of sub-committees. The postal survey for this research found that 19 per cent of TMOs responding did not have a management committee or board, but most of these managed less than 100 properties. All the case-study TMOs had management committees or boards but committee size and structure varied, as did the number and roles of office bearers.

7.27 The number of officer bearers and complexity of committee structure was found to be inversely related to size. The largest TMOs (Family and World) had fewer office bearers and no sub-committees. In both cases many of the functions of a committee secretary and treasurer, such as taking minutes, preparing agendas and book-keeping were carried out by staff. The smallest TMO (Tower) had only the three office bearers but had four sub-committees, three of which met fortnightly and one (the Allocations Sub-committee) which met when necessary to consider applications. The committee also had floor representatives who were responsible for keeping in contact with ordinary members.

7.28 The second smallest TMO (Hilltop), with a committee of 12 members, had eight office bearers including Chair, Vice-chair, Secretary, Assistant Secretary, Treasurer, Assistant Treasurer, Chair of repairs and Chair of social events. The executive committee of five met monthly and three sub-committees met fortnightly. This group administered their structure without staff support. They were however planning to employ an estate manager, but it was not clear whether the job description would include servicing the committee.

7.29 This variation in functions and roles of the committee meant that the 'job descriptions' for office bearers and ordinary committee members varied from organisation to organisation. A composite key task analysis for the post of Chairperson, Secretary, Treasurer, Chair of allocations and Chair of repairs sub-committee was drawn up and is shown in Appendix 5. This distinguishes between those tasks which all the office bearers said they were responsible for carrying out, and those which only some carried out, depending on the division of responsibilities between committee and staff.

Table 7.4 **Staff and Committee Structures in Case Study TMOs**

	Tower	Hilltop	Five Streets	Bungalow	Family	World
No. of staff	2	1(p)	NIL	1	10	25(p)
No. of office bearers	3	8	3	4	3	2
Size of committee	10	12	18	15	20	12
No. of sub-committees	4	3	NIL	4	NIL	NIL

P = planned

CHARACTERISTICS OF TMO MEMBERS
Establishing characteristics

7.30 The extent to which office bearers and ordinary committee members need training to carry out their duties effectively will depend on their previous skills and knowledge. The interviews with committee members explored the individual's background, previous and current employment, previous education, training and qualifications, trade union and other voluntary activities. Interviews with other key actors also sought views on the individuals at the outset of the TMO development process.

Age, sex and ethnic origin

7.31 Almost all the committee and board members interviewed were mature adults, aged 40 and upwards and a number were retired. The oldest committee member interviewed was over 80 years old. This reflected the findings of McCafferty and Riley (1989) that three-quarters of office bearers in tenant management co-ops were aged over 30. There were slightly more men in the sample than women. The arrangement of office bearers found some gender bias: the Chairperson and Treasurer were more likely to be male and the secretary was more likely to be female. Although several of the estates had ethnic minority households, five of the six case-study committees were all white. Only one, in the most ethnically mixed area, had black people on the committee.

Previous experience

7.32 None of the committee members had previous work-experience or qualifications in housing, though a number had formerly been active members of tenants' associations. Occupations, past and present, were very varied. These included accountancy, retail management, a foreman in industry, an army officer, a cabinet maker, a care assistant, a nurse and a miner. Office bearers appeared to be more likely to have had management or supervisory experience, although there were some committee members with very little work experience and a few who had low literacy skills. Four of the six Chairs had previous committee experience through union or management activities. Two Chairs did not have experience of this role. Most secretaries had previous administrative skills, but ordinary committee members had varied backgrounds. It was not surprising, however, that the research found committee members with management or supervisory experience were more likely to be office bearers. In young community organisations, people with existing skills are more likely to be put forward for positions of greater responsibility. There were also links between occupational experience and particular posts. For example those with office or existing administrative skills were more likely to be the secretary. Personality however also played a part. The chairpeople generally had strong personalities and were articulate and outgoing while some of the ordinary committee members had little to say.

> 'She's got a big mouth. She knows what to say. You've just got to have a mouth to talk to people and she's the right one.'
>
> Ordinary resident - Group interview

7.33 Table 7.5 shows the key skills, knowledge and attitudes which the Chairpeople in the six TMOs were thought to have before undertaking training. To protect confidentiality they have not been identified by organisation. It should be noted that gaps in the table may be because neither the individual nor other observers commented on a particular area of existing skills and knowledge rather than the individual lacking a particular ability at the outset of training. Having said that, the table clearly shows that while the Chairs had little of the knowledge required, five out of the six had considerable skills. Attitudes were mixed but most had confidence and a desire to increase their skills and knowledge.

Table 7.5 **Existing skills, knowledge and attitude of Chairpersons**

Topic	Chair A	Chair B	Chair C	Chair D	Chair E	Chair F
Knowledge						
Aims of TMO						
Management agreement						
How the council works	*					*
Rules/constitution						
Policies/Procedures						
Staff management	*	*				*
Skills						
Chairing	*	*	*	*		*
Team-working		*	*	*		*
Public speaking	*		*	*		*
Assertiveness	*		*	*		*
Negotiation		*	*	*		*
Decision-making	*	*	*	*		*
Attitudes						
Positive view of TMOs		*				
Non-discriminatory					*	*
Confidence	*	*	*	*		*
Desire to increase skills/knowledge	*		*	*	*	*
Importance of good performance	*	*	*			*

TRAINERS' SKILLS AND KNOWLEDGE

7.34 There were a number of trainers involved in the six case studies, including local authority staff, trainers from TMO training agencies and independent trainers. An analysis of the trainers' skills and knowledge at the outset of training is given in Table 7.6. This table is based on the trainers' own assessments, corroborated where possible with the views of other participants and the researchers' observations. It must be stressed that, as with the analysis of tenants' skills and knowledge, a 'missing' area may simply mean that this attribute was not mentioned or observed. The table should, therefore, be regarded as illustrative.

7.35 The first three trainers worked with TMO A. Trainer 1 was a consultant who worked intensively with the steering group in the promotional stage and occasionally thereafter. This trainer had extensive experience of community development but only an awareness of tenant management. Trainer 2 worked for a training agency which did occasional work with the steering group. This trainer had teaching, co-op and local authority experience and had extensive knowledge of co-ops. Trainer 3 was from a local authority background and was engaged to work full-time with the group. This trainer had good knowledge of housing and practical skills but little knowledge of co-ops. The weakness of this mix was that the trainer with the greatest knowledge of TMOs did the least work with the group and was only brought in at critical points.

Table 7.6 **Analysis of case-study trainers' key skills and knowledge**

TMO	A			B			C		D		E	F
Trainer	1	2	3	4	5	6	7	8	9	10	11	12
Knowledge												
What TP involves	*	*	*	*	*		*	*	*	*	*	*
What TMOs involve		*		*	*		*	*	*		*	*
How the council works	*	*	*	*		*			*	*	*	*
Housing legislation	*	*	*	*		*	*	*			*	*
Housing finance		*	*	*		*					*	*
Housing management		*	*	*		*	*				*	*
Training methods	*	*	*	*				*	*	*	*	
Practical skills	*	*	*	*				*	*	*	*	*
Rules and constitutions		*		*	*		*	*	*		*	*
Management agreement		*		*			*	*				*
TMO policies		*		*	*		*	*			*	
Committee work		*	*	*	*	*	*	*	*	*	*	*
Section 16 grants	*	*		*			*	*			*	*
TMO Finance		*		*	*		*				*	
Financial control		*	*	*	*	*	*			*	*	*
Employment law		*		*			*			*	*	*
Staff management		*		*			*			*	*	*
Office procedures		*	*	*	*		*			*	*	*
Repairs and maintenance			*				*			*		*
Evaluating training	*	*		*			*		*		*	
Monitoring performance	*	*		*			*		*			
Skills												
Communication skills	*	*	*	*	*	*	*	*	*	*	*	*
Public speaking	*	*	*	*	*		*	*	*	*	*	*
Team-building	*	*	*	*			*	*	*		*	
Assertiveness	*	*	*	*	*		*	*	*	*	*	*
Negotiation	*			*		*	*	*			*	*
Planning	*	*		*	*		*	*	*	*	*	*
Financial skills	*	*		*		*	*			*	*	
Interviewing		*		*		*	*		*	*	*	*

7.36 The second group of trainers worked with TMO B. Trainer 4 had extensive co-op experience and carried out some of the training for the group. He also trained Trainer 5, who did most of the day-to-day training with the TMO. Trainer 5 had some previous knowledge of housing co-operatives but learned a lot on this job. The trainer felt that the biggest gaps in his knowledge were on team-building and using a range of training methods. The third trainer was a local authority officer who attended the steering group meetings in the later stages. With no specific knowledge of TMOs, this officer nevertheless provided considerable informal training on council policies and housing management issues. This mix of trainers appeared to work well. Although the most experienced trainer did only a small amount of training he played a key role in providing advice to the council and the day-to-day trainer.

7.37 Trainers 7 and 8 worked with TMO C. Trainer 7 was appointed for the later stages of development, after the original trainer left. The original trainer appeared to have much less knowledge than either of the subsequent trainers. Trainer 7 had considerable skills and knowledge but due to the late stage of development, acted more as an advisor and independent consultant to the group. Trainer 8 was appointed by the council and worked with the group throughout their development. This trainer had knowledge of both co-ops and local authorities and, in addition to providing some training, brought in other local authority officers to give more specialist sessions. The mix appeared to give a broad base of skills and knowledge, though the tenants were scathing about the input from the original trainer.

7.38 Trainers 9 and 10 worked with TMO D. Trainer 9 had previous experience of community work and undertook a short training programme on TMOs before starting work with the group. The agency also provided more experienced staff for particular sessions. Trainer 10 was a local authority officer with a broad knowledge of housing management and tenant participation. This partnership of trainers covered almost all the skills and knowledge required.

7.39 Trainer 11 worked with TMO E and had previous training and co-op experience but found some difficulties, initially, with the council structures. Much of the knowledge needed for training tenants to form a TMO was learnt on the job and this trainer brought in a repairs officer to cover specialist technical areas. All the tenants at at this TMO spoke appreciatively of the support they had received.

7.40 Trainer 12 worked with TMO F and had both local authority and TMO experience. This person did most of the training, bringing in other trainers occasionally 'more for a change of face'. While tenants appreciated this support, it was clear that the trainer was over-stretched with other commitments and not able to devote sufficient time to the initiative in its later stages. The support and training given by the trainers in two of the TMOs, therefore, appeared to be good, but were more mixed in the others.

SUMMARY

7.41 This discussion of the backgrounds and characteristics of the case-studies shows that there were a number of factors which may have had an impact on the development of the TMO and the success of training. One of these factors was the wider local authority support, which can be deduced from the origins of the TMO and motivations of councillors and officers. The length of the development process may also be an indicator of problems such as avoidable delays. The physical environment and socio-economic factors may contribute to the ease or difficulty of management and the structure of the TMO, and the degree of involvement in day-to-day operations will affect the depths of knowledge and skills required. Finally, the experience and support provided by the trainers and the existing skills and knowledge of the tenants can be important factors. These factors can be summarised for each of the six case studies in Table 7.7 below.

Table 7.7 **Summary of contextual factors in case study TMOs**

Factor	Tower	Hilltop	Five Streets	Bungalow	Family	World
LA support	Good	Poor	Mixed	Good	Good	Mixed
Length of development (months)	22	48+	48+	34	31	36+
Environment	Good	Good	Poor	Mixed	Mixed	Poor
Socio-economic	Good	Poor	Poor	Good	Poor	Poor
Trainers support	Good	Good	Mixed	Mixed	Good	Good
Tenants skills and knowledge	Good	Good	Mixed	Mixed	Mixed	Mixed

7.42 Tower TMO was in an area with few problems. The properties had been modernised and were occupied mainly by working households. The office bearers had previous relevant skills and knowledge from work experience and political support was good. The agency gave considerable support during development. The properties at Hilltop were modernised during the development period, the office bearers were committed and had previous experience from their tenants' association and the agency trainer gave close support. However, few people in the area were in work and political support was ambivalent. The tenants felt that they had suffered delays as a result of staff changes. Five Streets had a poor environment and high unemployment. The council was split over support and although the key tenant activists were highly motivated, the majority had few previous skills. This TMO also appointed a trainer with no previous experience of TMOs. Bungalow TMO began with the skills and knowledge from a strong residents' association. However two of the key office bearers left towards the end of the development period. The majority of residents were elderly and the area had few environmental problems but the properties had not been modernised. The group had had some difficulties with the secondary agency and the first trainer left. However, support from the council officer was good.

7.43 The Family TMO estate was also modernised during development, though some work remained to be done. Despite high unemployment and high arrears the political support was good and office bearers had some previous skills. The agency had considerable previous experience and was able to provide tenants with wide contact with other groups. Finally, World TMO had a large area and poor environment, although improvements were being carried out. Rent arrears levels were high and there were considerable social problems. Political support from the council and senior officers was, initially, weak, although this changed with the appointment of a new director. Support was initially provided by the council officer. Although there were considerable skills in the group, there had been a high turnover of office bearers. The following chapters of the report explore the extent to which these factors had an impact on the effectiveness of training and the performance of the TMO.

Chapter 8   Inputs and reactions to training

8.1   This chapter examines the inputs to training in the case study TMOs. It begins by identifying who received training and then assesses the training programmes received by each TMO, looking first at the topics of training and then at the methods and media used. The assessment compares the topics to the 'ideal' model built up in Chapter 3 and notes tenants' reactions, from the in-depth interviews, to both topics covered in training and methods used by trainers.

WHO RECEIVED TRAINING?
During development

8.2   The case-studies tended to confirm the findings of the postal survey, that most training for tenant management was concentrated on the steering group and committee or board members. In some of the TMOs, the promotional stage began with a series of small group meetings which gave basic information to a wide range of residents. In Family TMO, 150 residents attended such meetings; in World TMO, it was estimated that over 500 people attended. As a result, fairly large groups of tenants started feasibility training (30 in one area and 50 in another) in these two areas. During the development period, however, whilst Family TMO continued to attract an average attendance of 17 people at these wider meetings, in World TMO the group dwindled once a steering group was formed, and wider training ceased. In the oldest case study, (Tower TMO) small group meetings were held throughout the development process and involved most of the residents. These groups discussed the rules of co-op and the management agreement, although only the steering group received training sessions on housing management.

8.3   Several of the TMOs said that they had tried to broaden training to a wider group of people. Two TMOs published the dates of training events in a newsletter with an open invitation for people to attend and in two other areas committee members said that they encouraged people to join training or go on study visits. This was confirmed by a few of the ordinary residents in group interviews. However, generally the ordinary residents did not express a great desire to become involved. Whilst a small number had attended training at some time, they appeared to have obtained most of their knowledge about the TMO's business from newsletters, letters, leaflets, public meetings and casual chats with their neighbours or in the estate office. Some commented that they did not have the time to commit themselves to regular meetings or that they were too old, too ill, or had too many family responsibilities to attend training. One TMO had established a creche to help people with family commitments to attend and another had thought of this, but had insufficient funds.

8.4   In three of the TMOs most of the tenants who originally formed the steering group to consider a TMO were still involved but in the others there had been higher turnover in participants. At the time of the research both Five Streets and World TMOs were attempting to attract new committee members and planned to train them before becoming established. In some cases it was also clear that individual office bearers had received additional training though most of this seemed to be informal and consisted of one-to-one counselling and coaching. There were few records of this informal training and it was very difficult to assess how important it was, retrospectively, but comments made by office bearers about support and advice received from trainers suggested that it was significant. Office bearers appeared to be more likely to attend external training courses than other committee members. In Bungalow TMO, for example, the Chair had attended a number of external seminars in the early stages of the TMO and brought information back for the rest of the committee.

Established organisations

8.5   In two of the three established case study organisations the committee members had only occasionally attended any training after taking over responsibilities. They regarded themselves as being trained and suggested that training might be useful for new members. However, the new members in those organisations did not appear to think that training was important either. They tended to 'pick it up' as they went along.

> 'I don't think they have any interest in being trained ... they see the role of committee member as ... rolling along every month ... and listening to what other people have got to say and voting at the end of it.'
>
> Co-op worker

8.6   In the third organisation training had continued at a fairly high level. This group continued to send members to conferences and seminars and had also had more in-house training from the local authority housing staff. They had helped to form a network with other TMOs and often received visits or went to meetings in other areas. Committee members also attended events as speakers.

8.7   Interviews at national level found a similar picture. Some TMOs were outgoing and keen to seek out ideas but many did not take part in training outside their own areas after they had become established. This may be due to lack of funds, but seems more likely to be due to the negative attitudes of committee members and staff towards training. Those TMOs which did provide ongoing training often used inexpensive methods such as 'networks', 'shadowing', booklets and training from their own workers.

TOPICS OF TRAINING

8.8   Training in the case studies included both formal and informal training methods. Establishing what training had taken place was not straight forward as informal discussions at meetings and practical learning were not always identified as 'training' by participants. In addition, the case studies did not follow a clear path through the promotion, feasibility and development model. The programmes followed by the case study TMOs varied significantly and covered a wide range of topics. Examples are given in Appendix 5 and a summary is shown in Table 8.1 below. However, neither detailed outlines of the training programme followed, nor the summary, can indicate the depth or extent of training on a particular topic. To assess this in more detail the research examined training material, where available, and interviewed both tenants and trainers. Topics are considered by stage of development, according to the 'ideal' model. However, as Table 8.1 indicates, this was not necessarily when training was received.

Table 8.1 **Topics of training**

	Tower	Hilltop	Five Streets	Bungalow	Family	World
Promotion						
What a TMC is	*	*	*	*		*(F)
What an EMB is		*	*	*	*	*
Priorities			*		*	*(F)
Tenant participation	*(F)	*	*(D)	*	*(F)	*(F)
How the council works	*(D)		*(D)	*(F)	*(F)	*(F)
Feasibility						
Overview of housing Management	*	*	*	*	*	
Responsibilities of a TMO	*	*	*	*	*	*
Team-work			*(D)		*	
Practical skills		*(D)	*	*(D)	*	*
Development						
Management agreement	*(F)	*(F)	*	*	*	*
Policies and procedures	*	*	*	*	*	
Committee work	*	*	*	*	*	*
Negotiating skills						
Staff management	*	*		*		*
Financial control	*	*	*	*	*(O)	
On-going						
Training for new members	*	na	na			na
Training for new Committee members		na	na		*	na
Up-dating skills and knowledge	*	na	na		*	na

Source: *Training programmes (Appendix 5) case study interviews.*

Notes: (F) = Training received during feasibility stage.
(D) = Training received during development stage.
(O) = Training received after TMO was established.

Topics at the promotional stage
Options for control

8.9 The 'ideal' model suggests that the promotional stage should develop awareness of the range of options available. It was clear that this had not happened in all the case studies. In Tower TMO, this was understandable as there were fewer options available when this TMO began the development process. Hilltop considered an estate committee before deciding to pursue a TMC, after visits to two TMOs. Five Streets appeared to have considered, and rejected, the possibility of a Housing Action Trust (HAT). An EMB was suggested to Bungalow TMO committee members but this group had already made up their minds to pursue a TMC. In Family and World TMOs, however, the tenants appear to have been presented with only one option at the outset - an EMB, and only became aware subsequently that there were other possibilities. In one area in particular some tenants expressed dissatisfaction that they had not been made aware of other possibilities at the outset.

> 'Nine months into our steering group we had a meeting ... about options for control of the estate. I think if that had been put on the table first ... this would have been a bit different, but we were given no choice, we were pushed into this.'
>
> Board member - TMO

Priorities

8.10 Only three of the case studies (Five Streets, Family and World TMOs) appeared to have received training on estate problems. Five Streets had the most comprehensive training with an independent consultant. This group then went on, at their feasibility stage to consider a range of extra facilities for the estate.

> 'We identified areas. What was lacking was facilities around us for young children so we started to provide out-of-school activities for the kids, as well as going along to meetings with the council.'
>
> Committee Member - TMO

8.11   World TMO had discussed environmental, social and economic issues at the feasibility stage while Family TMO considered employment training and economic development. However, although some of the other TMOs had not considered wider estate issues, this should be set in context. Tower TMO, as Chapter 7 has shown, had few problems and residents therefore had little interest in other priorities. Modernisation was the major issue at Hilltop and Bungalow TMOs. Hilltop had a programme of meetings on modernisation in parallel with the development of the TMO whilst the Bungalow TMO supported the council's unsuccessful bid for Estate Action resources.

Tenant participation

8.12   Hilltop and Bungalow TMOs appeared to have received some training on tenant participation at the promotional stage since both groups had carried out surveys of tenants to ascertain interest in a TMO.

> 'We did a lot of leg-work. We went and visited every tenant, we did quite a number of surveys before it ever went as far as it did.'
>
> Committee Member - TMO

8.13   In contrast training on consultation and representation was received at the feasibility stage in World and Family TMOs. Five Streets TMO had training on planning consultation with tenants at the development stage. Tower TMO did not appear to have received formal training on any form of participation, but participatory principles were demonstrated through small group meetings, public meetings, newsletters and distribution of minutes. In four of the six TMOs, some committee members had been members of existing tenants' groups and the in-depth interviews indicated that they had some understanding of the structures and processes of participation at the outset. Training was building, therefore, on previous knowledge.

How the council works

8.14   Although TMO members had some awareness of how the council operated at the outset, more detailed knowledge was developed at later stages. In Tower TMO, a senior local authority housing official attended meetings at the development stage and explained informally how various council policies worked. Tenants in this TMO, however, did not feel that they had sufficient knowledge about council structures.

> 'There was one big gap, ... we did not know who did what in the council. Fortunately we employed (a worker) who knew the council and knew where to go. (Otherwise) we would have needed some inroad into how the council worked.'
>
> Committee member - TMO

8.15   Council officers gave both formal and informal training to Five-Streets, Bungalow, Family and World TMOs on council policies and council structures. However in the Hilltop TMO, the tenants appeared to have learnt about the council largely from their other community activities, and through the process of negotiating the terms of the management agreement.

Topics at feasibility stage

8.16 The DOE description of the feasibility stage is further in-depth consideration of the options available leading to final choice of option. None of the case studies satisfactorily met this description since the option had already been chosen at the promotional stage, either by the tenants or by the council. However, the training provided at this stage did include the commencement of housing management, equal opportunities and general management, to a greater or lesser extent. The key skills and knowledge identified in the ideal model at the feasibility stage were an overview of housing management; a clear idea of the responsibilities of a TMO; developing team-work and practical skills.

Housing management overview and responsibilities

8.17 All the TMOs received some training designed to give an overview of what housing management involves and to introduce then to TMO responsibilities. In most of the case studies, the TMO had a short training course on a range of topics such as repairs, allocations, rent collection and arrears recovery. In World TMO, a large group was split into eight sub-committees each looking at a different subject area. The course at Five Streets was biased towards skills acquisition but responsibilities, lettings and housing policy were briefly covered. Tower TMO concentrated on rules and constitutions before going on to consider the management agreement. Finally, however, the programmes followed by Bungalow, Hilltop, and Family TMOs resembled the 'ideal model' more closely at this stage.

Team-work and practical skills

8.18 Only one TMO (Family) had a session specifically called team-building, but all the TMOs appeared to have learnt something about team-work, at the feasibility stage, through consideration of roles of committee members or training on skills in holding meetings. Five Streets TMO had the most extensive training on practical skills. The consultant carried out extensive team-building and community development work at the promotional stage and at the feasibility stage. Sessions included letter-writing, book-keeping, word processing and playgroup management. Both Family and World TMOs had sessions on designing a newsletter and all the groups had experience of holding public meetings, though it was not clear whether structured training took place on this.

Equal opportunities

8.19 Most of the TMOs' members mentioned that they had received training on equal opportunities. World TMO members had a two-day course, which included interviewing skills and employment of staff, while Bungalow and Tower TMO members appeared to have attended a more specific racial awareness course. Overall, the reaction to this equal opportunities training was mixed. Some thought that as a topic it had been over-stressed, while others thought it was very important. The 'racial awareness' type courses appeared to be the least successful and had some of the opposite effects to those intended. Equal opportunities appeared to be more successful when integrated into other topics such as representing the community, employment and tenancy allocations.

> 'I've been on equal opportunities training ... that was very useful. They taught you ... to be fair to each and everyone - not only race, class but incapacities as well.'
>
> Board Member - EMB

> 'I think the one that sticks in my mind was allocations ... on equal opportunities. I've got to say this, I hope it doesn't sound too wrong ... the gentleman (trainer) was coloured ... I felt the problem was more with him than it was with us.'
>
> Committee Member - Co-op

8.20 Current committee members' recollection of this early training varied. Some tenants we interviewed had not been involved at the feasibility stage and in other cases, people were unable to separate what they had learnt in the beginning, from later training. Those who had had training spoke appreciatively of the skills they had picked up in letter writing and word-processing but some parts of course appeared to be remembered better than others. For example, one tenant gave a fairly comprehensive account of how the repairs process operated but was much hazier about financial issues.

Topics at the development stage

8.21 The important topics at the development stage that were identified in the ideal model were the management agreement, TMO policies and procedures, committee work, negotiating skills, staff management and financial control.

Management agreement and policies

8.22 In some groups, discussions on the management agreement began during the feasibility stage and the patterns which the case study TMOs followed were varied. In Tower TMO consideration of the management agreement was carried out in small groups. In Hilltop TMO there were twelve sessions on the management agreement, followed by a block of training on policies, then further discussion of the management agreement. This pattern was partly because the Modular Management Agreement was introduced during the development period of the group. Bungalow TMO was similarly affected by this recommended new agreement. Family TMO set up a management agreement working party to develop their agreement while a wider group continued training on housing management and policies. Five Streets was the only case study which did not link training around the management agreement. Instead this group had an 18 month housing management and skills course. Tenants subsequently said that although they learnt a lot from this, in retrospect felt that training around the agreement would have been more focused and given a better understanding of TMO responsibilities.

> 'Some of it was quite good, some of it was a waste of time because it wasn't really housing management training that was needed, it was co-op training because we weren't going to be housing managers, we were going to be co-op managers.'
>
> Committee Member - TMO

Committee work

8.23 Formal training on committee skills appeared to be limited. However most groups had some previous experience of committee work and showed confidence in this area. Perhaps the most useful sessions were the 'interim' committees established at Hilltop, Bungalow and Family TMOs where participants gained experience, at the final stage of training, of the issues and decisions they would face when established. Some tenants felt that refresher training on committee skills would be useful, although others in the same organisation felt that training had been adequate.

> 'I think we've got sloppy ... we've had that many things to deal with ... things have got let go along the way, we are getting into bad habits.'
>
> Committee Member - TMO

Negotiating skills

8.24 Only two of the case study tenants interviewed mentioned receiving training on negotiation skills (Tower and Bungalow TMOs). However 'how to negotiate' appeared to have been only discussed informally at Hilltop and World TMOs during sessions on the management agreement. The extent to which strategies to ensure a 'win-win' situation, in which both the council and the tenants would gain, were properly discussed, was not clear. In our view, more of this type of training would have been useful in a number of the case studies as some tenants expressed unhappiness with their agreements, indicating that negotiations could have been improved.

Staff management

8.25 Training on staff management was also variable. Tower TMO had had meetings on drawing up a job description but no training on interviewing or managing a worker. In contrast, Bungalow and Hilltop TMOs had training on all three topics while World TMO members had received recruitment and interview training but did not appear to have received anything on managing a worker and office bearers had to learn 'on the job'. Family and Five Streets TMOs appeared to have received no staff management training. However, in the case of the former, the staff were employed by the local authority and in the case of the latter the office bearers had decided to run the TMO themselves.

Financial control

8.26 The extent to which financial knowledge is required by TMO members at this stage depends on whether they are administering the accounts themselves or employing staff to carry out this function. However, the ideal model does suggest that the committee members should understand the principles of financial control and be able to read financial statements. In Five Streets and World TMOs, the committee had received detailed training on book-keeping, while at Bungalow TMO two office bearers had attended a course at a local college. There were varying views about the usefulness of training on book-keeping. We felt that unless office bearers were intending to manage the accounts themselves, this detailed training was probably not necessary.

> 'I'm not interested in accounts. I like to see the books. I know the difference between what goes in and what goes out ... but I didn't really enjoy it .. I'm good on the office side.'
>
> Board Member - TMO

> 'I'm clumsy on sums. I didn't know what to do when I started the course. Now I can do it.'
>
> Committee Member - TMO

8.27 In Tower, Bungalow and Five Streets TMOs most committee members had received training on financial control and office bearers played a part in budgeting and monitoring expenditure. In World TMO some committee members appeared to have received informal training from their auditor but had only recently become involved in managing their budget. Family TMO appeared to leave financial issues to the staff and were just beginning to learn about budgetary control in the year after becoming established. Some of the TMOs had been developed before the change in Section 16 rules, which gave grants direct to the tenants, so they were not responsible for the majority of the finance received during the development period. We found that the tenants were unaware of the cost of training in these cases and there were several comments that training and advice were 'free' and some surprise at the cost of training when the TMOs became established. The change in the grant regime appeared to have made tenants more conscious of costs and budgeting.

METHODS OF TRAINING

8.28 The case study organisations used a variety of media and methods at all stages of development from lectures to examining the management agreement clause by clause. Ideally the training methods should take account of the purpose of the event and whether skills, knowledge or attitudes are being taught. Programmes should also accommodate different learning styles (see chapter 2). This section first examines training which took place locally and then training sessions which were held externally.

Local training

8.29 Most of the training carried out within the TMOs took place on or close to the estates and both trainers and tenants strongly stressed the need for training to be both locally based and locally relevant. And in fact, the majority of the training in the case study TMOs did appear to be focused on local issues and policies and procedures which the TMO could use. The main exceptions were some of the housing management training in Five Streets TMO and some sessions in Family and World TMOs where external speakers had been invited to present topics. The difficulty appeared to be that tenants thought that the training was too theoretical, not practical enough for their estate or that the speaker was trying to cover too much ground in a two-hour session. Feedback forms completed by one group after some presentations from external speakers suggested that participants found the sessions relevant but that insufficient time had been allowed to properly cover the topic.

> 'They couldn't do what they should have in an hour and a half ... it's impossible to take all that in.'
>
> Board Member - TMO

Some trainers, however, stressed the importance of an occasional alternative perspective and tenant or staff speakers from other TMOs seemed to be particularly popular.

Small group sessions

8.30 Most of the training received by the case study TMOs took place in small groups and used a variety of methods. Exercises, games and role-play appeared to be more memorable to participants than talks or lectures, though different respondents had different preferences, depending upon their particular learning styles. A number of tenants described the role-plays used during the interview skills training and suggested that these had been useful for learning how to ask questions and what to ask. Role-play did not, however, suit everyone.

> 'Somehow, it didn't really flow ... there were these set out documents of Mrs. so and so ... it didn't seem to get it over to me.'
>
> Committee Member - TMO

Games involving practical exercises appeared to be enjoyed by most participants, preferably when these were as realistic as possible.

> 'The training sessions were all talks. The best way to learn is putting into practice. On finance, we split into two groups and had to decide how much to spend on each thing ... I prefer that to the talks.'
>
> Board Member - TMO

Brainstorming was only mentioned by one group, but appeared to have been effective:

> 'Brainstorming, that's mostly what it was. If anybody had said "what do you specifically want?" I wouldn't have been able to answer them but when we all worked together ... we managed to build a picture up.'
>
> Committee Member - TMO

Public meetings

8.31 All the TMOs had held public meetings at some points in the development process. Tower, Bungalow and Five-Streets began their promotional stages with large public meetings while Family and World TMOs held a number of smaller public meetings during this stage. The main aim of the public meetings was to get information across to participants, usually in the form of a lecture, followed by questions and answers. As a rule, the smaller meetings appeared to have been better received than large meetings, since tenants were more willing to ask questions in a less formal setting. Meetings were usually preceded by leaflets or information about the purpose of the event.

> 'They put some leaflets out a day or two before and everyone was there. We went down and listened to what they had to say. They said it was a new thing. It was to take over the estate and run it ourselves where the services were concerned.'
>
> Board Member - TMO

Videos

8.32 Many committee members could not recall having seen any videos as part of their training and these did not appear to have played a large part in the promotion and development of the TMOs, possibly due to the lack of materials. Those who did recall having seen a video had varying opinions about its usefulness. One tenant said that videos were 'about estates elsewhere' rather than about problems in their own area. This was a difficulty mentioned by several trainers, who referred to the phenomenon of material which 'comes from another planet'. The John Cleese video on meetings was also mentioned by a few tenants. They had enjoyed it, and thought it was useful, despite the fact that it featured business men in suits.

Written materials

8.33 Written training materials were much more common than videos. Many tenants had large piles of material collected from both in-house and external training events. Some interviewees said that these were very useful, and helped them to retain what was learnt, though others who kept materials did not always read them after the event.

> 'All the time when you are sitting there and going through the seminars, I thought it was very valuable what you were hearing and learning but there is no way that you would be able to pass that on without literature.'
>
> Committee Member - TMO

> 'Oh yes, we had packs ... you came home laden with packs ... well some you read and some you didn't. Sometimes you got so much home that you just chucked it in a corner and forgot all about it.'
>
> Board Member - TMO

8.34 Leaflets and newsletters seemed more likely to be read than large piles of handouts and some tenants particularly mentioned that they enjoyed information about other TMOs. For example, one of the established TMOs in the case studies had produced a booklet, setting out the story of the TMO and describing the structure and functions of the organisation. This booklet was given to all new members, along with a copy of the rules and an information pack. This was the most comprehensive document of the materials produced by a TMO which we saw, that was produced by tenants themselves.

> 'You find it useful, because you see how other people are coping with the problems.'
>
> Board member - TMO

Practical skills training

8.35 Training by doing was carried out in most TMOs. This ranged from producing newsletters to operating as an interim committee. In some cases tenants appeared to have been thrown in to 'sink or swim'. This sometimes appeared to result in 'learning by bitter experience', how **not** to do things, and could be very demoralising. Structured practical training sessions appeared to be more useful. Some individuals and groups had received training on chairing meetings, public speaking, dealing with complaints and organising an open day.

Computer-based training

8.36 In two of the case study TMOs, members had used computer based training packages to learn computing skills. Although this enabled tenants to learn locally, and at their own pace, it appeared to be very slow. A co-op worker, who had helped one committee member to learn about computing, suggested that a training course may have been more efficient. In another co-op, tenants had been largely self-taught and then helped each other. While this gave confidence in using a computer, the results were mixed and initial practice followed-up with a course at a local college may have been more effective.

> 'One member ... comes in and uses the word-processor. We've had the machine for a year and only now am I in a position to get on with my own work without this committee member saying "What button do I press" ... training in computer skills ... would be very helpful for this co-op.'
>
> TMO worker

Shadowing

8.37 Shadowing is a training technique which involves participants learning by watching someone else carry out a task and then copying the technique. This is sometimes called 'Sitting by Nellie.' This was clearly in use in some TMOs, although trainers expressed some reservations where tenants were teaching other tenants;

> 'It's very haphazard ... some tenants are good at training, some are not. It's fair enough if you have got people with the time to do that - what happens if the post holder is leaving the area? ... Learning from others is not ideal.'
>
> Trainer - Secondary Co-op

8.38 There was evidence that some tenants were better at training others. In one area, the TMO had set up a structured induction programme which involved shadowing and practice at performing particular functions and this appeared to work fairly well. However, in two other areas there was a feeling that people 'learnt as they went along'. Our view was that these new committee members had not learnt all the skills and knowledge required and that shadowing as a training technique was flawed.

> 'As new members have come along we spend the time in the office ... The trainee now has gone and done a home visit with a committee member ... and come back and shown how to do a report ... they report repairs and we show them what to do ... I can show someone else how to sit down and type a letter ... there's a system in place ... of hands-on training.'
>
> Committee Member - TMO

Study visits

8.39 Five of the six case study groups had visited other organisations. Almost everyone said that they found study visits useful and that they learnt a lot from visiting other tenant management organisations. These visits seemed to be most valued for meeting other tenants, swapping problems and getting ideas. A number said that they gained confidence from seeing what other groups could do. Visits from other groups were also seen as a useful way to learn:

> 'We've had six or seven would-be co-ops visit us for the day. I think they have been useful. People get a lot from them by discussing the issues - the interchange between two tenants is what really works.'
>
> TMO worker

8.40 In some cases, specific things had been learnt from study visits. One committee member, for example, said that the major thing he had learnt was how important it was to cost out the services which the TMO wanted to provide very carefully and ensure that the necessary management allowances were sufficient to cover expenditure. He felt that the TMO he visited had not done this and were struggling with the budget they had. Only one tenant we interviewed thought that study visits were not useful as he felt the committee knew what they wanted on their estate and did not need to waste money seeing what other people had done. However, to be useful the study visit must be structured to allow tenants to meet and speak to others on a one-to-one basis. One tenant expressed disappointment that this had not happened:

> 'We were put in a hall and we didn't see any of the tenants, or even the estate. If you go ... you like to see the estate ... you want to hear what the tenants think.'
>
> Board Members - TMO

External conferences and seminars

8.41 In all but one of the case studies, some committee members had attended external events during development of their tenant management organisation. The only exception was the longest established TMO (Tower) and it may be that there were no conferences available at the time the TMO was developed. Tenants were generally enthusiastic about external courses although in most cases the value attached was not to the course content, but to meeting other tenants.

> 'You learn the rules and what you should do in workshops, but when you are actually talking to someone one-to-one you learn an awful lot more.'
>
> Board Member - TMO

8.42 There were some complaints from interviewees that there was too much packed into events. Several felt that they needed more time to think or to talk and more gently paced residential courses were preferred, although some found it a little disconcerting when there were few 'formal' lectures. In general, tenants had a better recall of residential events and felt that it had helped to broaden their horizons. Indeed, one tenant said that her first residential weekend had changed her life. In some cases, one-day external seminars on particular issues or tasks happened to take place at the same time as tenants were looking at the issue locally and participants seemed to be satisfied that their objectives were met. A particular example was a seminar on management agreements.

Local college courses

8.43 Some tenants involved in the case study TMOs had attended local college courses, either as part of the training for a TMO, or to enhance their skills and knowledge generally. Bungalow TMO had made greatest use of these types of facility. Two members had attended an eight-week book-keeping and accounts course, one had attended a computer course and the entire committee had attended a short course on managing staff. Other tenants interviewed during the research had attended secretarial skills and small business courses. All these courses, whether provided specifically for the TMO, or as part of the normal adult education provision were thought to be useful in increasing individual skills and knowledge. However, there was a difficulty that if only one or two individuals attended a course that this knowledge may be lost to the group if the tenants left.

SUMMARY

8.44   In terms of who received training the case studies found a similar pattern to that found in the postal surveys. Although some of the case studies had extended training to ordinary members, most training was concentrated on committee members.

8.45   The training programmes were found to be very varied. Some gave more emphasis to knowledge training and appeared to neglect skills, while others were more balanced. Again, a similar picture to that found in the postal surveys emerged. At the promotional stage some TMOs did not receive training on the range of options available and only three of the six discussed priorities for the estate. There was also insufficient training on how the council operates.

8.46   At the feasibility stage all the TMOs had received some training on housing management and the responsibilities of TMOs but team work and practical skills were neglected in some. Most of the TMOs had received some training on equal opportunities but this had not always been well received by tenants. Integrating this topic into other topics appeared to be more successful.

8.47   At the development stage, five of the six TMOs had spent a number of sessions discussing the management agreement but one had not focussed training around this. Policies and procedures and committee work were also covered, although some interviewees felt a need for refresher training. Training on negotiating skills appeared to be weak and training on staff management and financial control was variable.

8.48   All the interviewees emphasised that locally based, locally relevant training was vital. Sessions by external speakers were sometimes less successful, through training by people from other TMOs was appreciated.

8.49   Small group sessions, particularly those which involved games, role-play and exercises, appeared to be the most useful method of training, though participants had different preferences. Larger public meetings could get information across to a wider range of people and were used occasionally. Videos did not appear to have been well used but written materials were more common. Leaflets and manuals appeared to be more successful than bulky handouts.

8.50   Practical skills training appeared to have most impact when it involved structured learning, rather than learning from experience. Some TMOs had used computer-based packages but a number of trainers felt that local college courses providing tuition may have been more effective. Shadowing was used, but had variable results, and a more structured approach, with one-to-one counselling, seemed to be more successful.

8.51   Almost all tenants enjoyed study visits to other TMOs, and said that they learnt from these. External conferences were also found useful, particularly for meeting other tenants involved in TMOs. Some tenants had attended local college courses and these were also found helpful.

Chapter 9 — The outcomes of training

INTRODUCTION

9.1 In this section, the outcomes of training and effectiveness of the training received are evaluated with reference to the individuals, groups and organisations involved with the case study TMO. The section concludes by considering the impact of other factors upon training, such as the physical environment and political context. The aim of training in organisations is to help individuals to master particular skills and knowledge. Outcomes of training can be measured by looking at changes in skills, knowledge and attitudes of individuals, changes in group performance and changes in organisational performance (Warr, Bird and Rackham, 1970).

PERSONAL EFFECTIVENESS

9.2 In this study it was not possible to measure performance before and after training. We therefore asked participants what skills and knowledge they possessed prior to training and what they had learnt from training. These self-assessments were compared with the views of trainers and support staff about their performance. The research team also made their own assessments based on observation of key participants and the examination of records. This cannot be considered to be a comprehensive appraisal due to the limitations of the methods, and the short time span available. In some cases training had taken place several years previously and it was difficult to establish what had been learnt from formal sessions and what had been achieved from the experience of being involved in the TMO. Nevertheless, an attempt was made to assess the skills, knowledge and attitudes required by all Chairpersons, Secretaries and Treasurers. This is outlined in Appendix 6.

9.3 It must also be borne in mind that the roles of office bearers and committee members were affected by the structure of the TMO and the range of responsibilities taken on. In some TMOs the staff appeared to carry out most of the day to day administrative, financial and management functions. For example, three of the TMOs in the case studies did not have a Treasurer's post and book-keeping was carried out by the staff. Two of the TMOs were still at the development stage and had no staff. Both these TMOs had taken on some functions, such as ordering repairs, and the office bearers, in particular, were very involved in the day to day running of the TMO, but at this stage employed no support staff. The skills and knowledge required by these tenants were therefore greater than those required by TMOs where staff carried out day to day tasks.

Personal effectiveness of Chairpersons

9.4 Table 9.1 compares the key skills and knowledge which the chairpersons of the TMOs were thought to have before training, with those obtained from training.

Chairperson A

9.5 This chairperson was the driving force behind the original moves to form a TMO and was the dominant personality of the group. He had existing skills in chairing, public speaking and decision making and existing knowledge of staff management and how the council worked from professional and voluntary activities. The training he received was comprehensive, apart from negotiation skills and group-work, but this chair had a poor opinion of the trainers. He had gained knowledge from the training, although one interviewee commented that he was unwilling to take advice and learnt mainly from experience after problems arose. From observation, this chairperson appeared to have some competence in chairing meetings, public speaking and decision-making but the performance was marred by an authoritarian leadership style. He was observed by the team to be dealing with other committee members in an aggressive and inappropriate manner. There were also comments from ordinary residents that public meetings were heated and emotionally charged.

> 'I came (to meetings) when it first started and I was abused ... so since then I've not been to any meetings until a certain person apologises in public'
>
> Ordinary member - TMO

Table 9.1 **Key skills, knowledge and attitudes of Chairpersons of case study TMOs**

	A		B		C		D		E		F	
	H	O	H	O	H	O	H	O	H	O	H	O
Knowledge												
Aims and objectives of TMO				*		*		*		*		*
Management agreement				*		*		*				*
How the Council works		*		*		*		*		*		*
Rules/constitution				*		*		*		*	*	*
Policies and procedures				*		*		*				*
Staff management	*	*	*					*			*	*	*
Skills												
Chairing	*			*		*	*		*	*		*	*
Team working					*	*	*	*	*	*		*	*
Public speaking	*					*	*	*	*			*	*
Negotiation				*	*	*		*	*			*	*
Decision-making	*			*		*	*	*	*	*			*
Attitudes												
Positive view of TMOs			*	*			*		*		*	*
Non-discriminatory									*	*	*	*
Confidence	*	*	*		*	*	*	*		*	*	*
Desire to increase skills/knowledge				*	*	*	*	*	*	*	*	*
Importance of good performance	*	*	*	*			*		*		*	*

H = Had skills or knowledge prior to training.
O = Skills or knowledge obtained or enhanced by training.

Chairperson B

9.6 This person had previous experience which gave some of the skills necessary for a chairperson such as chairing, negotiation and decision making. The training for this TMO consisted mainly of small group work, discussing rules and constitutions and the management agreement. It appeared to include informal learning about chairing, negotiating and communication in groups. The TMO had been operational for some time so it was difficult to assess how much had been learnt from training during development and how much had been learnt 'on the job'. However, this chair had obviously gained knowledge and skills from training. He was well regarded by others and the committee meetings observed ran smoothly.

Chairperson C

9.7 It is likely that training had most impact on this chairperson. The training for this TMO seems to have been the most varied in terms of a mix of knowledge, skills and attitude training and local and outside events. This person had some existing skills for the role in the areas of communication and dealing with people. A confident and outgoing personality, her employment had given her experience of negotiation and people management. However, she had no previous knowledge of housing management or tenant activities. The training has not only increased her knowledge of TMOs and housing management, it has developed her personal skills in terms of public speaking, confidence, preparing and presenting reports. She had become a reasonably skilled chairperson in terms of conduct of meetings and general business of the TMO. However, much of this probably came during the period when the TMO was operating 'interim' committees. Overall, she displayed many of the skills and knowledge required by the key task analysis. Training seems to have had less impact on her attitudes with some evidence of stereotyping and judgemental views. The positive attitudes she displayed, such as the importance of good performance, training and confidence were closely linked to her own background and personality.

Chairperson D

9.8 This person was a confident and articulate individual who had had previous committee and management experience. The training received was strongly biased towards practical skills and word-processing and book-keeping skills had been developed which enabled this chairperson to combine the role of chair with that of treasurer. Extensive knowledge of housing had been learnt from the training, and existing skills had been enhanced. It was not possible to observe a committee meeting but others interviewed indicated that assertiveness skills were well developed.

> 'I've been to several meetings ... and she certainly doesn't lack any assertiveness ... she knows how to handle the system and speak to people. She's not reticent, she knows when to keep quiet as well'.
>
> Local authority officer

Chairperson E

9.9 This chairperson had the least previous skills and knowledge of those interviewed. The TMO had had some training in how the council worked, the management agreement, holding meetings, public speaking and negotiating but training was still underway. Some skills and knowledge had been learnt from the training, although this chair was hazy about details of policies and procedures on which further training was planned. Knowledge of how to chair a meeting and how to give a public presentation was shown in the interview. However, others interviewed indicated that this chairperson, who had only recently become an office bearer, was still weak at putting skills into practice and that more training was required.

> 'His heart is in the right place, he is enthusiastic but sometimes he pushes things through without the group's knowledge ... at times he runs off with an idea ... when I joined the committee ... it was more professional ... things have gone down hill in the way meetings are run ... they are going to need a lot of training to get them to do the business.'
>
> Co-op worker

Chairperson F

9.10 This chair had previous experience of voluntary group participation, some knowledge of local government processes and some committee and negotiating skills. His commitment to equal opportunities was probably present prior to training. The training received had enhanced skills but most had been learnt about housing management and TMO knowledge topics about which he knew little previously. Observers felt that he had always had enough self-confidence to chair the group and that training had made less difference than could be seen in other office bearers. He spoke positively about all the training events he had attended and was well organised, good at delegating and non-dogmatic in his role as chairperson.

Personal effectiveness of Secretaries

Table 9.2 **Key skills, knowledge and attitudes of Secretaries of case study TMOs**

	A		B		C		D		E		F	
	H	O	H	O	H	O	H	O	H	O	H	O
Knowledge												
Aims of TMO		*		*		*		*		*		*
Management agreement		*		*		*		*				*
Constitution of TMO		*		*		*		*		*		*
Legal responsibilities		*		*		*		*		*		*
How the council operates						*				*	*	*
Skills												
Team-working	*				*		*	*			*	*
Office skills	*					*		*			*	*
Letter-writing	*			*	*	*		*			*	*
Minute-taking				*				*			*	*
Report-writing	*							*			*	*
Decision-making	*			*	*			*			*	*
Attitudes												
Positive view of TMOs		*		*		*				*		*
Organised	*			*	*	*		*			*	*
Non-discriminatory								*				
Providing information		*		*				*	*			*

Notes: H = Had skills and knowledge previously.
O = Skills and knowledge obtained or enhanced by training.

Secretary A

9.11 This secretary brought considerable life skills to the job and a stint as assistant secretary may also have provided a 'run-in' period. The programme received by this TMO covered a wide range of subjects from committee and management skills, through all the housing management functions to negotiation, employing staff and interviewing skills. The secretary received most training 'on the job'. There was little recollection of any specific training sessions and more emphasis was placed on 'life skills'. From the researcher's observation and comments passed by others, this person seemed to have considerable team and communication skills. The secretary was seen as the 'voice of reason' by the local authority worker most connected with the TMO, with more listening and decision making skills than some other office bearers. Although significant knowledge of housing management and the TMO was shown, this person had little specific recollection of training events and expressed negative views about training in general. The skills did appear to have been present prior to training, although some may have been learnt from practical experience in the TMO.

Secretary B

9.12 This secretary had developed considerably as a result of the training programme for the TMO and attendance at external courses. Previously with only unskilled employment experience, this person was involved in the training for the TMO from the start. However, it is likely that some organisational and management skills were already present from domestic responsibilities. The training programme undertaken by this TMO included a mixture of sessions by the training agency staff and the local authority workers. Tenants also went on a number of regional and national events covering a wide range of topics. The programme thus covered personal skills as well as those on the housing management side. However, important skills such as negotiation did not seem to have been covered by training.

9.13   This person was organised and aware of the duties involved in maintaining the membership and other records. Awareness of the importance of keeping people involved and of providing information was also displayed during interview. These aspects of her skills were also the subject of comment by workers involved in the project. A very positive reaction to most of the training was expressed, particularly the results in terms of increased personal confidence and abilities.

9.14   Training has had a considerable impact in terms of knowledge, skills and developing positive attitudes. There was evidence of stereotyping of groups in relation to discussions about allocations and enforcement of tenancy agreements which were displayed by several members of this TMO. Training on these aspects of allocations and estate management had perhaps not been wholly effective. It is important to note that the duties of a Secretary in this TMO did not include taking minutes, setting agendas or preparing reports as these tasks were carried out by staff. The researcher was therefore unable to observe whether these skills were present.

Secretary C

9.15   This person was not the secretary of the TMO at the time of the interview but had been the secretary several times in the past. She had previous administrative and office employment experience but no previous voluntary committee experience. The training received was largely knowledge based and this person was able to talk knowledgeably about some aspects of housing management, particularly allocations. However, in this case study TMO staff carried out many of the possible duties of a secretary and it was not therefore possible to observe the skills claimed. The TMO worker criticised the abilities of secretaries of the TMO but had offered only limited training:

> 'We've never had a lady ... who had any secretarial experience, so most of the secretarial stuff passes them by because ... they don't know these tasks ... I produced sheets, item one, apologies for absence ... they could enter it ... but you get things like "You'll remember what happened here".'
>
> TMO worker

Secretary D

9.16   This secretary had extensive previous skills and knowledge from employment and voluntary activity and was involved in other tenants' associations on the estate. This had provided some knowledge of how the council operated and the skills required for the secretary's duties, although agenda setting and minutes were usually dealt with by the TMO worker. The training had included both knowledge and practical skills training, but little input specifically on the skills required by a secretary. This person demonstrated a knowledge of the aims of a TMO, the constitution and legal responsibilities and appeared to be astute about both the structure of the council and its politics. Knowledge on secretarial duties was also shown and letter writing and report writing ability was observed. It seems likely, however, that there had been little enhancement of secretarial skills which were already well developed and were probably not being fully exploited.

Secretary E

9.17 This secretary had had little training since leaving school and no recent work experience. The training received had involved extensive skills training including book-keeping, letter writing and computer skills along with housing management knowledge. During the training this person had learnt basic typing and office administration and felt that both skills and knowledge had increased substantially, along with confidence. This progress was also referred to by others interviewed:

> 'When I first started she wouldn't answer the phone. She organises training now and deals with benefits and fills (forms) in.'
>
> Committee member - TMO

Secretary F

9.18 The final secretary interviewed had previous experience in tenants' association activities but little relevant work experience. However, the voluntary activities had given committee skills such as minute-taking and campaigning though little knowledge of local government, housing management or negotiating. The training had covered both knowledge and practical skills, including housing practice and operating as an interim committee. This secretary felt that she had learnt a lot and increased considerably in confidence, particularly at public speaking.

> 'I have gained the experience and felt more at ease at each one I have gone to. The more you go to and the more work you do, the easier you feel able to speak out about something.'
>
> Committee member - TMO

9.19 Considerable knowledge of housing management and administrative skills were demonstrated both in the interview and in observation. Others interviewed also commented on this person's skills which appeared to have been enhanced by both training and by practice.

Personal effectiveness of Treasurers

Treasurer A

9.20 This treasurer had considerable skills prior to involvement in the TMO, from his employment, such as drafting and monitoring budgets, overseeing contracts, tendering procedures and managing staff. This person also had considerable voluntary experience and effective communication skills, confidence, decision making skills and organisational skills were all present.

9.21 The training programme for this TMO was very different because all of the original members had considerable life skills. Thus there was little committee or personal skills training as such. However the manner in which other training took place would have meant that effectively members did receive training in group work skills and negotiation. Knowledge was attained from the training in terms of housing management, housing finance and procedures for running the co-op. Book-keeping and accounting were learnt from the TMO auditor. No one in the TMO had anything but praise for this person's abilities and attitude to the job of treasurer. He appeared to be competent and knowledgeable about both financial issues and housing management. The concerns were that without this person the TMO would struggle.

Table 9.3 **Key skills, knowledge and attitudes of Treasurers in the case study TMOs**

	A		B		C	
	H	O	H	O	H	O
Knowledge						
Aims of TMO		*	*			*
Management agreement		*				*
How council operates						*
Finance for TMOs		*	*			*
Role of auditor	*	*	*			*
Financial planning	*					*
Tendering procedures	*		*			
Preparation of accounts	*					*
Skills						
Team work	*	*				*
Book-keeping		*	*			*
Planning/Budgeting	*					*
Decision-making	*					*
Public speaking	*					*
Attitudes						
Positive view of TMO		*	*			*
Trustworthy	*		*		*	
Value for money	*		*		*	*
Financial control	*	*	*			*

Note: H = Had skills and knowledge previously.
D = Skills and knowledge obtained or enhanced by training.

Treasurer B

9.22 This treasurer joined the TMO almost at the end of the development period. No formal training sessions were attended and indeed this person denied having had any training at all. Eventually, it was agreed that the assistance and guidance which had been received from the previous treasurer was 'on the job training'. No interest was expressed in going on formal training courses and no training needs were admitted. This person felt that the best way for any new group to learn was 'to come along here for a few days and see how we do it'.

9.23 However, from comments of the estate worker, and conversations observed by the team, it seems clear that this person's book-keeping and accounting skills were limited. The previous treasurer was still giving a lot of guidance and helping to keep the accounts in order. The current treasurer had no knowledge of the computer which was to be introduced for rent accounting. The estate worker identified finance as an area where the group, and particularly the treasurer, required training.

9.24 Evidence was displayed during the interview of a basic understanding of how to handle money, for example, attitudes relating to value for money and financial control were present. This was likely to stem partly from previous work experience, and partly from experience of dealing with contractors in the TMO. The previous treasurer appeared to have passed on some of the information about the financial controls and procedures which were in place and were rigidly adhered to.

Treasurer C

9.25 The third treasurer had little previous relevant experience but had attended all the training sessions. He was responsible for day-to-day book-keeping and maintaining the petty cash, but not for the preparation of the annual accounts, which were done by the TMO auditor. However, he presented the accounts to the AGM and explained financial statements at committee meetings. Training appeared to have been given on accounts and financial systems by the trainer through one-to-one and small group sessions of 'housing practice'. General financial issues for TMOs and financial control issues had been covered in more formal training and the treasurer showed knowledge and awareness of these. Since financial skills and knowledge were not present prior to training, the competence shown must have been developed through training and practice.

Effectiveness of office-bearers generally

9.26 While few of the office-bearers had much of the knowledge to run a TMO at the outset, a number had substantial skills. There was an indication that office-bearers had been chosen for particular posts because they had relevant previous experience. It was difficult to assess, retrospectively, whether these pre-existing skills had been enhanced, but some office-bearers, themselves, felt that the training received had been very beneficial. Chairperson D and Secretary F were good examples of this.

9.27 In other cases, however, there were office-bearers who had little previous experience and the impact of skills training was more marked. Secretary E and Treasurer C, in particular, had gained a high degree of competence from training and the experience of carrying out their duties.

9.28 All the office-bearers had improved their knowledge of TMOs. However, weak areas evident in some office-bearers in all the case study TMOs were knowledge of how the council operated, financial issues and wider tenant participation. There was evidence that equal opportunities training had not been successful in altering pre-existing stereotyped or discriminating views.

9.29 As individuals abilities, knowledge and attitudes varied there was no TMO where all the committee members interviewed matched the key task analysis completely. The office bearers in Hilltop, Five Streets and Family TMOs were the most competent on the widest range of tasks. All three of these organisations had had quite extensive skills and knowledge training. The office bearers in Tower were competent in 'core' skills and knowledge, such as chairing and financial overview but weak on wider issues such as training and participation. This TMO had no training on these areas. The office bearers in Bungalow and World TMOs were more mixed. This was partly due to turnover in these committees and training had not been completed. However, it was clear that competence was not due just to training, but also depended on previous skills and knowledge and the attitudes of both tenants and staff.

Personal effectiveness of committee members

9.30 The ordinary committee members' skills varied more widely. In some cases, there was a large gap between those interviewed and office-bearers in the same organisations. Those with previous committee skills tended to take a more active part in meetings. In one case study TMO, a committee member chaired a meeting fairly effectively in the absence of the Chair. In another TMO, ordinary committee members were supposed to take minutes of sub-committee meetings. However, the minute book revealed low standards, with a failure to record decisions or reasons for decisions.

9.31 In most cases, the tenants who had undertaken training were knowledgeable about housing management and tenant management. This knowledge appeared to have been developed from both formal and informal training. It was noticeable that more recent members, who had not had training, were less knowledgeable. One recent member felt that she was 'not qualified to answer questions' or deal with 'irate tenants', while tenants in the same organisation who had undergone training were considerably more confident. In one organisation, members were less knowledgeable about housing management policy and practice. However, this organisation still had a further year's training to undertake before taking over responsibilities and had been 'stalled' for some time.

9.32   Weak areas, evident in some committee members in all the TMOs, were knowledge of how the council operated, financial issues, attitudes towards equal opportunities, wider tenant participation and further training. Although some training on finance had been given in all TMOs, several committee members were less receptive to this. There were some views that equal opportunities had been over-emphasised. The committee which was most enthusiastic about equal opportunities training was also the most ethnically mixed.

9.33   A number of committee members spoke of 'apathy' and 'lack of interest' on their estate. Few committee members showed an understanding of reasons why people might not get involved, although all the case studies had some training on participation, either through training sessions or practical hands-on experience. Two quotes show the contrast:

> 'I've targeted ... the young mums and dads ... you don't seem to get through to them. It's their estate ... they ought to come and do a bit more than they do.'
>
> Board member - TMO

> 'There are things you have to take into consideration ... getting people away from a nice fire into the cold ... it's not on ... Everyone watches certain programmes ... If you have a meeting at that time you will lose more people ... on a Friday people are ... rushing to go out ... on a Saturday they are ... shopping and on Sunday there's ... the housework ... They're too busy ... You've got a problem.'
>
> Board member - TMO

9.34   The concern about attitudes towards further training was reflected in many of the interviews with trainers and local authority staff. Several said that they offered continuing support, and others had organised training events specifically targeted at established TMOs but had had poor attendance. A typical comment was:

> 'More extensive training is needed and we tried it last year. We organised training sessions ... and the response was abysmal ... some of them had to be cancelled.'
>
> Trainer - Secondary co-op

9.35   Lack of funding was cited as one reason why members of established co-operatives did not attend training, but a second reason, suggested by several trainers, was that committee members needed assistance in identifying their training needs.

> 'It's easy for the residents to become very arrogant and think they must have learnt everything there is to learn ... there needs to be someone to make a connection.'
>
> Trainer - National Agency

9.36 The interviews with committee members found many tenants who were open and receptive to new ideas and had an interest in continuing to learn as much as possible. One tenant with this view commented:

> 'Training is as vital as ever. Two reasons: one is that the new board members need knowledge ... but it's important for us to realise that training is always needed.'
>
> Board member - TMO

9.37 However, there were as many, if not more, committee members with the opposite view. The issue does seem to be one of organisational culture, as much as funding. In some organisations all the committee, co-op workers and local authority officers were suggesting that learning the skills and knowledge to run a TMO could be done 'as you go' and that committee members simply needed 'common sense'. In others, almost everyone was enthusiastic about training, meeting other groups and learning from others. There were also organisations which typified the trainers' views that some committee members thought they knew it all, though it was clear from the interviews that they did not. The quote below is from a committee member who recognised a training need for new members, but not for himself.

> 'New members coming on to the board will get training ... they will need all the training we have had.'
>
> Board member - TMO

GROUP EFFECTIVENESS

9.38 Group performance can be compared to 'ideals' of effective group functioning. Fowler (1988) identified the characteristics of an effective team as common goals; willingness to co-operate; mix of skills and personalities; seeing themselves as a team; effective leadership and self monitoring. These can be identified from perceptions of interviewees and from observation.

9.39 By the time the groups have completed training they should have acquired most, if not all, of these characteristics and be a 'mature' group in which members work together effectively. However, group cohesiveness was found to vary. In several of our case studies the committees were dominated by a small number of individuals. In one case, two members effectively ran the organisation between them and other committee members appeared to play no major role at all. This TMO did not appear to have committee meetings. Views from observers of this group were mixed. One felt, that although the group relied considerably on the Chair and Secretary, the group could continue if these people left. Other commentators had reservations and suggested that the key individuals were excluding others from the decision-making process.

9.40 In another group there were obvious tensions and conflicts between committee members. In committee meetings there was evidence of hidden agendas being played out and there was a tendency to 'nit-pick' and to fail to take decisions. One observer noted:

> 'The group ... has changed over time but has a hard core of members. They come from different directions, they've got different agendas, they are not homogeneous in any way ... it's difficult to hold a group like that together, it's a constant struggle.'
>
> Local authority officer

9.41 However, despite the tensions, the group had the common goal of establishing a TMO and a determination to achieve this aim was clear from all participants. This goal had kept the group together, meeting weekly for four years during which time, it was clear from minutes and interviews, a number of storms had been weathered, involving departing group members, lack of money and political indifference. They had resolved difficulties and had been adaptable and flexible. There was, therefore, a group spirit in shared adversity and, in our view, a willingness by most committee members to put group goals above individual interest. It was difficult to pin-point whether formal training had helped this process but there was evidence that informal training on conflict resolution had helped the group to overcome some problems.

9.42 In another group, although the committee meetings appeared to run well, there had been conflict with 'outsiders'. This group appeared to be fairly elitist, viewing themselves as the knowledgeable and important members of the estate. Some ordinary members suggested that the committee was a clique, not interested in sharing power. Some committee members voiced concerns that the group did not see itself as 'running a business' and an observer of this group felt that though they appeared to operate well, members did not have full commitment or understanding of the responsibility.

> 'The co-op is run ... in many respects ... as an extension of the tenant's association ... votes are taken ... then instead of keeping order and saying "that is the decision..." or speaking up ... they vote even if they disagree with the thing. This leads to huge problems where tenants say "I spoke to a member of the management committee and they don't agree with it".'
>
> Co-op worker

9.43 The other three groups appeared to be operating well with no visible conflicts and observers all felt that these groups worked well together. In one of the groups, the board meetings were led by officers and councillors. Overall, observers felt that it was too early to judge whether residents would really control the board and challenge council policy 'if it came to the crunch'. In another group, the major problem may be staleness. This group had remained substantially the same for a number of years and while the committee meetings were smoothly and competently run, there were few problems and little evidence of innovation or a desire to move into other areas of work. Observers generally felt that the committee relied on staff to run the organisation and make day-to-day decisions.

> 'they ... attend meetings ... they listen to others, they receive information but truthfully, most of them do not do a lot with it ... the committee meets once a month and in between meetings I doubt ... whether they even chat to one another ... I'm not entirely sure they all understand the aims and objectives of the co-op.'
>
> Co-op worker

9.44 This group had little training on team building or committee skills and most skills were learnt on the job. Committee members had attended few training sessions since becoming established and had not visited other organisations. In this case, therefore, the lack of training and on-going stimulation may be a factor in why they had not developed. However, the co-op appeared to run smoothly, they had few problems and competent staff. The committee had a clear idea of what they wanted and appeared to be happy with this. The final group appeared to be well organised, with business-like meetings and clear aims. The committee members all spoke well of one another. The three most effective groups were Tower, Family and Hilltop TMOs. These two latter TMOs had training on committee skills and group work. Tower TMO had little training but had been operating for a number of years and group skills may have been learnt 'on the job'.

ORGANISATIONAL OUTCOMES

9.45 Since the organisation did not exist prior to training, it is not possible to compare 'before' and 'after'. However, where possible we aimed to compare performance with that of the local authority as a whole, and gained participants', observers' and ordinary tenants' views on whether the TMO was more effective than the local authority at providing services. The key indicators of effective performance were taken to be repairs, voids, rent arrears and levels of participation. Since three of the case studies had not taken over responsibilities, and two had only been operational for a year, it would be unfair to draw hard and fast conclusions. In addition, organisational performance will be affected by the environment and the competence of staff.

Repairs

9.46 Table 9.4 shows that Tower TMO had the lowest number of repairs per dwelling while Family TMO had the highest number. However, it must be noted that properties in Family TMO were undergoing modernisation and repairs were carried out by the Council DLO. Tower TMO also completed all its repairs within target time using a caretaker/handyman and private contractors. Tenants were encouraged to carry out their own minor repairs. Bungalow TMO also used private contractors. Training on repairs had taken place in all three organisations. In Tower TMO and Bungalow TMO, committee members sometimes assisted staff to inspect repairs and deal with emergencies, although this was due more to previous occupational interest than training on repairs. The good performance on repairs can be ascribed to staff competence, committee interest and quality environments.

Table 9.4 Comparison of performance in case study TMOs

	Tower	Hilltop	Five Streets	Bungalow	Family	World
Average no. of repairs per dwelling	2.2	M	M	2.8	3.4	M
% completed in target time	100	M	M	97	M	M
% of stock void at March 1992	0	0.7	5.5	1	5.5	4.0
% of tenants in arrears	15	M	M	10	54	M
% of tenants on Housing Benefit	43	M	c75	60	74	c75

M = Missing
C = Estimate by local authority

Voids

9.47 The lowest void rate was found in Tower TMO but two others also had void rates below the average found in local authority tenant management organisations in an earlier study (McCafferty and Riley, 1989). Two TMOs which had not taken over management had high void rates, though the statistics for World TMO showed that the local authority had been working to reduce the number of voids. Voids in Five Streets TMO were also reducing, as the committee had begun to let previously empty dwellings. Both these areas had poor environments and were regarded as unpopular. In Family TMO, a number of voids were held for modernisation or temporary housing purposes and the figure was, therefore, artificially high. The 'true' void rate of this organisation was 1.6 per cent. Reports suggested that the estate has changed from being unpopular to one with a reasonable demand level.

Arrears

9.48 Arrears figures were only available for the established TMOs. Comparison between TMOs show that Bungalow had the lowest number of tenants in arrears while in Family TMO over half the tenants owed rent. Both these areas had a high proportion of tenants in receipt of Housing Benefit:

60 per cent in Bungalow TMO and 74 percent in Family TMO. However, the majority of tenants in Bungalow TMO were elderly, while Family TMO had a broad range of households, including many with children. Studies of tenants in arrears have found that elderly tenants are least likely to have rent arrears while families with children and single people are more likely to be in debt (Scott and Kintrea, 1992). In fact, the true level of arrears in Bungalow TMO was even lower than the statistics indicate as the co-op estimated that in the majority of cases, arrears were due to local authority delays in paying Housing Benefit. Reports from Family TMO showed that arrears fell in the first year that the TMO took over responsibility and had only a small increase in the second year. The estate had previously had the worst arrears rate in the district but appeared to be improving in relative terms. In all three areas, detailed work on arrears was carried out by staff, with TMO committees making decisions on action to be taken at committee meetings.

Tenant participation

Table 9.5 **Indicators of participation in the case study TMOs**

	Tower	Hilltop	Five Streets	Bungalow	Family	World
% of residents voting in ballot	84	90	98	97	61	28
% in favour of TMO	100	92	99	87	97	82
Newsletter issued	Y	N	Y	Y(oc)	Y(oc)	Y(oc)
Public meetings	Y	Y	Y	Y	Y	Y
Members as a % of households	126	158	112	118	101	10
% of members attending AGM	34	32	32	40	4	35
Participation policy	N	N	N	N	N	N

(oc) = occasionally

9.49   In all six case study TMOs, the local authority had carried out a ballot during the development process to ascertain interest in tenant management by ordinary residents of the area. The steering groups had assisted in this consultation exercise and the level of response can therefore be seen as an indicator of tenant participation. In the four smaller TMOs a high proportion of residents voted. However, in Family TMO only 61 per cent of residents took part in the ballot and in World TMO only 28 per cent of residents voted.

9.50   Once the TMO is established, the committee or board should ensure that residents are well-informed, have a say in making decisions, and participation is seen by many as central to the co-operative spirit (McCafferty and Riley, 1989). Five of the six case study organisations had produced newsletters, though only two did regularly. In the TMO which did not produce a newsletter, committee members said that they kept residents informed through door knocking, letters and informal means.

9.51   In most of the TMOs, membership exceeded the number of households. This may be because several residents in some households are members or because potential residents are members. The lowest membership was found in World TMO. However, this organisation was the furthest away from taking over responsibility and intended to carry out a membership drive during its final phase of development. All six held public meetings and in most, the average attendance was between 30 and 40 per cent of the membership. This level of attendance is fairly high. The level of attendance at meetings in Family TMO had dropped and committee members expressed concern over this.

9.52 We were surprised to find that none of the case study TMOs had formal tenant participation policies or agreed methods of consulting tenants. Formal participation policies, newsletters and meetings do not guarantee effective participation and previous studies have found that the processes of participation are more important than the structures (Cairncross, Clapham and Goodlad, 1989). However, we were concerned that lack of evidence of participation was coupled with weak knowledge, by some committee members, of the mechanisms of participation and attitudes toward non-participation such as complaints of 'apathy'. The views of ordinary members are, therefore, an important indicator of the success of participation.

ORDINARY RESIDENTS' VIEWS

9.53 Ordinary residents provide a barometer of the effectiveness of change and of resident satisfaction. Rather than carry out a door-to-door survey, qualitative evidence of residents' views was obtained from group interviews in each area. Residents were asked their views on services from both the local authority and the TMO and on participation issues.

9.54 In three areas which had not yet taken over control, the residents generally felt that the services they received from the landlord were poor. Repairs services were particularly berated along with the attitudes of some council staff.

> 'It's the simple things they don't do ... I've been asking for a socket for six months. I've been through the system so many times, and just nothing. People just get frustrated.'
>
> Ordinary resident - Group interview

9.55 However, in two of the three case studies, ordinary residents still had to be convinced that a tenant management organisation could be better. In Hilltop TMO, a resident expressed the view that the TMO would flop because residents' behaviour would not improve. In World TMO, the residents in the group interview were concerned that an unprofessional committee would not be able to handle the task.

> 'I think it would be very difficult to manage an estate like this ... it worries me that control might be passed to people who are well-intentioned but when it comes to the practice they are going to have a hard job, just like the council.'
>
> Ordinary member - Group interview

9.56 In Five Streets TMO, the ordinary residents were more positive about the prospect of a tenant management organisation. They felt that the service received from the council, particularly with regard to repairs and allocations, was poor and there was a general consensus that the TMO would do better.

> 'They (council) tell you nothing ... shove anyone next to you.'
>
> Ordinary member - Group interview

> 'We took a chance with the co-op because the council were doing nothing at the time. We felt they were better. They were offering so much more than what the council were.'
>
> Ordinary member - Group interview

9.57 In the three established TMOs, views on the services provided were mixed. In Tower TMO, all the tenants were complimentary about the services received. The repairs service was particularly praised as being quick and good quality. The committee were said to be organised in an emergency, the caretaker was courteous and efficient and cleanliness was good. They thought the service was value for money, and might be prepared to pay more if it was properly explained what for, and generally thought that they were lucky compared to other council tenants round about.

> 'We get our repairs done within a short period of time and they do give you their time when they come here.'
>
> Ordinary member - Group interview

9.58 In both the other organisations, residents had complaints. In Bungalow TMO there was a view that 'personalities' decided everything, although most thought that the service provided was an improvement on that provided by the council.

> 'If you need a repair, it comes to the personality of the person, rather than what the repair is.'
>
> Ordinary member - Group interview

9.59 The tenants on this estate valued the local office but were concerned about the lack of privacy because committee members would walk in when they were 'talking private'. They were worried about committee members interviewing applicants and felt that the co-op worker should carry out allocations. One ordinary member (who turned out to be related to a committee member) was more supportive of the difficulties of running a TMO on a voluntary basis.

9.60 In Family TMO, ordinary tenants were definitely not satisfied with the repairs service and several tenants thought that things were no better since the TMO took over, with poor response times and poor quality of work. This was not surprising as the repair system had not changed. Most committee members and some ordinary members did not think that the TMO had enough control over who was allocated a house. Some tenants thought that the TMO did not pay sufficient attention to wider issues on the estate, such as traffic management.

9.61 Views of ordinary residents also varied on whether they were kept informed and consulted over issues which affected them. In three areas, all small organisations, the residents felt that they were well-informed. They said that their TMOs sent leaflets, letters or minutes and some members in each group had been to meetings. In two areas, the TMO office also served as a drop-in centre and some residents said that they used this and would call in 'for a chat'. It was fairly clear from the interviews that the ordinary residents were quite well-informed. They knew at least some of the committee members and had a reasonable grasp of what the TMO was, or would be, responsible for. They felt that views were listened to and that there was encouragement to get involved.

> 'They are quite willing to listen and if there is anything you want to say, you just say it'.
>
> Ordinary member - Group interview

9.62 However, in the other three areas, residents were rather more scathing. None thought that they got regular information and there were accusations that the committees were 'secret societies'. In World TMO, the majority could not remember whether they had taken part in a ballot and there was only a vague recollection of newsletters. None had been to a meeting and most were unaware that any had been held. Of those who knew committee members there were comments about the average age of the committee:

> 'They had a board of geriatrics. They should have more young people involved. Their values come from the 1930s. They don't understand anything of today at all.'
>
> Ordinary resident - Group interview

9.63 Several of the participants in this group interview were unaware that a TMO existed and had never heard of the idea of tenant management. It was also clear, from a door-knocking exercise we carried out on the estate, that many residents were unaware of the TMO. This TMO also had the smallest proportional membership of those we visited and a very low response in the ballot to establish whether residents were interested in being managed by a TMO. This was a cause for concern. However, this TMO was some way off becoming established and had been dormant for some time. The committee intended to carry out a membership drive, hold an AGM and produce some newsletters. There was an indication from the other case studies that membership increased substantially in the run up to taking over responsibilities. Despite this, worries remained about participation in this area. Turnover on the estate was high and many residents did not speak English, but no information was produced in other languages. The estate was also very large and several committee members and ordinary residents suggested that they identified with their particular block, rather than with the estate. The role of the board was seen more as a 'mini council' by local authority officers. While it may be possible to have TMOs which manage very large estates, their role will be very different to that of a small co-operative and either there will be less participation or substantially more resources will be needed to ensure that residents are informed and consulted.

9.64 However, problems of participation are not confined to larger estates. In Bungalow TMO residents complained about lack of information, though they knew the committee members (and generally had poor opinions of them) and had been to meetings. The co-op worker in this area also felt that ordinary members were not well informed and did not think that residents really understood the role and responsibilities of the TMO. Members of the committee of this TMO acknowledged that contact with members had slipped because they had been so tied up with getting the co-operative established. There seemed to be a view that things were settling down and that they could pay attention to such issues.

> 'I spend a lot of time explaining to tenants how the co-op runs, and why it runs that way ... a lot of them are not aware of the concept behind a co-op ... I am very dubious about how well-informed the tenants were when they were required to vote on forming a co-op ... I am not sure they had all the facts. They were told "we will be doing our own repairs, we will get them done quicker." They were not sure what it would mean to them.'
>
> Co-op worker

9.65 Several trainers and workers suggested that information and training should be provided much more extensively to ordinary residents and should cover issues of concern to them and answer questions about security of tenure, ownership of the property, what happens if people have arrears and what would happen if the TMO closed. In Family TMO, which was a large estate, there were similar concerns that many residents did not really understand the nature of the TMO or its responsibilities. A project worker who had been responsible for producing information, holding meetings and organising training had been withdrawn from this area when the TMO was established and committee members confirmed that they had had difficulties in keeping activities going themselves.

9.66 It appeared that the case study TMOs which were less successful at promoting participation had made only sporadic attempts to involve a majority of tenants, with most activity in the early stages and around the ballot. The lack of information and involvement made ordinary residents suspicious, leading to the accusations of 'secret societies'. There may also be a relationship between the size of the area and satisfactory participation, as both the larger TMOs had members who felt less well-informed.

SUMMARY

9.67 The effectiveness of each of the TMOs is summarised in Table 9.6 below. This shows the relative effectiveness of personal, group and organisational outcomes. Overall, the most effective organisation was Tower TMO. Hilltop TMO may be effective when it is fully operational. Five Streets TMO had some trained committee members but had a high committee member turnover and did not hold meetings. Bungalow TMO appeared to be performing effectively in providing services but other indicators of performance were mixed. In Family TMO the individuals and the group were effective but services and participation were less effective. World TMO was performing less well on all indicators.

Table 9.6 **Summary of effectiveness in case study TMOs**

	Tower	**Hilltop**	**Five Streets**	**Bungalow**	**Family**	**World**
Effectiveness						
Office Bearers	Mixed	Good	Mixed	Mixed	Good	Mixed
Group	Good	Good	N/A	Mixed	Good	Mixed
Organisation	Good	N/A	N/A	Good	Poor	N/A
Participation	Good	Good	Good	Mixed	Mixed	Poor
Members' view	Good	Mixed	Good	Mixed	Mixed	Poor
Context						
Environment	Good	Good	Poor	Mixed	Mixed	Poor
Socio-Economic	Good	Poor	Poor	Good	Poor	Poor
LA support	Good	Poor	Mixed	Good	Good	Poor

9.68 The performance in Tower TMO was assisted by a problem-free environment. It is also important to note that committee members in this organisation played a minimal role. Day to day running of the TMO was carried out by the co-op worker. The largely knowledge-based training which this group received was adequate for this role. Hilltop TMO and Five Streets TMO did not have staff at the time of research and duties were carried out by committee members who had received both skills and knowledge training. Some functions in Five Streets TMO appeared to be performed well, but administration was below standard. Bungalow TMO had good organisational performance, though this was assisted by an organised and efficient TMO worker. This TMO had received training but committee members did not always use the skills and knowledge they had gained. They did not think that further training was necessary apart from a few specific knowledge topics such as building construction.

9.69 The organisational performance of Family TMO was affected by the environment and socio-economic factors. This TMO was, in practice, overseeing the running of a local housing office and operating local authority policies. The ordinary members did not notice much difference in services. It may be that if the TMO had been allowed more autonomy it might have been performing more effectively. The training was provided by both the local authority and an agency, but local authority views prevailed. Participation declined when the support worker was withdrawn. World TMO was struggling with mixed individual and group performance, due to committee turnover. The environment was also problematic. However, since modernisation was underway and a new local manager and a new training agency had been appointed, it did appear that the final year of training might have significant impact.

The impact of other factors

9.70 From the analysis of the context, inputs and outcomes of training in the case studies outlined above, and in Chapter 7 and 8, it is possible to identify factors which appear to have had a major impact on the effectiveness of training. These are outlined below.

Political context

9.71 The attitude of the local authority towards tenant management was of critical importance. Some councils took an active interest, with support from senior officers and involvement from individual officers allowed to play a key part in development. In others, commitment from councillors and officers was limited. These TMOs were more likely to experience avoidable delays.

9.72 Lengthy development times, caused by delays in funding or signing the management agreement sapped the confidence and morale of committee members. Long periods of hiatus wasted a significant amount of training as tenants forgot the skills and knowledge they had learnt without practice, leading to a need for 'refresher' courses. Working intensively most TMOs should be able to achieve operational status in three years, some in less.

Physical environment

9.73 In most areas the properties had been modernised either before or during the development of the TMO. It was evident that this had an impact on the satisfaction levels of ordinary members and affected their views of the performance of the TMO, whether or not training had been good. The standard of the physical environment also had an impact on the tasks which the TMO carried out. Properties in poor condition may have a higher need for repair than those in good condition, which may affect performance in this function.

9.74 A related environmental factor may be the type of property which the TMOs manage. Tower TMO and World TMO both operated in areas where multi-storey flats predominated. Both these areas had less sense of community and less social interaction between neighbours than street-level estates, where residents were more likely to find out about activities during casual contact.

Size of TMOs

9.75 The larger estates were less effective at communicating with ordinary tenants, who were more likely to complain that they did not know what was going on. It may be that more attention needs to be paid to wider tenant participation training in larger TMOs.

Socio-economic factors

9.76 Socio-economic factors also appeared to influence performance as, in the established TMOs, the areas with high levels of unemployment were less effective at reducing arrears. Particular communication problems were evident in the TMO with a high proportion of ethnic minority households.

Skills and knowledge of trainer

9.77 Stable, long-term support from one or two trainers, from both councils and training agencies appeared to be more effective than broken patterns, and personnel changes. The ability of the trainer and the support from the agency was critical. One case study TMO had received inappropriate training from a trainer without knowledge of TMOs and, in another case, a TMO, which had a council officer as their main trainer, queried whether this training was 'independent'.

Skills and knowledge of TMO members

9.78 In some cases, members had little management experience and fewer basic skills. These individuals needed skills based training in addition to knowledge orientated programmes. The impact of training on the skills of more experienced committee members was less noticeable, although their knowledge had clearly increased. In some cases, involvement in the development of a TMO had released previously untapped skills and knowledge. Many tenants said the process had increased their confidence.

Financing

Chapter 10 Cost effectiveness and value for money

10.1   This section begins with an overview of spending nationally on tenant training and identifies sources of finance. The costs of training in the case studies are then examined and compared to the effectiveness of different types of training at each stage. Details of how costs were calculated are given in Appendix 1.

NATIONAL SPENDING

10.2   The postal survey asked both local authorities and training agencies how much they spent on training for tenants. The results provide only a partial view as not all councils and agencies were able to answer this question. However, 51 local authorities who did respond between them spent £429,000 on tenant training. Most (63%) spent more than £20,000 in the previous year. Forty-two per cent of the money was given in grants to tenants' groups and a further 30 per cent was attributed to staff time. Only £64,000 was paid in fees to other agencies. It is clear from the postal survey results that the majority of spending was on training for tenants' associations.

10.3   The response from 13 training agencies found that they had provided a total of £645,000 worth of training. This ranged from £400 in one agency to £270,000 in another. The mean expenditure was £50,376. The major source of income, for agencies, was DoE Section 16 grants (56%) followed by Housing Corporation Section 87 grants (24%). Only 12 per cent came from landlords. Agencies were asked whether the income derived from training covered their costs. Of the 21 agencies who answered this question, eight said that it did, and 13 said that it did not. Eight said that they financed the shortfall by cross-subsidy from other activities.

10.4   As Chapter 2 indicated, spending on tenant training by government has increased dramatically in the last few years from less than £1 million to almost £5 million in 1992/93. Department of Environment promotional grants were paid to 30 advice agencies working with approximately 120 local authorities. Ninety-eight feasibility studies were concluded and 44 TMOs received funds for the development stage (DOE 1992). The grant funded up to 100 per cent of costs at the promotion and feasibility stages but at the development stage the local authority was asked to contribute 25 per cent of costs.

10.5   The responses to the postal questionnaire, from a small number of potential TMOs, suggested some unhappiness with the level of grants. Four out of five potential TMOs said that they spent too little on training. However, the in-depth interviews found that most tenants and agencies felt that funding during development was adequate to meet training needs. Some agencies felt that there was insufficient recognition that some groups, perhaps starting from a lower base level of skills and knowledge, needed more support and training.

> 'We are worried that we have to push groups to take on things before they are ready.'
>
> Trainer - Secondary co-op

There were also concerns that the grant regime did not take account of the problems of developing tenant management in severely deprived areas. These issues were explored in the cost-effectiveness analysis of the case studies.

SOURCES OF FINANCE IN CASE STUDIES

10.6   Tower TMO was developed before grants for tenant management were available and was financed by the local authority. In addition to the 'thousands of pounds' paid to the development agency, the authority also invested a considerable amount of senior officer time in the later stages of development and negotiating the management agreement. They also refurbished and equipped the co-operative's office. The total cost, at 1991 prices, was estimated to be around £40,000.

10.7   The total cost of development at Hilltop TMO was around £57,500, of which the Section 16 grant contribution was £25,200 (44%). The local authority, therefore, bore more than half the cost contribution including direct financial assistance, staff time in the development, and refurbishment of the TMO's office. Five Streets TMO had had £82,000 from the Department of the Environment and, in addition to its Section 16 contribution direct to the TMO, the council had invested considerable officer time in the development. In Bungalow TMO, the council appointed a co-op development officer who spent 25 per cent of her time on the development of the TMO for three years and substantial contributions were also made by three senior staff. The local authority bought and equipped the co-op's office and funded the salary of a co-op worker for three months prior to the co-operative taking over responsibilities. A Section 16 grant was paid to the agency working with this TMO in the form of a block grant, and it was not possible to assess the full level of financial support for this group because the agency did not record how much time was spent with the group.

10.8   In World TMO, Section 16 was only claimed for one year and amounted to £12,000. In comparison, the local authority contributed one-quarter of a local authority officer's time and converted a shop premises at a cost of £40,000. The total local authority contribution was estimated to be in the region of £70,000 with further expenditure required for the final year of development. These findings in the case studies suggest that the local authorities were committing considerably more than 25 per cent of the development costs. In addition to paying a contribution to the development costs, all the councils invested staff time and provided office accommodation.

10.9   Not all the funds in developing a TMO are spent on training. Grants can be claimed for staff, office administration, office equipment, travel, consultant's fees and external seminar costs. In practice, the majority seemed to be spent on staff salaries and consultant's fees, but staff and consultants may perform a wide range of tasks in addition to training. The in-depth interviews found that development workers may help groups to apply for funds; deal with letters and office administration; organise meetings; assist in negotiations and provide general support and advice. This research was concerned only with the cost of training and, to gain more detailed information on the cost-effectiveness of training, we carried out an analysis of the costs and benefits of training in the case studies. This is given below for each stage of the development process.

COST-EFFECTIVENESS AT THE PROMOTION STAGE
Costs

10.10 The training programme followed by each of the six case study organisations were very different, as Chapter 8 has outlined. It was difficult in some cases to establish a true record of promotional training because groups had been established and working with community development staff for some years. We took only the events which led to the decision to consider tenant management further, but true costs may be very much higher than this. The activities at promotional stage, which can be identified, are detailed below. Table 10.1 shows that the costs of the promotional stage varied from £1875 in Tower TMO, most of which was for two public meetings, to £15,700 in World TMO. The majority of this cost was for 74 small group meetings across this large estate. However, it must be borne in mind that the tenants in Tower TMO had already expressed an interest in joining a co-operative and had been selected for flats on this estate with that express purpose. In other areas, the motivation for tenants to become involved must be sought at the promotional stage.

Table 10.1 Costs of promotional stage in case studies

Event	Staff £	Fees £	Other £	Total £	Opportunity cost (hours)	Cost per dwelling £
Tower						
Letter	100	250	20	370		
2 x Publicity Meetings	400	580	260	1240	240	
1 x Steering Group	-	245	20	265	20	
				1875	260	£24.00
Hilltop						
1 Seminar	135	100	40	275	20	
4 x study visit	540	160	300	1000	285	
1 x public meeting	200	-	70	270	120	
Survey	150	-	150	300	150	
Appoint trainer	270		20	290	20	
				2135	595	£14.00
Five Streets						
2 x public meetings	400	-	100	500	60	
20 x training		3200	800	4000	400	
1 x study visit	135	20	30	185	20	
				4685	480	£26.20
Bungalow						
2 x Seminar	-	220	30	250	27	
2 x study visit	370	100	100	570	40	
2 x public meeting	140	300	200	640	160	
2 x steering group	-	300	100	400	50	
Survey	70	70	150	290	150	
				2150	427	£11.60
Family						
Feasibility study	200	2500	100	2800	20	
12 x small group meetings	-	3360	440	3980	360	
				6780	380	£8.40
World						
Seminar	150	120	20	290	12	
1 x meeting	280	-	90	370	24	
74 x small group meetings	13885	-	480	14365	1200	
1 x public meeting	280	-	400	680	120	
				15705	1354	£9.30

Study visits

10.11 In Hilltop TMO and Bungalow TMOs, there were a combination of seminars, study visits and meetings. Study visits are an inexpensive way of letting residents see for themselves how a tenant management organisation works. The major costs are staff time and travel costs. Most TMOs did not charge for visits but there is, nevertheless an opportunity cost which was included as a fee. Visits cost between £200 and £700 a time, depending on distance and staff involved. Tenants' reaction to study visits (examined in Chapter 8) was positive and they appeared, in most cases to be more effective than attending an external course or an in-house session in gaining a basic understanding of TMOs. They had additional benefits in providing an opportunity for staff to acquire an understanding of TMOs, and for the 'host' TMO to meet and talk with other groups.

External seminars

10.12 External one-day seminars on tenant management options were found to be a good way for tenants to meet others, and gain a wider view of the issues, though in some cases tenants complained that there was too much information to take in. It did appear, from the session which the researchers attended that the lecture-style format was aimed more at officers than at tenants. However, the seminars attended by tenants in Bungalow and World TMOs provided a catalyst for pursuing interests, and materials were brought back for dissemination to a wider group of tenants. The costs for tenant attendance, at around £100 per person, including travel, were subsidised but thought to be value for money by participants.

Community development support

10.13 Five Streets TMO had a consultant working with the group for a considerable period of time. It was estimated that 20 sessions cost £4,000. Although this looks expensive (see Table 10.1), it must be borne in mind that other groups had the support of community workers whose input has not been costed. The tenants also identified a number of issues which led to other community initiatives on the estate. This was, therefore, more cost-effective than it appeared.

Small group meetings

10.14 Family TMO and World TMO had a large number of small group meetings to promote tenant management. In the case of World TMO, this was very expensive, although it reached around 500 residents. However, the impact of these meetings on those who did not attend subsequent meetings was probably small. There were factors in the design of the estate which led to the decision, taken by the tenants and the trainers, to hold meetings for each 'landing' of tenants but this extensive campaign may not have been the most effective means of informing residents as many of the residents did not speak English.

COST EFFECTIVENESS AT FEASIBILITY STAGE

Costs

10.15 Table 10.2 shows the cost of training at the feasibility stage in the six case study TMOs. The costs ranged from £8,600 at Tower TMO to £24,990 in Family TMO. However the content varied widely. Training in Tower TMO concentrated on producing the rules and beginning discussion on the management agreement, including a wide range of residents sessions in small group meetings. Hilltop had a small number of training sessions and then began to discuss the rules and management agreement. Hilltop concentrated on skills training. Bungalow, Family and World TMOs all had a number of training sessions on housing management and co-operatives. The providers also varied. In Tower, Hilltop and Five Streets training was provided by external agencies while in Bungalow and Family, both local authority officers and agency trainers were involved. Training in World TMO was provided mainly by local authority officers.

Table 10.2 **Costs of training at feasibility stage**

Event	Staff £	Fees £	Other £	Total £	Opportunity cost (hours)	Cost per dwelling £
Tower						
8 x rules		3000	500	3500		
8 x MA		3000	500	3500		
5 x steering group		1500	100	1600		
				8600	800	£110.25
Hilltop						
4 x TMO training	-	1600	200	1800	120	
4 x study visit	-	600	400	1000	200	
1 x conference	-	580	50	630	40	
4 x rules	-	960	200	1160	120	
12 x MA	-	2880	640	3520	290	
1 x public meeting	-	400	100	500	150	
				8610	820	£56.70
Five Streets						
14 x skills	-	3400	740	4140	200	
5 x accounts	-	1400	250	1650	120	
5 x study visits	-	900	500	1385	100	
8 x TMO training	-	3360	400	3760	160	
1 x openday training	-	1400	500	1900	350	
				12835	930	£71.70
Bungalow						
1 x HM training	4110	4550	450	9110	430	
8 x accounts		500	30	530	25	
2 x study visits	390	-	100	490	100	
2 x conference	100	200	50	350	15	
1 x public meetings	270	270	100	640	150	
				11120	720	£59.80
Family						
19 x HM training	4000	8700	1600	14300	500	
6 x MA	2500	3000	450	5950	100	
3 x study visits	-	1300	600	1900	120	
3 x conference		1000	1600	1600	100	
1 x residential	-	1040	250	1240	120	
				24990	940	£30.90
World						
28 x HM training	11900	1000	1260	14160	560	
4 x accounts	50	500	120	670	80	
1 x 2 day	1280	-	400	1680	110	
1 x residential	50	480	200	730	100	
1 x seminar	200	-	200	400	70	
1 x study visit	320	160	200	680	100	
1 x fun day	600	-	1500	2100	200	
4 x newsletter	1200	-	2000	3200	200	
				23620	1420	£14.00

Notes: HM = Housing Management training.
MA = Management agreement training.
Staff = Local authority officers or directly employed staff.
Fees = Training agency fees and fees for external events.
Others = Travel, materials, accommodation costs.

10.16   On a per house basis, Tower TMO with the smallest number of properties was the most expensive at £110.30 per dwelling, but the large number of residents involved meant that the estimated cost per 'tenant hour' of training was £10.75. Bungalow and Hilltop TMOs had similar costs per dwelling (£56.70 and £59.80) though the Bungalow cost per hour was higher, at £15.50 compared with £10.50 in Hilltop. This was due to greater use of external events which only a few tenants attended.

10.17   The two larger TMOs also had similar costs, but because the World TMO estate was twice the size of the estate at Family TMO the cost per dwelling at 'World' TMO was only £14.00 compared with £30.90 at 'Family' TMO. Some tenants commented that there was insufficient depth in the training at World TMO and despite training to produce newsletters and hold a 'fun-day' there was a low ballot turnout. The initially high number of tenants involved in training dropped rapidly as sessions progressed. Comparing inputs, it appeared that World TMO had insufficient support at the feasibility stage. Most of the TMOs had either dedicated support from one trainer, or considerable input from several trainers and local authority staff. However, the trainer at World TMO was only able to devote one day per week of support after the initial intensive training period. This was insufficient for the size of the estate and complexity of its problems.

Housing management training

10.18   Looking at the individual elements of the training programmes, training on housing management topics appeared to vary from none in Tower TMO to 28 sessions in World TMO. However, both Tower and Hilltop residents did discuss housing management topics during their rules and management agreement training, so direct comparison is misleading. The programmes in Bungalow, Family and World TMOs were more similar. Bungalow TMO had 18 sessions costing £9,110, Family had 19 sessions costing £14,300 and World had 28 sessions costing £14,160. In all three, there were a combination of local authority and agency trainers. The 'hourly rates' of local authority staff, including overheads, were often less than the rates of agency trainers. For example, an officer on a salary of £17,000 per annum had an hourly rate of £18.86 per hour including overhead costs compared with a agency trainer's hourly rate of £35.00 per hour. Where training was given by local authority staff it might therefore be less expensive than training given by an agency trainer. Local authority staff were not always less expensive, however, as training given by a senior officer (£30,000+) would cost £45.30 per hour and sessions where both a senior local authority officer and an agency trainer attended could cost £80.00 per hour (Appendix 1 gives details of calculations). Although attendance at training sessions by local authority staff and trainers was more expensive than attendance by one person there were several benefits. Tenants had two viewpoints, local authority staff learnt about TMOs and training agency staff learnt more about the authority. Sessions varied in price from £750 per session at Family TMO to £430 at Tower TMO.

Accounts

10.19   Three TMOs had training on book-keeping and accounts. In Five Streets and World TMOs this training was given to the full committee but in Bungalow TMO, two tenants attended a local college course of 8 sessions at an estimated cost of £250 per person. This compared with £150 per person at Five Streets and £67 per person at World TMO. In both Bungalow and Five Streets no accounts training had been put into practice but in World TMO, book-keeping was carried out by the TMO worker. Chapter 8 indicated that participants had mixed views of accounts training and indicated that more general training on financial control may be more useful for most committee members, with specialist training provided, if required, to office-bearers taking responsibility for accounts.

Skills training

10.20 Five Streets TMO had the greatest number of sessions on skills, mostly on letter writing, office administration and word-processing. These 14 sessions cost around £590 per person. However, the group included a number of participants with little previous office experience and committee members who undertook training were subsequently able to pass basic skills on to the others. None of the other TMOs had such training, though the research found some committee members with low literacy skills for whom such training may have been useful. However, most committee members were able to write letters, take minutes and keep records without the need for further training.

10.21 Other skills learnt by the TMOs included holding a public meeting, organising an open day and producing a newsletter. TMO members at Five Streets had a week's training on organising an open day at a cost of £1,900 while a sub-committee at 'World' TMO produced two newsletters at a cost of £3,200, and organised a fun-day at a cost of £2,100. These costs include the costs of materials which could be considerable. For example the newsletter production cost £2,000 while the training cost £1,200. However, the open days and newsletter served a wider purpose of informing ordinary tenants and were therefore a cost-effective use of the monies. The training components were good examples of structured practical learning.

External conferences and seminars

10.22 Members of four of the six groups attended external seminars and conferences. The events which had the most positive reactions were the residential courses attended by members of Family and World TMOs, though other one-day events on specific topics were also thought valuable. Most participants appeared to have brought back fresh ideas and the conferences, which cost around £100 per person for a one-day event and £200 per person for a weekend, depending on travel costs, were good value for money. External events often produced copious handouts but Chapter 8 found that tenants often preferred shorter leaflets, which would cost no more to produce.

COST EFFECTIVENESS AT THE DEVELOPMENT STAGE
Costs

10.23 Costs at the development stage ranged from £19,900 in Tower TMO to £49,900 at Five Streets TMO. Table 10.3 shows that on a cost per dwelling basis Five Streets TMO was the most expensive at £283.50 and World TMO was the cheapest at £21.80 including planned expenditure.

Management agreement

10.24 Both Tower and Hilltop TMOs began training on the management agreement at the feasibility stage and Tower TMO had only the final negotiating sessions during the development stage. Costs of training on the management agreement varied depending on the number of sessions and trainers involved. Bungalow and Hilltop had the greatest number of sessions (23 at Hilltop and 18 at Bungalow) and highest cost (£8,750 at Hilltop and £11,330 at Bungalow) but this included time for retraining when the new Modular Management Agreement was introduced. Ten to 12 sessions appeared to be more usual. Family TMO had the smallest number of sessions but other training on the agreement was included in housing management training. The amount of training required on the agreement depends on whether discussions on housing management issues are incorporated into this training or held separately.

Table 10.3 **Costs of training at development stage**

Event	Staff £	Fees £	Other £	Total £	Opportunity cost (hours)	Cost per dwelling £
Tower						
18 x TMO training	-	5670	1000	6670	360	
2 x MA	1120	500	200	1820	54	
6 x staff management		2940	200	3140	90	
7 x interim committee	1400	3430	70	4830	170	
6 x public meeting	1200	1470	800	3470	600	
				19930	1274	£255.50
Hilltop						
11 x HM training	-	4800	730	5530	270	
5 x repairs		1200	150	1350	120	
6 x conferences		4975	2390	7365	235	
6 x policies		3355	260	2615	145	
11 x MA	1750	3000	480	5230	130	
6 x interim committee		1170	200	1370	140	
10 x housing practice		2730	500	3230	280	
1 x public meeting		400	100	500	150	
				28910	1470	£185.50
Five Streets						
200 x HM training	30000	-	2000	32000	1300	
72 x skills	2000	-	1500	3500	280	
3 x residential	930	-	1200	2130	72	
3 x study visit	320	-	450	770	96	
2 x seminar	260	-	600	860	20	
10 x MA		3200	460	3660	72	
6 x finance		900	200	1100	120	
20 x housing practice	4000		600	4600	420	
Induction	780		500	1280	420	
				49900	2800	£283.50
Bungalow						
15 x HM training	3250	3355	400	7005	360	
18 x MA	9630	1000	700	11330	320	
2 x staff management		1200	-	1200	120	
3 x study visits	540	120	50	710	100	
2 x conference	50	200	40	290	40	
1 x office visit	380	-	-	380	20	
12 x interim committee	1130	1470	200	2800	280	
10 x housing practice	1900	2500	500	4900	250	
1 x public meeting	270	270	100	640	150	
				29255	1640	£157.30
Family						
18 x HM training	5400	7200	1800	14400	600	
5 x study visits (from)	-	1000	500	1500	75	
7 x conference		3380	720	4100	600	
10 x steering group	1500	2000	300	3800	200	
6 x MA	2400	1200	300	3990	90	
9 x interim committee	3120	2600	330	6050	300	
1 x public meeting	350	350	500	1200	160	
				25040	2025	£43.30
World						
12 x MA	4620	-	480	5100	190	
12 x TMO training	2800	850	400	4950	240	
2 x accounts		250	80	330	24	
1 x residential	100	840	200	1140	175	
1 x study visit	320	160	200	680	64	
1 x public meeting		300	400	700	100	
4 x newsletter	1200	-	4000	5200	200	
Interviews	500	-	1000	1500	40	
Planned training	(4000)	(11300)	(2000)	(17300)	(800)	
				36800	1803	£21.80

Notes: HM = Housing management training.
MA = Management agreement training.
Staff = Local authority officer and directly employed staff.
Fees = Training agency fees and external events fees.
Other = Travel, materials and accomodation costs.

Housing management

10.25 The most unusual, and the most expensive, programme was followed by Five Streets TMO who employed a trainer full-time for 18 months. The direct employment of a trainer was less expensive per session (£160) but this course was not value for money as the course was not focused on TMOs but covered housing management more generally. The £32,000 total cost of the course compares poorly with the £7,000 spent at Bungalow TMO and £14,400 spent at Family TMO where sessions were given by local authority staff and agency trainers and geared towards TMO needs. Some trainers used role-play, games and exercises and these methods appeared to have more impact than 'talks'. These sessions were more expensive than talks.

Practical learning

10.26 Both World and Bungalow TMOs had training on interviewing skills and employing staff. At World this was given by local authority staff during the feasibility stage while at Bungalow the sessions were given at the development stage by staff from a local college. In both TMOs the committees employed staff shortly after and found the training very useful. These sessions cost around £1,500, or around £125 per person and were considered good value for money as they assisted the TMO to make staff appointments and gave skills in interview technique.

Interim committees

10.27 Four of the TMOs had practice at running a TMO by holding interim or shadow committees. World TMO intended to have this training. The costs ranged from £1,400 at Hilltop TMO to £6,000 at Family TMO. The cost difference was due to the cost of support. Hilltop, Five Streets and Bungalow TMOs also had a number of sessions of structured 'hands-on' practice, operating office systems, speaking to tenants and ordering repairs. Costs ranged from £3,200 at Hilltop to £4,900 at Bungalow TMO. Both these types of experiences were felt to be useful in ensuring that the TMOs could manage their functions providing practice in the skills and knowledge learnt and enhancing the theoretical learning.

OVERALL COSTS

10.28 The overall costs for all three stages of development in the six case-study TMOs are shown in Table 10.4. These ranged from £76,100 in World TMO to £30,405 in Tower TMO. On a cost per 'tenant training hour' basis, Hilltop was the most economic with a cost of £12.30 per hour and Tower TMO was next lowest cost per hour at £13.00, while Family TMO was the most expensive at £20.00. Tower TMO was the most expensive on a cost-per-dwelling basis at £389.80 per dwelling, and Five Streets TMO was the next most expensive at £378.70 per dwelling. The larger TMOs were considerably cheaper at £82.50 per dwelling in Family TMO and £45.20 in World TMO. Their 'per tenant hour' and 'per unit' costs do not necessarily mean, however, that the effectiveness of training was similar.

10.29 Chapter 9 found that the office bearers who had received training during the development of the TMO had all increased their skills and knowledge and that some attitudes had changed. It was difficult, retrospectively, to attribute particular training sessions to these improvements since learning was a cumulative experience. In four TMOs some training had been received by ordinary members as well as by committee members and this additional participation had a cost, though there may have been other benefits.

Table 10.4 **Costs of training for promotion, feasibility and development in case studies.**

TMO	Promotion	Feasibility	Development	Total
Tower				
Cost	£1875	£8600	£19930	£30405
Opportunity cost (hours)	260	800	1274	2334
Hilltop				
Cost	£2135	£8610	£28190	£38935
Opportunity cost (hours)	595	820	1470	2885
Five Streets				
Cost	£4685	£12825	£49900	£67410
Opportunity cost (hours)	480	1050	2800	4330
Bungalow				
Cost	£2150	£11120	£29255	£42525
Opportunity cost (hours)	427	720	1640	2787
Family				
Cost	£6780	£24990	£35040	£66810
Opportunity cost (hours)	380	940	2025	3345
World				
Cost	£15705	£23620	£36800	£76125
Opportunity cost (hours)	1356	1420	1803	4579

10.30 The six case study TMOs had received very different patterns of training and this section aims to assess the cost-effectiveness of the programmes at each stage for different sizes of estate, taking into account the different skills and knowledge which participants had at the outset.

PROMOTION

Small estates

10.31 The skills and knowledge required at the promotion stage, varied from group to group, and from individual to individual. For areas with an established tenants' group on a smaller estate, a combination of a leaflet drop, a door-to-door survey, and a public meeting might assess initial interest. The steering group might then have a study visit, an external seminar and a number of meetings to discuss problems and outline options. The costs of Hilltop and Bungalow at £2,100 each indicate that this was sufficient to achieve tasks at the promotional stage.

Large estates

10.32 The feasibility studies and 14 small group meetings at Family TMO, accompanied by a leaflet drop does not seem excessive at £6,800. World TMO cost £15,700 but the estate was twice the size of Family TMO. While the researchers felt that some of the cost could have been more effectively spent on provision for ethnic minority households this would be unlikely to make the cost of promotion less expensive.

Severely deprived estates

10.33 Five Streets TMO required considerable input at a pre-promotional stage as some of the tenants in this area lacked the skills and knowledge of tenant activists in other TMOs. Spending an additional £2,500 on provision of basic skills and knowledge appeared good value for money.

FEASIBILITY
Small estates

10.34   Costs for the smaller TMOs ranged from £8,600 at Tower TMO to £12,800 at Five Streets TMO for training at the feasibility stage. Tower TMO included wide participation of ordinary residents through small group meetings. Training only the steering group would have decreased costs. However, this group did not visit any other TMO or attend any external conferences. The programme followed by Hilltop, for the same price may represent a minimum for a small TMO. The additional costs at Five Streets were mainly due to the high level of skills training and may be justified due to the low skills base.

Large estates

10.35   Little ineffective training was identified in Family TMO and £25,000 appeared to be a reasonable cost for an estate of over 800 houses. However, the researchers felt that 'World' TMO had been inadequately resourced for the size of the estate and would have benefited from additional expenditure.

DEVELOPMENT

10.36   Costs in Hilltop and Bungalow may have been lower if it had not been necessary for tenants to train on the management agreement twice while Tower TMO could have benefited from more skills training and external conferences. The housing management training at Five Streets was, however, not good value for money. An overall cost, for smaller TMOs, of around £26,000 seemed more reasonable. Both Family and World TMOs spent, or planned to spend around £35,000 on training at the development stage. These costs seemed adequate for the TMO committee but further provision would help to ensure that ordinary residents were kept informed.

STAFF TRAINING

10.37   These costs do not include local authority staff training, although some staff did accompany tenants on study visits, and others may have learnt 'on the job' while negotiating the management agreement and attending meetings. Chapter 6 indicated that a wide range of staff needed training on TMOs and suggested that this should be carried out in parallel with training for the tenants involved in TMOs. None of the case study TMOs had carried out extensive staff training on TMOs and it was beyond the remit of the researchers to calculate such costs. However, as the commitment of senior staff and councillors is vital to the promotion of a TMO and staff turnover and delays were found to cause problems, particularly at the development stage, provision for funding a staff training programme would assist the effective development of a TMO.

SUMMARY

10.38   Although only a minority of councils spent money on tenant training, those which did spent significant amounts. The local authorities whose TMOs were included in the case studies made significant contributions, both in direct financial support and in kind.

10.39   All the TMOs had locally based training programmes, though five of the six also had study visits and external sessions and all included some training by local authority officers and some by agency trainers. Sessions varied in cost depending on the number and 'hourly rates' of trainers, the cost of accommodation and, for external events, the distances travelled. The least expensive local sessions were those delivered by a single trainer, however in some instances both local authority trainers and training agency workers attended sessions. This was more expensive but may have resulted in enhanced training.

10.40   The training programmes had tried to take into account the skills and knowledge of the tenants and difficulties in the areas, such as size of the estate. Additional training to compensate for low skills and knowledge and training for a wider group of residents was more expensive, but was thought to be beneficial. Locally based housing management training varied in cost from £160 per session to over £750 per session. The methods used appeared to have an impact on effectiveness. Trainers who used role-play games and exercises appeared to be more effective than those who did not. Most of the case studies learnt about the management agreement by considering it clause by clause. Ten to twelve sessions on this seemed to be usual. Costs depended on the trainers involved and whether sessions incorporated some housing management training.

10.41   Study visits were found useful at all stages of development. These varied in cost from £200 to £700, depending on staff support and distances travelled but on a 'cost per tenant' basis these were good value for money. External residential conferences were more expensive, usually around £200 per tenant but thought worthwhile for those who attended. Tenants often brought back copious quantities of reading material but it appeared that well-designed leaflets were more likely to be read and would cost no more to produce.

10.42   Structured practical learning sessions on organising events and producing newsletters were more expensive than 'learning by experience' but were probably better value for money. Housing practice sessions were used by three TMOs and ranged in cost from £3,200 to £4,000. 'Interim' committees were also a useful learning tool and costs for this ranged from £1,400 to £6,000, depending on the number of sessions and staff involved.

10.43   Overall, it was felt that the costs of promotion for a small estate were cost-effective at around £2,100. However, additional expenditure would be required for additional skills training, ethnic minority languages and large estates. The minimum cost of training at the feasibility stage was £8,600, while a budget which would allow a reasonable training programme at the development stage would be around £26,000. Larger estates and more complex problems would require additional funding as at the promotional stage. There were a few examples of badly targetted training. These included the £32,000 spent at Five Streets for an intensive housing management programme and the large number of small group meetings at World TMO at the promotional stage. There were also doubts about whether book-keeping and accounts training was necessary or effective for most committee members.

Chapter 11   Self-financing and commercial development

SELF-FINANCING
TMO funding for training

11.1   The research was intended to address the issues of whether training for established TMOs might become self-financing. This was interpreted as the ability of TMOs to pay for their own training or failing that, use resources other than those provided by central government. In most cases, once a TMO is established, an allowance will be received from the local authority for management and maintenance costs. The levels and formula for calculating allowances are decided in the final stages of negotiating the management agreement. Section 16 grant funding is not available for established TMOs and most TMOs need to find money for training from their allowances.

11.2   Around half (31) of the TMOs responding to the postal survey said that they had training budgets and EMBs were more likely to have one than co-ops. Budgets of established TMOs ranged from £300 to £3,000. Potential TMOs, at the development stage, had budgets ranging from £2,500 to £39,000. Not surprisingly, training represented a small proportion of expenditure in the longer established TMOs and a high proportion of expenditure of TMOs at the development stage.

11.3   The levels of allowances are usually based on the costs which the local authority would have spent to manage the stock itself. Allowances to TMOs were found to vary considerably. Some TMOs, as the postal questionnaire found, had quite generous training budgets, while others had very little.

> '(The budget) reflects what the local authority was spending on management. The proportion of that which goes on training ... is very small and tenants are faced with the same problem.'
>
> Trainer - National agency

> 'The money that is in our budget (for training) is very limited ... it's a breakdown of the city budget ... which is peanuts - just about pays for a weekend ...'
>
> Board member - TMO

11.4   When asked for their views on training expenditure, 56 per cent said that they were spending too little and only one said that they were spending too much. Forty-one per cent said that they were spending about the right amount. Most (95%) said that the training they had received was good value for money. Of the three case studies which were established, only one (the largest) had substantial training, whilst the other two attended few training events.

Attendance at external events

11.5   Although 63 per cent of established co-ops replying to the postal survey said that they had undertaken some training since becoming established, this was only 31 TMOs. Trainers commented that demand for courses was low and where programmes have been tried, many courses had to be cancelled. This lack of interest may be partly due to the attitudes in some TMOs that continued training is not necessary but cost was also found to be an important factor. Many tenants thought that commercially priced training sessions were expensive, and pointed out that travel and accommodation costs had to be added to the fee for the course.

> 'Some of them, you just can't believe them, we are talking in the region of £150-£250 per person and most of the conferences are held in London, so you are talking about the cost of travel and the cost for accommodation, even if it's only B and B.'
>
> Committee member - TMO

11.6 Even at £65 for a day seminar, agencies said that sessions did not attract sufficient delegates to cover costs. The conclusion which must be drawn is that TMOs either need bigger training budgets or that external courses require subsidy, to bring them within the reach of TMOs.

> 'Our initial intention for one-day seminars was 50 or 60 delegates. We actually got 20 to 40. That doesn't cover the staff cost in putting training events on.'
>
> Trainer - National agency

> 'If it's just a general training course, we're talking in the region of £30-£40 ... (some agencies) cover everything and usually at a reasonable cost.'
>
> Committee member - TMO

Better financing by local authorities

11.7 A number of possible solutions were suggested to assist training to become self-financing. First, some trainers and tenants suggested that local authorities might improve support. Many local authorities appeared to fix the allowances on a 'no-extra' basis. This means that the budgets are based on what the authority would have spent on management and maintenance on the estate. Some have made specific provision for training but most do not. In the case-studies two of the authorities offered training in addition to the budget but in the third there was no training budget and little assistance from the authority.

11.8 There is an issue here about the proposals for Compulsory Competitive Tendering. The proposed Right to Manage suggests that local authorities must be satisfied that a TMO is competent and cost-effective. In order to remain competent the members should have continuing training. There is a case to be made for specific budgetary provision for on-going training in TMOs in addition to allowances for management and maintenance to assist in ensuring competence.

> 'There should be a sum of money, specifically identified within the budget, for training ... The tenants need to negotiate for a reasonable sum. It needs to be built in. It's like building a house and having no maintenance - it will fall down eventually. A management committee needs on-going training if you want it to succeed.'
>
> Trainer - National agency

Local authority co-op units

11.9 Some local authorities had specialist co-op officers, or co-op units, whose job was to assist in the development of new groups and provide support to established groups. In most cases this involved liaising between the TMO and local authority sections and the provision of training. The in-depth interviews found that tenants valued such specialist staff. Other local authorities with several TMOs, or plans to develop TMOs may find the appointment of specialist staff assists good relations between TMOs and their landlord.

Support to agencies

11.10   A number of training agencies said that they offered on-going support and advice to established TMOs for which there was no specific payment. Some trainers suggested that provision might be made, within Section 16, for one-day 'review days', at six monthly intervals, throughout the existence of a TMO. This review would be flexible so that, if a TMO had a specific problem, the agency could respond.

> 'The role of secondary co-ops is now a service agency. Co-ops do phone with their problems and ask for advice, which we provide but there are the limitations of funding. We're thought of as having a public face - public responsibility - but that's not reflected in the funding - we can't say (to the co-op) this will cost you £500. Do the DOE want us to act as a private consultancy or a regional service agency?'
>
> Trainer - Secondary Co-op

Tenants levy

11.11   There was little support for the idea of a levy on tenants in the TMO to fund training for committee members. There may be Housing Benefit problems with a voluntary levy and TMO comittee members felt that an additional rental charge would be seen as a penalty by residents.

> 'I'd be totally against (a training levy). The members pay sufficient in their time and commitment and voluntary work. It's an absurd idea. The money that the government puts into training courses, its pennies compared to the billions they waste ... I'd like to see the percentage of people who get a job after ET.'
>
> Committee member - TMO

Finance from other sources

11.12   The postal survey found that six TMOs had raised money on their own. Four of these have raised less than £1,000, though groups said that they had had money from 'other' sources, including three TMOs who had received funds from charitable sources, although none had had more than £5,000. The postal questionnaire was not detailed enough to establish the source or purposes of these funds. Some groups levied a small charge to other organisations who visited them. This was used to provide funds for training.

> 'We try to do these talks and have people down on the estate because we do generate some income and that all goes back into training, which is good ... That's why I give up my time to do it ... we're aware that there's an on-going training need and training is expensive so we try and solve funding.'
>
> Board member - EMB

Networks

11.13   The case studies and in-depth interviews found that some TMOs had formed regional networks with other TMOs to share problems and experiences. This was obviously considerably less expensive than commercially organised courses but may need initial start-up funding to a training agency until it becomes established. The existing networks had had such support but at least one had become self-sufficient.

> 'Co-op links ... is for co-ops to meet and discuss problems ... we felt it was important to have a regional network - to get together as a body - to lobby. The individual co-ops pay a nominal amount for letters etc. Each meeting is held at a different co-op. The co-op hosting the event organises the venue ... and visiting co-ops pay to spread the costs.'
>
> Committee member - TMO

Training by tenants themselves

11.14 A small number of respondents to the postal questionnaire indicated that they used their own members to train other committee members. This is not always possible since, if office bearers have left, there may be no-one who can pass on the skills and knowledge.

11.15 As Chapter 8 indicated, only one of the groups in the case studies had an induction programme for new committee members. The costs involved were the opportunity costs of committee members who would have to spend a little more time than usual carrying out tasks. Another group had produced a comprehensive information pack for new residents and sent newsletters and minutes out regularly. Ordinary residents in this TMO felt they were particularly well-informed and consulted about decisions. This pack would not have been expensive to produce. The newsletters would involve the opportunity cost of committee members and photocopying, while distribution of minutes, which would be produced anyway, costs only the price of photocopying and distribution.

COMMERCIAL DEVELOPMENT
Gaps in provision

11.16 The review of training, and training material, is described in Chapter 5 found that the major gap in training at promotional stage was information on how councils operate. Tenants interviewed said that they would welcome more information on how their council operates and on variations on policy and practice between local authorities. Although the postal surveys and case studies found that councils are involved in providing training, much of this was informal. Tenants were also concerned with wider issues on their estates. However, there was little information on problems such as dogs; crime; security; repairs and neighbour nuisance.

11.17 There were few materials available for the feasibility stage for specific skills, such as presentation, campaigning, holding a public meeting or producing a newsletter. Evidence from the case studies found that much of this skills training was carried out by hands-on learning. The research suggested that tutored guidance was a more effective way of learning practical skills and that trainers may welcome check-lists and case study examples to help them provide support.

11.18 Many trainers used the Modular Management Agreement as a basis for training but some interspersed sessions on the agreement with formal and informal training sessions on topics such as allocations, rent arrears and employment. We felt that this was more effective and that more agencies could work this way. There were surprisingly few training materials on these topics, although some agencies had produced unpublished training packs. Financial knowledge and negotiating skills also appeared to be poorly covered.

The market

11.19 One of the reasons for the gaps was that the market for training and training materials for tenant management organisations was small and, even if every established and potential TMO attended a particular course or bought a publication, this would not produce a 'best seller'. One of the reasons why most published materials were aimed at the promotional stage is that participation, committee skills and options for control had a much larger market.

11.20 In addition, whilst many established TMOs had small training budgets, one-third of TMOs had no training budgets. Few committee members read books on TMOs, although some said that they would read leaflets and booklets about specific issues of interest and about other TMOs. TMOs did not have extensive libraries of materials, other than materials they had brought back from training courses. Agencies and educational institutions tended to buy one copy and then plagiarise or photocopy. Although there were gaps, any materials produced were likely to need subsidy and free or low cost distribution.

> 'We had 1000 copies printed. I have sold it to about 40 different organisations, but I've only sold 100 copies ... We sold 4 copies to polytechnics. Why isn't the DOE prepared to subsidise certain things, for colleges at least half a dozen copies in the library?'
>
> Trainer - Secondary co-op

11.21 There is scope for development of some materials for a much wider market. Tenant participation officers in local authorities and housing associations use materials produced by others and may be willing to pay for trainers' packs on a wide range of issues. The introduction of Compulsory Competitive Tendering means that tenants in local authorities will need training on how the council works, setting standards, drawing up contracts and monitoring. They will also need knowledge of a variety of housing management functions, local authority finance and estate problems. Skills such as negotiating, reading tender documents and financial statements and committee skills would also be useful.

Materials by consortia

11.22 One of the disadvantages of a competitive market is that agencies saw training material they had produced as their 'bread and butter' and were unwilling to publish or share ideas with other organisations. A number of trainers said that much time was invested in 're-inventing the wheel'. There were some examples of co-operation such as the 'Southside' training courses produced by a consortium of secondary co-ops, and the TMC development handbook produced by Chisel, Hexagon and Lewisham LBC. The Tenant Participation Workers' Groups and the Tenant Management Training Group also brought trainers and support workers together to share ideas. Such consortia might be commissioned to produce published material.

> 'I have produced quite a lot of material in the last two years. We have done a book and a series of leaflets ... The problem is that ... we are in competition and don't want to give away information we have spent two years developing. On the other hand, it is material that could be used by other agencies. It remains to be seen whether (the DOE) would support small agencies producing material on a national basis, to use the expertise that's available.'
>
> Trainer - Secondary co-op

Word-processor disk material

11.23 Both trainers and tenants stressed the importance of materials tailored to local situations. There was also a problem of keeping material up to date. Materials on housing legislation and employment law date rapidly. The problems of making information locally applicable and keeping it up-to-date limit commercial possibilities and dictate the kind of materials produced. One suggestion was to make material available on word-processor disk, so that trainers could update, amend and bespoke as required.

Skills videos

11.24 Material which does not date and is widely applicable, such as knowledge of how to run a committee, producing a newsletter, negotiating skills and public speaking can be used with little adaptation for local circumstances. There is particular scope here for video materials designed for, and featuring, tenants.

Presentation

11.25 The standard of many handouts from training courses was disappointing. It may be that insufficient time is available for preparation but much of the material would have benefited from desk-top publishing. Trainers may need more time to invest in maintaining their files of materials, and in training in desk-top publishing. This would increase the cost of training, but might produce better quality products which tenants can use afterwards. In some cases, the problem was too much material, written in a non-user friendly way. There may be a need for a guide for trainers on how to write and present training materials. Some trainers said that they had never had any training on how to train. 'Training for trainers' courses might be useful, with adequate provision for training time.

Materials from TMOs

11.26 Tenants can also learn from other TMOs. A few had produced materials about themselves but there is scope for more, to be used alone or in conjunction with study visits. Such materials would also be useful for on-going groups to give induction training for new members. Groups reaching the end of development could be encouraged to produce materials about their experience. Some trainers were already doing this:

> 'I was just doing it on the tenants' basis for development themselves. We are going to produce a project report of the whole thing, how long it took, how it was set up, why we developed the training structure we did. Things like that will be more useful in the long run ... than a load of training material.'
>
> Trainer - Secondary co-op

Materials from local authorities

11.27 Local authorities did not appear to produce much material. Only the council, perhaps in conjunction with tenants, can produce material on 'How the council works'. More councils could be encouraged to provide information for tenants such as handbooks and regular newsletters and more could be encouraged to provide training themselves.

Good Practice Guide

11.28 The Modular Management Agreement has helped tenants to understand their responsibilities and options but we feel that there are better ways of learning than simply going through this clause by clause. The TMC *Development Handbook* (Williams and Swailes, 1991) was a good first step in providing an outline programme around the management agreement. However, there is scope for further development. We suggest production of a *Good Practice Guide* for tenants and trainers setting out a logical training programme, effective training methods, sources of materials and a guide to agencies.

Co-ordinating lists of events

11.29 One complaint, which a number of TMOs made, was that it was difficult to budget for training. Information on external courses was received throughout the year. There were several suggestions that a co-ordinated list of events should be available in advance so that expenditure could be planned. It might be possible to produce such information in conjunction with a newsletter for TMOs, with agencies and TMO contributing articles and advertising.

> 'We are budgeting all the time. We don't get the information at the beginning of the financial year, so we can't balance it out. You could send ten people on one course - and then in the middle of the year, three or four courses may spring up that are really good - you want to send people on them but the finances are not there.'
>
> Committee member - TMO

Training the trainers courses

11.30 A number of tenants had become experienced speakers at seminars and conferences and some had begun to offer training programmes for other groups. TMOs which did this successfully had put considerable effort into it, attending 'training for trainers' courses and producing business plans. More 'training the trainers' courses would help tenants to train others both in their own organisations and externally.

> 'We hope to do the majority of training in our initiative centre ... There's a lot of skill in communities, training the community for the community. We see the initiative centre for training groups in basic skills. We hope to employ one or two workers ... to create employment. We're drawing up a business plan.'
>
> Committee member - TMO

Certificates

11.31 Many tenants told us that they felt they ought to get a certificate for the training they have received. Some trainers did give certificates and this appeared to offer additional motivation to tenants to attend. An American trainer interviewed indicated that USA community training often used certificates for attendance and for 'successful completion', that is achieving learning outcomes. This could be more widely adopted in Britain.

Qualifications

11.32 The National Certificate in Tenant Participation, run by a number of colleges and universities in England, was mentioned by a number of trainers and tenants as a potentially useful course both during development and for on-going TMO committee members. Some local colleges also ran courses in communication skills, accounts and book-keeping, running a small business, and computer skills. Some tenants in TMOs had attended such courses and found them useful. Certain office bearers may need more in-depth skills and knowledge on particular topics and local colleges may be able to provide tuition at reasonable cost.

SUMMARY

11.33 Once a TMO is established, it receives an allowance for management and maintenance to meet on-going costs. These allowances were found to vary considerably. EMBs were more likely to have a budget specifically for training (9 out of 11) than co-operatives, where only one-third had a budget. Over half the established TMOs (56%) said that they spent too little on training. We felt that there was a case for writing an allowance for training into the management agreement.

11.34 Some local authorities were found to be providing training to established TMOs through specialist support staff, or funding external training. Although a number of agencies said that they provided on-going support and advice to TMOs, both trainers and tenants felt that TMOs could not easily afford to pay for such services. Some trainers suggested that provision might be made, within Section 16, for 'review days' at six monthly intervals throughout the existence of a TMO.

11.35 There was little support for the idea of a levy on tenants in the TMO to fund training for committee members. Most tenants were totally against the idea.

11.36   Some TMOs had raised money from other sources, including charitable funds, though the purpose of such grants was not clear. Others raised money by charging other organisations who visited them. This was thought to be a useful way of raising additional funds.

11.37   Forming networks with other TMOs was also thought to be a useful and inexpensive way to share problems and experiences. There was support for the formation of more regional networks, perhaps facilitated by regional or national training agencies, though this may need 'start-up' support.

11.38   Some TMOs indicated that they used their own members to train others and a small number of tenant managers had undertaken 'training the trainers' courses. This form of training relies on the voluntary efforts of tenants themselves and needs to be more systematic in some organisations than is presently the case.

11.39   The market for training and training materials aimed specifically at TMOs was small and the importance of materials tailored for specific situations was stressed by both trainers and tenants. However, there is scope for development of materials and training packs for a much wider market. This market includes local authority tenant participation and tenants who will be involved in CCT.

11.40   The 'core curriculum' of skills and knowledge is wide. Training was only available in any quantity on committee skills. There was evidence that there would be considerable demand for materials on the wider range of topics.

11.41   The quality of many of the materials produced was disappointing. One suggestion was that material might be made available on word-processor disk, so that trainers could update, amend and bespoke as required.

11.42   It was also noted that there were no videos, featuring tenants, on skills such as committee meetings, interviewing or negotiating. The use of videos intended for industry suggests that video materials on skills would be a useful supplement to training.

11.43   There is also a need for more materials specifically for training for tenant management. Some agencies provide training, and have produced material, geared around the Modular Management Agreement but a Good Practice Guide and more comprehensive set of training materials would be useful.

11.44   Materials produced by TMOs themselves, about their experiences were also appreciated by other groups and could be useful for induction training for new members. More TMOs could be encouraged to produce such materials, perhaps as part of their development programme.

11.45   The introduction of certificates for the training which tenants undertake in developing a TMO may assist motivation and reduce turnover of TMO committee members.

Chapter 12 Conclusions and recommendations

INTRODUCTION

12.1 The preceding chapters of the report have set out the findings of the research. This final chapter draws the different elements of the project together, to address the aims and objectives which were outlined in Chapter 2. The chapter looks in turn at the:

- Extent of tenant management
- Provision of training for tenants
- Staff training
- Topics of training
- Training for ordinary members
- Gaps in material
- Commercial development
- Methods of training
- Effectiveness of training on the individual
- Organisational effectiveness
- Value for money
- Self financing
- Other issues

At the end of each section, the key policy issues arising from the research are identified and recommendations, to improve training for tenant management in the future, are made.

EXTENT OF TENANT MANAGEMENT

Policy stimulus

12.2 Chapter 2 described the slow growth of tenant management in the early 1980s and policies which were intended to stimulate the formation of TMOs. These included the introduction of Section 16 grants, encouragement of tenant involvement in Estate Action initiatives and the introduction of the Estate Management Board model (para 2.3).

12.3 The research suggests that these measures have had some success, as over half (54%) of the local authorities responding to the postal questionnaire said that some of their estate-based initiatives had developed from Estate Action programmes (para 4.8). In addition, the research found that the number of local authorities who had taken steps to develop a TMO had increased from one in ten in 1986/87 to one in five in 1992 (para 4.9).

12.4 The introduction of the Section 16 grant regime also appeared to have had an impact as there had been a considerable increase in the number of TMOs established, especially since 1990 (para 4.16). There was particular interest in the EMB model and 44 local authorities nationally had considered this compared with 33 who had considered a TMC (para 4.11).

12.5 Other government policy was also found to have played a part in the motivation of tenants and their landlords to form a TMO. In four of the six case studies, tenants mentioned that fear of being taken over by a private landlord or a Housing Action Trust, as a result of provisions in the 1988 Housing Act, had been a factor in their decision to set up a TMO (para 7.7). More recently, government proposals to introduce Compulsory Competitive Tendering to housing management had spurred some local authorities into action. However, it was clear that some landlords had pursued tenant participation initiatives without the encouragement of government policy, as two-thirds of the estates, where joint management was taking place, were not part of an Estate Action proposal (para 4.8) and 70 per cent of councils claimed to have at least one participation initiative in their area (para 4.22).

Distribution of interest

12.6 The research found that interest in tenant participation and tenant management had developed unevenly. Metropolitan councils were most likely to have taken steps to develop a TMO but only 12 per cent of district councils had done so (para 4.9). Most of the established TMOs were in London, with clusters in the North-West and West Midlands. However, there were none in the East or South-East and only one in the East Midlands and South-West regions (para 4.18). Larger local authorities were most likely to have developed participation initiatives but it appeared that smaller councils had not given this issue priority.

12.7 Although interest in tenant management had increased, there was considerable potential for further development as local authorities named 253 estates which had tenants involved in joint-decision making (para 4.5). There were indications however, that many of the initiatives were linked to modernisation or environmental improvement projects and may only be temporary arrangements (para 4.7).

12.8 It was clear from the research that, in most cases, the idea of forming a TMO had come from the council (para 6.2). A number of the trainers, who were interviewed as part of the research, felt that many tenants' groups were unaware of the options available or the existence of Section 16 funding. Knowledge of funding and training available may encourage tenants to approach their landlord to discuss the possibility of tenant management.

Issues

12.9 The issues arising from the research findings on the extent of tenant management are that:

a) Government policy has had an impact but interest in tenant management is unevenly distributed.

b) Many estate-based initiatives may be temporary arrangements.

c) Many tenants' groups may not be aware of the existence of Section 16 or the training available.

12.10 **RECOMMENDATION 1 - Promotion of Tenant Participation and Tenant Management**

a) **The DoE should sponsor the production of leaflets on the availability of Section 16 funding and local training agencies and ensure that these are widely distributed to local authorities and tenants' groups.**

b) **The DoE should seek to monitor the prevalence of tenant participation and tenant management to assess the extent to which tenant involvement increases.**

PROVISION OF TRAINING FOR TENANTS

Local authority support

12.11   Provision of training was seen as an important prerequisite for tenant involvement and the research found 88 councils (34% of respondents) who said that they provided or assisted in the provision of training for tenants. This was a considerable increase in activity since the 1986/87 survey found no English authorities who provided training (para 4.24). However, support for training was uneven and the distribution of types of authority and their geographic location was similar to the distribution of those who had taken steps to develop tenant management.

Training agency provision

12.12   Forty-five agencies, who were involved in the provision of training for tenants, were identified. Twelve of these could be described as national agencies who were willing to work anywhere, while the remainder served a regional or local catchment area (para 4.25). There were more local and regional training agencies in regions where a higher proportion of authorities supported training, such as Inner London, North-West and Yorkshire and Humberside and few in some regions where there was little local authority support, such as the South-West. However, despite the fact that there were 5 training agencies in the East region, only one in five of local authority respondents from the area supported training (para 4.26).

Training for TMOs

12.13   Most training supported by local authorities was, in fact, given to tenants' associations (para 4.28). However, the research found 56 local authorities and 30 training agencies who said they were involved in the provision of training to potential TMOs (para 5.1). It was clear that most training was actually carried out by training agencies as 82 per cent of authorities, who supported training at the promotional stage, used external trainers. PEP and TPAS were the most frequently mentioned providers (para 5.2).

12.14   Tenants involved in TMOs also played a significant part in the provision of training for developing TMOs and were mentioned by 21 per cent of local authorities and 30 per cent of agencies (para 5.3). Much of this training may have been in the form of study visits although some tenants involved in TMOs visited other groups to give talks or spoke at conferences and seminars.

Issues

12.15   The issues raised by the research findings on the provision of training are:

    a)   The lack of support for tenant training by many district councils.

    b)   The uneven geographic distribution of local authority support for tenant training.

    c)   The uneven geographic distribution of training agencies.

    d)   That some local authorities took little active part in training.

    e)   Tenants involved in TMOs could potentially play a greater role in training others.

12.16   **RECOMMENDATION 2 - Tenant Training**

    a)   **Local authorities should provide training for tenants and support tenant attendance at external events.**

    b)   **The DoE should consider the merits of supporting the establishment of additional local and regional training agencies in the North and South-West of England.**

12.17 **RECOMMENDATION 3 - TMO Training**

a) **Local authority staff should play a more active role in training for tenant management organisations.**

b) **Local authorities and training agencies should work in partnership to support and train TMOs.**

12.18 **RECOMMENDATION 4 - Tenants as Trainers**

a) **Local authorities and training agencies should encourage tenants involved in TMOs to attend 'Training for Trainers' courses, to enable them to train tenants in other TMOs and their own new members.**

b) **Local authorities, potential TMOs and training agencies should extend the use of tenants involved in TMOs as trainers.**

STAFF TRAINING
Local authority staff

12.19 Housing staff were found to be an important source of initial information and support and lack of knowledge about TMOs could cause delays in the development process. Chapter 6 detailed the training provision for local authority staff and concluded that, although many local authorities had provided training for staff on tenant participation and tenant management, this was mainly of an introductory nature and needed to include a wider range of staff.

Training agencies

12.20 Many trainers had learnt 'on the job' - an unsatisfactory arrangement for them and for tenants - and many felt that there was inadequate time available for training. Support networks were valued and the National Certificate in Tenant Participation was thought to be a useful qualification for new trainers.

TMO workers

12.21 Training provision was varied and some TMOs encouraged staff training, while others made little provision. This was, potentially, a very isolated group of staff.

Issues

12.22 Ensuring the local authority officers and agency staff have the skills and knowledge to assist in the development of a TMO was felt to be critically important. The key issues were:

a) Wider training provision on tenant participation for staff.

b) Adequate training and support for staff in training agencies.

c) The lack of training opportunities for TMO workers.

12.23 **RECOMMENDATION 5 - Training For Local Authority Staff**

a) **Local authorities should ensure that all staff working on housing functions have received training on the implications and benefits of tenant participation.**

b) **The promotional/feasibility stages for TMOs should include training for local authority staff to develop their understanding of tenant management and awareness of the impact of their activities on potential TMOs.**

c) **Local authorities should ensure that a range of key local authority staff have training at the development stage for TMOs on the management agreement and its implications for the council and the TMO.**

12.24 **RECOMMENDATION 6 - Training Agencies**

a) The DoE should ensure that financial arrangements for payment of agencies include provision for staff training.

b) Training agencies should ensure that trainers have adequate time for learning new skills and knowledge and for updating. The Audit Commission guide of 10 days training per member of staff per year is recommended.

12.25 **RECOMMENDATION 7 - TMO Workers**

a) TMOs should ensure that TMO workers are encouraged to plan their training needs and should provide adequate resources to ensure that needs are met.

b) Local authorities should ensure that management allowances for TMOs include adequate financial provision for staff training.

c) Local authorities should offer places to TMO workers on appropriate internal staff training courses.

TOPICS OF TRAINING
Promotion

12.26 Chapter 3 detailed the tasks which a steering group needs to carry out from the initial idea of establishing a TMO to taking over functions. At the promotional stage the key skills and knowledge required were:-

- Options available
- Estate issues and priorities
- Tenant participation
- How the council works

(para 3.25).

12.27 Although there were many training materials and events available on the options for control and tenant participation, the research raised concerns that some groups were presented with only one option and did not receive information on other possibilities, as only 4 (36%) of the established EMBs responding to the postal survey had been given training on tenant management co-operatives (para 5.7).

12.28 Only two of the six case study TMOs had discussed estate issues and priorities at the outset, although others may have discussed these prior to training for tenant management (para 8.10). Less than half (46%) of the postal survey respondents had received training on 'how the council operates' (Table 5.3) and, although five of the six case study TMOs received this training at some stage, not all tenants were happy with the depth of knowledge obtained (para 8.14).

Issues

12.29 The issues raised by the comparison of promotional training received with the ideal model are:

a) Concern that some of the tenants may not have received information about all the options available.

b) Insufficient information about how the council works.

c) Lack of discussion about estate issues and priorities.

12.30 **RECOMMENDATION 8 - Promotional Training**

The promotional stage should take account of the existing skills and knowledge of tenants and should aim to ensure that by the end of this stage tenants have a basic understanding of:

- a) **the different options available (e.g. Tenants' Associations, TMCs, EMB)**
- b) **estate issues and priorities (e.g. repairs, security, neighbour problems)**
- c) **the benefits and implications of tenant participation**
- d) **how the council works (e.g. structures, policies, finance).**

Feasibility

12.31 The key skills and knowledge identified at the feasibility stage were:-

- Overview of housing management
- Responsibilities of TMOs
- Team-work skills
- Practical skills

(para 3.25).

12.32 The coverage of training on housing management topics and the responsibilities of a TMO was generally good. Almost all the respondents to the postal questionnaire and all the case study TMOs had received training on these issues. However, training provision of team-work and practical skills was more mixed. Although 70 per cent of respondents to the postal survey had received training on team-work, only 41 per cent received training on public speaking and even fewer (37%) received training on writing letters and reports (Table 5.3). Indeed, some trainers said that they did not hold with 'community development' training and concentrated on teaching facts and knowledge (para 3.6). Four of the six case study TMOs had some practical skills training but the amount varied widely. For example, one TMO had received extensive skills training but three others appeared to have learnt public speaking and team work skills 'on the job' (para 8.18).

12.33 The researchers were concerned that the system for Section 16 funding at the development stages placed a lot of responsibility on the tenants' groups to decide their training programme. The research found examples of inappropriate training, due to the lack of knowledge by tenants of the skills and knowledge they needed.

Issues

12.34 The issues raised about training at the feasibility stage are:

- a) Lack of emphasis by some trainers on practical skills and team work.
- b) Lack of knowledge by tenants of the skills and knowledge required to run a TMO.

12.35 **RECOMMENDATION 9 - Feasibility Training**

Training at the feasibility stage should ensure that by the end of this stage tenants have:

- a) **developed an overview of housing management functions**

b) an understanding of the nature of the responsibilities of a TMO

c) an understanding of a TMO's legal status in relation to the local authority and the relevance of Section 27 of the Housing Act 1985

d) developed team-working and practical skills

e) an understanding of the skills and knowledge needed at the development stage.

Development

12.36 A wider range of skills and knowledge were needed by groups who continued to the development stage. The ideal model suggested that the key areas were:-

- Management agreement
- Policies and procedures
- Committee work
- Negotiating skills
- Staff management
- Financial control.

12.37 The Modular Management Agreement was widely used as the basis of training at the development stage and most (87%) of the TMOs in the postal survey had received some input on the management agreement but only two-thirds (65%) had received training on finance for TMOs and only half (50%) had training on how to negotiate. The six case study TMOs had all received training on the management agreement although the number of sessions on this varied from 12 in one TMO to 23 in another. It should be noted, however, that some of this latter training was re-training on a new agreement (para 10.24). None of the case study TMOs had received formal training on negotiating skills and only four out of the six had received training on staff management or financial control (para 8.25 - 8.27).

Issues

12.38 The issues raised about training at the development stage are:

a) Lack of training on negotiating skills

b) Patchy provision of training on staff management and financial control

12.39 **RECOMMENDATION 10 - Development Training**

Training at the development stage should ensure that by the end of training tenants have:

a) **an understanding of their management agreement**

b) **developed and understood their policies and procedures**

c) **developed skills in running meetings and operating as a committee**

d) **developed negotiating skills**

e) **an understanding of the role and responsibilities of an employer and basic knowledge of employment law**

f) **an understanding of local authority and TMO finances and financial control issues.**

Training for office bearers

12.40   While all potential committee or board members of TMOs need basic skills and knowledge, the ideal model also identified a need for specific individuals to gain a wider and more fully developed range of abilities (para 3.21). The research found that many of the office bearers in the case studies had some existing skills and knowledge (para 7.33). However, specific training to develop critical areas did not always appear to have taken place (para 9.29).

Issues

12.41   The issue raised by the examination of training received by office-bearers is that not all of these individuals had received appropriate training.

12.42   **RECOMMENDATION 11 - Training for TMO Office Bearers**

In addition to the key skills and knowledge identified in Recommendations 8, 9 and 10, the training programme should ensure that:

- a) **office bearers understand their roles and responsibilities**
- b) **the Chairperson has developed chairing, leadership and public speaking skills**
- c) **the Secretary has developed skills in written communication and an understanding of the legal responsibilities of a TMO**
- d) **the Treasurer has developed financial skills and an understanding of accounts and financial control**
- e) **other office bearers have developed specific skills and knowledge relevant to their roles and responsibilities.**

TRAINING FOR ORDINARY MEMBERS

12.43   The evidence from both the postal surveys and the case study TMOs suggests that, in most cases, training was concentrated on the steering group or committee rather than being spread to other residents of the estate (para 5.13). Most of the committee members interviewed were mature adults (over 40) and ethnic minorities appeared to be under-represented. There were slightly more men than women among the office bearers (para 7.31).

12.44   Although several of the case study TMOs had tried to broaden training to a wider group of people this had often been unsuccessful. Some ordinary members interviewed felt that they had too many family responsibilities to attend regularly (para 8.3). The lack of creche facilities at local training sessions may have been a barrier to some potential participants. There was also a lack of information available in other languages and particular communication problems were evident in World TMO which had a high proportion of ethnic minority households.

Issues

12.45   The findings on the lack of wider involvement in training raise concerns about the provision of facilities for some groups, particularly younger people and people from ethnic minorities, to participate in training.

12.46   **RECOMMENDATION 12 - Wider Training**

- a) **Potential TMOs, local authorities and training agencies should provide training and information for ordinary tenants as well as the steering group.**
- b) **Section 16 grants and local authority support for TMOs should take account of the need for provision of materials in ethnic minority languages, use of interpreters and creche provision.**

GAPS IN MATERIALS

12.47 The research included a major review of materials which might be used for training, including both published and unpublished materials. The topics covered by the materials were described in Chapter 5. The review found that there were many training materials on the options for control, tenant participation and committee work. However, there was surprisingly little on:

- How councils operate
- Estate problems
- Financial issues
- Specific housing management functions
- Structured practical skills training
- Negotiating skills

(para 5.14).

12.48 It was difficult to assess whether there was a lack of materials on these topics because they were not emphasised in training, or whether they were not taught because there was a lack of materials.

12.49 Equal opportunities principles were emphasised by many trainers but some tenants felt that this had been over-stressed. The best materials were publications which discussed the importance of equity and equality in TMO policies and practice on, for example, allocations, participation and recruitment. However, many materials were concerned with changing attitudes rather than stressing policy and practice.

12.50 A further concern was the standard of many of the handouts. The researchers felt that investment in desk-top publishing and preparation time would improve materials greatly (para 11.25). Trainers pointed out that they had to tailor material for each TMO individually so preparation time was almost always required.

COMMERCIAL DEVELOPMENT

12.51 The research found that there was limited scope for true 'commercial' development due to the small size of the market (para 11.16). However, there was scope for the development of some materials for a wider market of tenant participation officers in local authorities, and tenants' associations. The need for tenant training for involvement in Compulsory Competitive Tendering was felt likely to create demand for further materials in the future.

12.52 Chapter 11 outlined opportunities for development. These were:

- the production of material by consortia of training agencies and TMOs
- producing material on word-processor disk, which could be updated and customised by trainers
- scope for videos on skills for tenant management featuring tenants
- encouraging TMOs to produce their own materials
- 'Training the trainer' courses (see Recommendation 4)
- Encouraging local authorities to produce materials

12.53 **RECOMMENDATION 13 - Materials**

a) **The DoE should encourage consortia of training agencies and TMOs to produce training packs on estate problems, financial issues, specific housing management functions, practical skills and negotiating skills.**

b) These training packs should be made available, at low-cost, to local authorities, training agencies and TMOs. Provision of training material on word-processor disk should also be considered.

c) The DoE should consider supporting the production of videos on the range of skills needed for tenant management such as negotiation and effective meetings.

d) TMOs should be encouraged to produce materials on their development experiences and activities, perhaps in the form of illustrated booklets, which can then be used to generate income.

e) Local authorities should provide information and training material on 'How the Council Operates'.

f) Training agencies should ensure that they have quality training materials on all key areas of skills and knowledge as set out in Recommendations 8, 9, 10 and 11.

g) Training agencies should invest in desk-top publishing equipment and ensure that trainers have adequate preparation time to produce customised material of quality.

h) The DoE should ensure that financial arrangements for training agencies include payment for adequate preparation time.

METHODS OF TRAINING

12.54 Chapter 5 described the methods of training used nationally. Single training sessions, which might be in-house events or external seminars, were the most frequently mentioned form of training provision overall, while a series of sessions was the most popular form of training used at the development stage. Study visits to other TMOs were used particularly at the feasibility and development stages while residential meetings were the least used form of training.

12.55 Chapter 8 assessed the methods of training used in the case study TMOs in more depth. This found that the most effective methods were:-

- Local training
- Small group sessions
- Structured practical skills training
- Study visits
- Residential courses
- Local college courses
- Use of manuals and leaflets.

Local training

12.56 All the interviewees stressed that training should be locally based and locally relevant and, in fact, most training was delivered on site. However, some videos, external events and sessions by guest speakers were seen to be less relevant to local problems and issues.

Small group sessions

12.57 Most training was also delivered to small groups and these sessions were thought to be a more useful way of informing wider groups of residents than larger public meetings. Role-play was used by some trainers to enhance communication, interviewing and meeting skills and those tenants who had undertaken this training appeared to be more effective than those who had not. Games involving mock budgets and fake money appeared to be an effective means for committee members to learn financial skills and knowledge.

Practical skills

12.58   Some of the case study TMOs had received structured training sessions on how to chair meetings, public speaking, producing a newsletter or holding an open day. These sessions appeared to be more effective than learning by 'bitter experience' which sometimes had a demoralising effect. Four of the six case study TMOs operated interim committees prior to taking over functions and found these useful.

Study visits

12.59   Study visits to other TMOs were cited as a key factor in the decision to proceed by two of the case study TMOs and were found useful by others. They were also appreciated at later stages of the development process. Some groups had visited their local housing office and this had given tenants a better insight into how local authority systems operated than classroom learning.

Residential courses

12.60   External events were appreciated mainly for the opportunity to meet other tenants. However, the content of residential courses appeared to have a greater impact.

Local college courses

12.61   One group had made extensive use of local college courses and facilities and some tenants from other TMOs had attended secretarial, finance and small business courses. Although many of these were not explicitly designed for TMOs, those attending felt that they provided more depth and were particularly useful for office-bearers who wished to improve their skills and knowledge.

Manuals and leaflets

12.62   Many tenants had copious quantities of handouts from training events, but manuals and short leaflets seemed to be most likely to be referred to after the event.

Ineffective methods

12.63   Few tenants enjoyed lengthy lectures without the opportunity for participation and found ploughing through the management agreement clause by clause very dry, unless it was relieved by group discussion. Shadowing, that is learning by observing other TMO members, had mixed results and was most effective when it was organised as a structured induction course. However, some tenants were clearly better at training than others and it was not always possible for office-bearers to instruct their successors.

Issues

12.64   Although many trainers used a wide mixture of methods to suit the learning styles of tenants there were examples of ineffective methods.

12.65   **RECOMMENDATION 14 - Methods of Training**
   a) **Trainers should use a wide variety of training methods.**
   b) **Training agencies should implement quality control systems to ensure that trainers have skills and knowledge in a wide range of training methods.**

EFFECTIVENESS OF TRAINING ON THE INDIVIDUAL

Training required

12.66 The training required by a particular TMO was found to depend on the existing skills and knowledge of tenants, the functions they intended to take responsibility for and whether they intended to employ staff. Although many of the office bearers had some existing skills and knowledge, in some cases tenants had little experience of office or committee work. In such cases more skills-based programmes were required. There was evidence that some training programmes had been tailored to suit the needs of the particular group of tenants but it was also clear that there were gaps in almost all the programmes.

Skills and knowledge gained

12.67 All participants in training had gained specific knowledge about TMOs and some had gained skills or had existing skills enhanced. Training had given positive views of TMOs and had increased confidence in most cases. But not all office-bearers had a desire to further increase their skills and knowledge, and training appeared to have little effect on attitudes towards equal opportunities. Knowledge of financial issues and wider tenant participation were also thought to be weak areas.

12.68 Not all office-bearers had the opportunity to practise the skills and knowledge they had learnt as many of the tasks, which might be considered part of a secretary's or treasurer's duties, were carried out by staff. In contrast, office-bearers in other TMOs were closely involved in the day to day running of the organisation and carried out many of the operational tasks themselves.

Other factors

12.69 In addition to the existing skills and knowledge of participants there were several other factors which appeared to have an impact on the effectiveness of training. The motivation of tenants was clearly important and both trainers and tenants suggested that certificates for successful completion of training programmes may help to maintain interest and reduce the drop-out rates.

12.70 The attitude of the local authority was also very important. Where commitment from councillors and officers was low there had been delays leading to a loss of morale and a need for 'refresher courses'. Wider staff training and the inclusion of staff in feasibility and development training may assist this problem (see Recommendation 5).

Issues

12.71 The issues arising from the evaluation of the impact of training on individuals are:-

   a)   Training must be geared to the needs of a particular group.

   b)   Demotivation and loss of morale was a problem for some groups.

12.72 **RECOMMENDATION 15 - Effectiveness of Training**

Trainers and potential TMOs should carry out a training needs analysis at beginning of the feasibility and development stages and base training programmes on this.

12.73 **RECOMMENDATION 16 - Provision of Certificates**

   a)   **Training agencies should give certificates to tenants who achieve the key skills and knowledge at each stage of the development process.**

   b)   **Local authority associations and the Housing Sector Consortium should explore whether National Vocational Qualifications (NVQs) could be extended to tenant managers.**

ORGANISATIONAL EFFECTIVENESS

12.74 The latter part of Chapter 9 looked at a number of key indicators of effective performance in the case study TMOs and obtained the views of ordinary residents. There was a relationship between the physical and socio-economic problems in an area and performance on arrears and repairs. To some extent, this also affected residents' perceptions and satisfaction with the TMO. However, training alone will not change a poor environment or solve unemployment problems.

12.75 It was more surprising to find that none of the case study TMOs had a tenant participation policy, though most held public meetings and issued newsletters. Fewer residents had voted in the ballot in the larger TMOs and turnout at the AGMs had dropped dramatically in Family TMO. In the two larger TMOs, and in Bungalow TMO, tenants felt that they were not kept informed. The researchers felt that the size of some estates was a barrier to effective communication and that large TMOs needed to put considerable additional resources into keeping ordinary members informed and involved, both during feasibility and development and once they were established.

Issues

12.76 The findings on organisational effectiveness raise issues about wider participation.

12.77 **RECOMMENDATION 17 - Organisational Effectiveness**

a) **All TMOs should have policies and procedures for wider participation.**

b) **Local authorities should ensure that TMO management allowances include adequate resources to encourage and support wider participation.**

VALUE FOR MONEY

12.78 Chapter 10 provided a detailed analysis of the costs of training in the case study TMOs. This found that the overall costs of training varied from £76,100 at Five Streets TMO to £30,405 in Tower TMO (para 10.28).

Good value for money

12.79 The analysis of the costs of different training methods found that those which were effective were good value for money.

- Study visits cost between £200 and £700 per visit but often included the entire steering group. The cost per tenant was therefore low.

- Residential courses cost around £200 per tenant but included around 15 hours of training.

- Role-play, games and structured practical learning were no more expensive than more traditional methods.

- Producing manuals and leaflets cost little more than forests of unread handouts.

- Training sessions involving local authority officers and the training agency were more expensive than attendance by only one trainer, but gave a broader view.

- Interim committees were also expensive, from £1,600 at Hilltop TMO to £6,000 at Family TMO, but were felt to be very useful by trainers, tenants and local authority officers.

Poor value for money

12.80 There were some examples of poor value for money, for example, Five Streets TMO employed a full-time trainer for 18 months to deliver a housing management training programme. Although this cost £32,000 it did not give the participants the knowledge they needed about TMOs.

12.81 A second example was the 74 small group meetings held by World TMO at the promotional stage, which cost £14,000. Although these sessions were attended by 500 residents, expenditure on leaflets in ethnic minority languages and interpreters may have reached a wider audience.

12.82 Detailed training on accounts was provided for all committee members in some of the case study TMOs, but tenants' reactions to this were mixed. It may be better value for money for interested tenants to attend local college courses.

12.83 To some extent the inappropriate training experiences were experimental and, as each group of tenants has different needs, some failures may be inevitable. If these are not expensive they may be considered to be part of the learning experience - you may not know that you do not like accounts training unless you try it - and some training tapped previously unused skills. However, expensive failures might be avoided if trainers have appropriate skills and tenants are more aware of training needs.

Costs at each stage

12.84 There were differences in the cost of training at each stage, depending on the size of the estate and other factors. The analysis suggested that a small TMO (less than 200 properties), with no additional factors, should be able to achieve the tasks at each stage for a **training** cost (at 1992 prices) of:

- £2,100 at the promotional stage
- £8,600 at the feasibility stage
- £26,000 at the development stage.

Larger estates, areas with high ethnic minority populations and committees with few existing skills would need more.

Issues

12.85 The major issues raised by the assessment of value for money were that:

a) Some TMOs had used methods which were poor value for money.

b) Cost-effective methods had not always been explored.

12.86 **RECOMMENDATION 18 - Value for Money**

a) **Local authorities, training agencies and TMOs should assess the cost-effectiveness of different training methods and programmes.**

b) **Local authorities, training agencies and TMOs should consider whether local colleges can assist in meeting training needs in a cost-effective manner.**

SELF FINANCING

12.87 Financing training was a problem for established TMOs, as Section 16 funding ceased to be available once the management agreement is signed, and the TMOs receive an allowance for management and maintenance. Since the research was completed, the DoE has recognised the problems of newly established TMOs and has agreed to provide limited additional Section 16 support for the first year of operation. However, longer term problems of financing for training remain. Chapter 11 addressed the issue of self-financing in some detail and the points are briefly reviewed here.

12.88 Two thirds (67%) of established TMOs responding to the postal questionnaire, had identified training needs and 63 per cent had received some training. EMBs were more likely to have received training than TMCs and were more likely to have a specific training budget.

12.89 Some local authorities were assisting by providing training, producing videos and manuals and funding external training but over half the established TMOs felt that they spent too little on training.

12.90 Some TMOs had found effective and inexpensive ways to train new members and update existing members. These included:-

- Structured induction training by other tenants
- Training by TMO staff
- Producing information packs
- Forming networks with other TMOs.

12.91 A few TMOs had found other sources of funding and others raised money by charging other organisations to visit them.

Issues

12.92 Resources for training were a problem for many established TMOs but many interviewees felt that continued training was vital. The issues are that:-

a) Some established TMOs received no further training.

b) Some had no training budget.

c) Local authority support was varied.

12.93 **RECOMMENDATION 19 - Financing Training in Established TMOs**

a) **Local authorities should ensure that arrangements for earmarked and adequate training budgets are included in the management agreement and are paid in addition to management and maintenance allowances.**

b) **Local authorities should ensure that they have adequate arrangements to support and monitor TMOs in their stock.**

c) **The DoE should consider the provision of pump-priming support to establish regional networks for TMOs to meet, exchange views and share training.**

d) **Established TMOs should be encouraged to raise additional funds by charging for study visits from developing groups and producing materials on their history and activities.**

e) **The DoE should consider providing support for a regular newsletter for established TMOs which would include details of forthcoming training events.**

OTHER ISSUES

12.94 The research raised a number of other issues about the effectiveness of training. One key area of concern, expressed by both trainers and tenants, was that the system of monitoring, used by the DoE, was largely aimed at recording the number of training sessions run. Information on the topics and methods of training was not requested and it was, therefore, difficult for the DoE to assess whether appropriate training had been received. There was also no method of assessing the quality of training.

12.95 A second and related issue was that the choice of trainer was critical. Tenants appeared to receive little guidance about skills and knowledge required and this had resulted in one TMO selecting a trainer who lacked knowledge of TMOs. Although there were some materials which outlined training needs, there was no comprehensive manual which tenants and trainers could use to ensure they obtained effective training.

Issues

12.96 The issues arising from the research are that:

a) trainers must have appropriate skills and knowledge

b) systems of monitoring the quality of training are inadequate.

12.97 **RECOMMENDATION 20 - Quality Control of Training**

a) **The DoE should investigate systems, such as accreditation, which would ensure that trainers have appropriate skills and knowledge.**

b) **The DoE should examine its system of monitoring Section 16 grants with the aim of ensuring that key topics have been covered at each stage of development.**

c) **The DoE should investigate how systems of monitoring the quality of training can be implemented.**

d) **The DoE should consider developing a system of quality assurance to monitor the effectiveness of training.**

12.98 **RECOMMENDATION 21 -** *Good Practice Guide*

The DoE should initiate the production of a *Good Practice Guide* which would give guidance on:

a) **the selection of trainers and agencies**

b) **the key skills and knowledge required to run a TMO**

c) **assessment of training need**

d) **effective methods of training**

e) **evaluation of training**

f) **value for money in training.**

The Guide should be made available to local authorities, trainers and tenants considering the development of a TMO.

OVERALL

12.99 The broad conclusion of the research was that the Section 16 programme, to provide training and support for tenants wishing to develop a TMO, was successful. The number of TMOs had increased and one in five of local authorities had taken steps to promote a TMO. Generally, training has been effective and good value for money. There were many examples of innovative and imaginative methods, being pursued by enthusiastic trainers, and tenants felt that the time spent had been well worth-while. Ordinary residents were also supportive of the idea. There were, however, areas which could be improved and the implementation of these recommendations should improve effectiveness and ensure value for money from the programme.

Appendices

Appendix 1 Research methods

The research used a wide variety of methods. In the first stage the research aimed to establish a national picture of training provision for tenant management. This involved:

- a postal questionnaire survey of all local authorities in England
- a postal questionnaire to agencies providing training for tenants
- a postal questionnaire to all established TMOs in England and those who had reached an advanced stage of development
- a review of materials which might be used as a basis for training
- attendance at training events
- in-depth interviews with local authority officers, trainers and tenants involved in TMOs.
- group discussions with trainers

Postal questionnaires

A postal questionnaire was sent to all 365 local authorities in England. The overall response rate was 77 per cent as Table A.1 shows. The response rate was slightly higher for London boroughs (84%) than for metropolitan boroughs (81%) and district councils (76%).

Table A.1 **Response from questionnaire to local authorities**

Type of LA	Total	All stock transferred	With stock	Number of responses	Number of refusals	Response as % of all LAs with stock
London Borough	33	1	32	25	2	84%
Metropolitan District	36	-	36	29	-	81%
District Councils	296	17	279	203	9	76%
	365	18	247	257	11	77%

A similar questionnaire was sent to 67 training agencies. Thirteen were sent to invalid addresses, nine said that they did not provide training to TMOs, leaving an effective total of 45. In total, 34 questionnaires were returned, which was a response rate of 76 per cent.

The TMO questionnaire was sent to 117 tenant management organisations identified through information provided by the Department of the Environment, supplemented by information from local authorities and training agencies. Of the 117 TMOs identified, six were subsequently removed from the list, because the organisation had been duplicated on the address list, or was not involved in managing council housing or was a secondary housing co-operative. Out of an effective total of 111 there were seven refusals and 66 questionnaires were returned completed. This represented a total response rate of 60 per cent.

Table A.2 **Response to questionnaire to TMOs**

	TMC		PTMC		EMB		PEMB		Other		Total	
	No.	%	No.	%	No.	%	No.	%	No.	%	No.	%
Total	68		14		14		14		7		117	
Deleted	0		0		0		0		6		6	
Effective total	68	100	14	100	14	100	14	100	1	100	111	100
Refusals	5	7	0	0	0	0	2	14	0	0	7	6
Non-responses	22	33	8	57	3	21	5	36	0	0	38	34
Responses	41	60	6	43	11	79	7	50	1	100	66	60

TMO = Tenant Management Organisation
TMC = Tenant Management Co-operative
PTMC = Potential Tenant Management Co-operative
EMB = Estate Management Board
PEMB = Potential Estate Management Board

Review of training materials

The aim of the review was to identify and analyse material which was available for use by those involved in training for tenant management. The material was identified and gathered through a combination of visits to training agencies and tenant management organisations, responses to requests to provide information along with the postal surveys and sources identified in the directory produced by Brunel University (Birchall, 1992).

The review of materials included both published and unpublished materials. In total, 251 examples of materials produced by 66 organisations were assessed. The largest producers of relevant information were training agencies. However materials were also received from 15 local authorities, 3 tenants' federations and 6 tenant management organisations.

In order to evaluate the material a classification framework was devised. This included classification by topic, producer, format, who the material was aimed at and which stage of the development process it was suitable for. The material was also assessed on three aspects - content, presentation and needs met, from a method devised by Goodlad (1986) and then described and marked in these categories.

The content was judged by virtue of what it covered, its nature and accuracy. The presentation mark took account of several aspects: whether the material attracted attention with its use of colour, headlines, illustrations and overall effect; whether the style was empathetic, patronising or authoritarian; how well the material was organised and produced, for example whether there was a content guide; whether the material was intelligible; and whether it was legible.

When the aim of the material was specified, it was evaluated according to whether these needs were met. When aims were not specified, how well the material met the needs of a tenant management organisation was a significant factor. Factors which were taken into account in the needs met category were: whether the skills, knowledge and attitudes relevant to the topic were covered; whether equal opportunities were acknowledged; and whether the learning methods were appropriate. The material was also assessed in the light of whether it was intended for direct use by a tenant or whether it was intended for use by a trainer in a training session.

The review includes both published and unpublished material. As some organisations were reluctant to provide us with their unpublished material, it can not be considered to be completely comprehensive. A number of training agencies also informed us that, as much of their material is being constantly up-dated and revised, some of the material included was, at the time of the research, out-of-date to some extent.

Attendance at training events

In order to assess training at first hand, researchers on the project attended 10 training events. These represented a range from national conferences, regional promotional events, sessions on specific topics and events for trainers. The events were assessed using a checklist covering the purpose of the event, the content and quality of presentation the reaction of participants and whether the event met training needs.

In-depth interviews

In-depth semi-structured interviews were carried out with staff in local authorities, training agencies and tenant management organisations, and with tenants involved in TMOs. In total, 99 people were interviewed during the course of the research. This included 11 local authority officers, 24 staff in training agencies, 7 co-op workers and 59 tenants involved in TMOs.

The interviews covered a wide range of topics including: information about the previous experience of the person interviewed; history of the TMO; skills, knowledge and attitudes required at each stage in the development process; training received; reactions to training; training needed for on-going TMOs; funding for on-going TMOs; roles of committee members; training for new committee members; training and information for new members and ordinary members; views on training agency role; views on local authority role; views on Section 16 grant regime.

The interviews were tape-recorded and transcribed and were analysed manually. Inevitably such a process imposes the researchers' own structure. Considerable use was made of the transcript material to allow participants' own views to be apparent. However, to ensure confidentiality neither the names of the interviewees, or their organisations were identified.

Group discussions

The group discussions were held during a training event for trainers. The 30 participants, from a wide range of organisations were asked to discuss the role of tenant participation officers, the skills knowledge and attitudes required and to identify training which might meet gaps.

Case studies

The second stage of the research identified six case study TMOs for more in-depth study. The evaluation followed the CIRO model described in Chapter 2.

Context

The context of each organisation was examined through an organisation survey looking at the structure and functions of each TMO. A task analysis was carried out for each of the office bearers' posts and for ordinary committee members. An environmental survey aimed to assess whether the type of property, density, physical appearance and standard of maintenance had an impact on effectiveness. Ideally a full house condition survey would provide information on the physical environment but simpler techniques provided an indication of physical factors. Similarly, ideally a full social survey would be carried out but in this research rent arrears and housing benefit statistics were used as an indicator of poverty, along with ethnic variation, to evaluate social context. The examination of political context included an assessment of the local authority's attitude towards the organisation, as well as tenant management in general.

Inputs and reactions

Inputs were explored through in-depth interviews with trainers, assessment of training programmes and training materials. As it was not possible to observe training events in the case studies, a small number of national and regional events were attended, to gain a flavour of content and methods. Reactions to training were explored through in-depth interviews with tenants.

Personal outcomes

Personal outcomes of training were assessed by observation of committee meetings, an examination of records, views of committee members on their own personal performance and the views of others.

Organisational outcomes

Organisational outcomes were assessed by an analysis of performance indicators, the views of ordinary residents in group discussions and the views of trainers and staff. The time constraints of the research meant that it was impossible to measure personal and organisational outcomes before and after training. Therefore, the research depended on cross-sectional analysis (comparing different organisations at one point in time after training) and on the perceptions of members of organisations and outside observers, of changes over time.

Defining training

The task of establishing what training had taken place and fitting this to the promotion, feasibility, development and ongoing model was not straightforward as prior to the promotional stage, tenants groups may have been involved in promoting participation, identifying problems on the estate and deciding priorities for action. Some work may also have been done on gaining an understanding of the options for tenant management.

Drawing a line between feasibility and development stages was also difficult as these stages may not be clear. In order to analyse the training, we imposed a framework for the four stages and drew lines at what appeared to be appropriate points. In some cases this was after a major event, such as a consultation exercise or 'fun day', in other cases it was where training changed and became more detailed.

Even where clear training programmes had been set out these were not always followed precisely. Changes might be made for a variety of reasons. In some cases speakers were unavailable, in others the tenants decided that they wanted something different part-way through, or outside influences meant that training focused round these rather than the agenda.

> 'The beauty ... of working there regularly on the doorstep ... was that if somebody had a query ... they didn't have to wait a week to find out and have lost the impetus, one could cover it at the time.'
>
> Independent trainer

In some TMOs training sessions were quite clearly labelled as such, but in others training took place much more informally during sub-committee discussions on the management agreement and policies. Often there was a combination of external conferences, study visits, meetings and training sessions, many of which involved learning the skills, knowledge and attitudes required.

We used minutes of meetings, handouts and the interviews to make decisions about what to include as training. Purely 'housekeeping' meetings about general business were excluded, as were some of the negotiating meetings, if these did not cover new ground. However, some 'learning by doing' was included.

In a number of cases, capital improvement works took place at the same time as the development of the tenant management organisation and tenants received training on design issues. As this was an extra set of skills and knowledge we did not include these.

Cost effectiveness analysis

The inputs to training are personnel, time, training material, accommodation and, in some cases, travel costs. There is also an opportunity cost to participants who give time voluntarily that might be spent on other activities. Having identified the training which took place in each case study, each element of each training event was costed.

Where it was not possible to obtain actual costs these were estimated from information from the accounts and comparison with other TMOs. It was felt to be too complex a task for this study to unravel hidden subsidies, such as DoE funding to agencies to subsidise external training for tenants, or cross-subsidies within agencies. The analysis costed external events on the basis of the fee charged and the cost of consultants on their hourly rate. To allow comparison, costs were updated to 1991 levels.

The cost of local authority officers' time was obtained by calculating an hourly rate, based on salaries but taking into account items such as national insurance, superannuation and employers' overhead costs. In some cases, speakers did not charge for their time. However, to avoid ignoring this type of hidden subsidy, a similar hourly rate calculation was applied. Details of this calculation are given below.

In-house training calculations

1. The calculation began with the **salary** of the local authority officer, to which Employers National Insurance and Superannuation contributions (26%) were added.

2. This was then converted to first a daily, then an hourly rate. Potentially, there are 260 working days per year. However, from this must be subtracted

   - holidays (30 days)
   - sickness (8 per cent or 20 days)
   - training days (varies from NIL to 30 - average assumed 5)
   - public holidays (13 days).

   This gave **192** actual working days.

3. There is no definitive answer to the question of **overheads**. Overheads include office accommodation, finance, personnel and computing functions. They also include an allowance for 'non-productive' time and the 'costs of democracy' (servicing council committees). None of the local authorities studied had service level agreements sufficiently detailed to calculate overheads precisely. However, discussions with auditors suggested that an overhead of around **80 per cent** was reasonable.

4. The calculation for costing in-house staff time was therefore:

$$\frac{(A+N)+O}{Ad} = Rd$$

$$\frac{Rd}{Hd} = RpH$$

A = Annual salary
N = NI & Superann (26%)
O = Overhead (80%)
Rd = Rate per day
Ad = Annual available days (192)
Hd = Hours per day (7)
RpH = Rate per hour

Example

$$\frac{(£17,106 \times 26\%) \times 80\%}{192} = £202$$

$$\frac{£202}{7} = £28.86 \text{ per hour}$$

In order to carry out a training event, trainers have to plan and prepare materials. Preparation time varied from event to event and where trainers were undertaking an event for the first time, materials would need to be prepared from scratch. More experienced trainers might have materials from a previous event which could be adapted and updated for use with a particular group. Where possible, the actual preparation time was used. Where the information was not available, an average of two hours preparation time for each hour of 'tenant contact' was taken. This meant that a two-hour training session would require four hours of preparation.

It was difficult to assign a monetary value to the participants' time. Some committee members had full-time jobs, others were pensioners or long-term unemployed. Some worked voluntarily in the TMO office virtually full-time. Notional 'hourly rates' for training would vary from individual to individual, depending on their 'normal' employment. We therefore calculated opportunity cost separately and gave the cost in terms of hours spent on training.

Summary

The research methods used for the case studies can therefore be summaried as:

Organisation survey

Physical environment survey

Collection of data from the local authority

Task analysis of key roles in the organisation

In-depth interviews with committee/board members

In-depth interviews with trainers

In-depth interviews with local authority support staff

In-depth interviews with TMO support staff

Assessment of training programmes and training materials

Observation of committee meetings

Examination of records and minutes

Analysis of key performance indicators

Group interviews with 'ordinary' members

Cost effectiveness analysis.

Appendix 2 Tenant management organisations in England in 1992

LONDON AND SOUTH EAST

Name and LA	Date established	Size	Support Agency	Stage of development
BRENT				
Chalkhill EMB		1800	TPAS	Development
Kilburn Square Co-op		268	CATCH	Development
CAMDEN				
Kilburn Vale TMC	1991	205	CATCH	Ongoing
South Hampstead TMC	1991	704	CATCH	Ongoing
Abbey Road TA	1992	279	CATCH	Ongoing
Godwin and Crowndale	1992	173	PEP	Ongoing
Maiden Lane	1992	479	PEP	Ongoing
Carol Street	1992	36	White & Co	Ongoing
HACKNEY				
Trowbridge		123	Tenant action	Development
Clapton Park EMB		1724	PEP	Development
De Beauvoir EMB		877	PEP	Development
HILLINGDON				
Rabbs Mill TMC	1986	78	CDS	Ongoing
ISLINGTON				
St. Pancras Ct TMC		49	CATCH	Development
Arch Elm Co-op	1980	95	GLSHA	Ongoing
Charteris Neighbourhood TMC	1976	123	HM	Ongoing
Islington Community HC	1986	45	Islington	Ongoing
Brooke Park Co-op	1980	115	GLSHA	Ongoing
Elthorne First Co-op	1980	133	GLSHA	Ongoing
Penton Street HC	1977	6	Islington	Ongoing
Newbery House HC	1976	54	Islington	Ongoing
Half-Moon Crescent Co-p	1986	192	GLSHA	Ongoing
Harry Weston Co-op	1980	124	GLSHA	Ongoing
Newington Green Co-op	1976	71	Islington	Ongoing
Holbrook Co-op	1979	89	GLSHA	Ongoing
Islington Green Co-op	1978	33	Islington	Ongoing
New Arts HC	1987	9	Islington	Ongoing
Islington Gay HC	1987	8	Islington	Ongoing
Grimaldi HC	1986	4	Islington	Ongoing
Co-Action HC	1987	2	Islington	Ongoing
Clerkenwell HC	1991	10	Islington	Ongoing
Moonshine HC	1989	13	Islington	Ongoing
Concrete HC	1986	14	Islington	Ongoing
Wholenut HC	1987	3	Islington	Ongoing

Name	Year	Units	Agency	Status
Samovar HC	1987	8	Islington	Ongoing
Pluto HC	1988	6	Islington	Ongoing
Not Another HC	1987	4	Islington	Ongoing
New Moon HC	1986	6	Islington	Ongoing
Northern Line HC	1988	4	Islington	Ongoing
New Roof HC	1988	12	Islington	Ongoing
Hornsey Lane EMB	1992	173	Islington/own worker	Ongoing

KENSINGTON AND CHELSEA

Name	Year	Units	Agency	Status
Lancaster West EMB		900	PEP	Development

LEWISHAM

Name	Year	Units	Agency	Status
Excalibur TMC	1991	186	CHISEL	Ongoing
Ewart Road TMC	1981	190	GLC	Ongoing
Crusaders HC		1220	PEP	Development

SOUTHWARK

Name	Year	Units	Agency	Status
Tabard Gardens TMC		1433	Tenant action	Development
Haddon Hall	1981	169	GLC	Ongoing
Juniper House	1981	75	GLC	Ongoing
Browning TA		433	English Churches	Development
Woolwich Common RAG		1220	PEP	Development
Kennington Park House	1992	40	HEXAGON	Ongoing
North Peckham Estate		1429	PEP	Development
Copper Close TMC	1987	63	GLC	Ongoing
Applegarth TMC	1992	53	CDS	Ongoing

LAMBETH

Name	Year	Units	Agency	Status
Wellington Mills	1975	138	GLC	Ongoing

TOWER HAMLETS

Name	Year	Units	Agency	Status
Stephen & Matilda TMC	1978	132	GLC	Ongoing
Birchfield TMC	1979	16	GLC/SOLON	Ongoing
Dennis Central	1980	76	GLC	Ongoing
Samuda EMB	1992	505	PEP	Ongoing
Bancroft TMC		628	SOLON E	Development

WANDSWORTH

Name	Year	Units	Agency	Status
All Saints Tenants' Co-op Ltd	1979	54	BCHT	Ongoing
Convent Co-op	1981	110	Wandsworth	Ongoing
Felsham Road		88	Wandsworth	Ongoing
Chatham Court	1988	18	Wandsworth	Ongoing
Wimbledon Park	1990	280		Ongoing
Totteridge House	1991	138	Wandsworth/CDS	Ongoing
Farnhurst & Langhurst	1991	32		Ongoing
Angell Town TA		844	PEP	Development
Oslo Court		16	SOLON W	Development
Old and New Loughborough		1209	PEP	Development

WESTMINSTER

Name	Year	Units	Agency	Status
Martlett Court TMC	1991	125	Westminster	Ongoing
Torridon House TMC	1991	98	Westminster	Ongoing
Thurso & Dundee TMC	1992	77	Westminster	Ongoing

BROMLEY KENT
Nightingale Corner Co-op		34	CHISEL	Development

CHELTENHAM
St Pauls TA (EMB)		370	ECHG	Development

MIDLANDS

BIRMINGHAM
Bloomsbury EMB	1990	988	PEP	Ongoing
Pavillions	1978	24	Birmingham	Ongoing
Mount Glen	1987	51	Birmingham	Ongoing
Mill View	1987	44	Birmingham	Ongoing
Holly Rise	1989	59	Birmingham	Ongoing
South Aston	1989	150	Birmingham	Ongoing
Bardfield Co-op	1978	24	Birmingham	Ongoing
Sutton Street		174	Birmingham/own worker	Development
Wigan Tower		120	Birmingham/own worker	Development
Park Lane		143	Birmingham/own worker	Development

WOLVERHAMPTON
New Park Village RA		415	PEP	Development

WALSALL
Chuckery EMB		213	BCHS	Development

NOTTINGHAM
Cartergate TMC	1992	53	CHS	Ongoing

STOKE-ON-TRENT
Chell Heath EMB	1990	810	PEP	Ongoing

NORTH-EAST

MIDDLESBROUGH
Langridge Crescent Co-op	1987	73	BOW	Ongoing
Alderwood	1992	20	BOW	Ongoing
Rothbury Road		16	BOW	Development
South Bank		865	PEP	Development

HARTLEPOOL
Wyncote TMC		15	BOW	Development

NORTH TYNESIDE
Action 5		200	Own worker	Development

NORTH-WEST

CARLISLE
Botcherby RAG		538	BOW	Development

WYRE
West View Estate		1128	PEP	Development

YORKSHIRE AND LANCASHIRE

SHEFFIELD
Alpha TMC		152	YCHS	Development

LEEDS
Belle Isle EMB	1990	1468	PEP	Ongoing
Halton Moor	1992	1319	PEP	Ongoing

BLACKBURN
Shadsworth EMB	1990	1200	PEP	Ongoing

BRADFORD
Parkwood Rise HC		192	YCHS	Development
Church Ct HC		32	YCHS	Development
Ridings Way HC		135	YCHS	Development

BURNLEY
West End Estates EMB	1991	950	PEP	Ongoing

WEST LANCASTER
Digmoor EMB	1991	960	PEP	Ongoing
Tanhouse	1992	1063	PEP	Ongoing

SALFORD
New Barracks TMC	1990	91	CHS (NW)	Ongoing

ROCHDALE
Cloverhall TMC	1984	243	PEP	Ongoing
Hollin EMB	1992	1200	PEP	Ongoing
Freehold EMB	1991	500	PEP	Ongoing

KIRKLEES
Staincliffe TARA		628	PEP	Development

STALYBRIDGE
Carrbrook TMC	1992	115	CHS (NW)	Ongoing

OLDHAM
Higginshaw Village		401	PEP	Development

ROSSENDALE
Bacup and Stacksteads EMB	1990	1200	PEP	Ongoing
Haslingdon EMB	1992	1460	PEP	Ongoing
Whitworth Valley	1992	827	PEP	Ongoing

MERSEYSIDE

SEFTON
St James Village Co-op		40	CDS	Development

Information sources: DoE Data, Islington TMC Handbook, questionnaire returns, Power (1988), PEP Newsletters

Appendix 3   Training agencies in England 1992

Aldbourne Associate
Ulmus
Osbourne St George Road
Aldbourne
Wiltshire
SN8 2LD

Contact: Lesley Andrews
Tel: 0672 20090

Banks of the Wear CHS
3rd Floor
Mea House
Ellison Place
Newcastle on Tyne

Contact: Alison Coupe
Tel: 091 232 6446

Offices **also** in Ashington, Sunderland & Middlesborough

Birmingham CHS
510a Coventry Road
Birmingham
B10 0UN

Contact: Julie Fisher
Tel: 021 773 3583

CATCH
2 West End Lane
London
NW6

Contact: Tony Bloor
Tel: 071 328 4438

Centre for Active Citizenship
Fircroft College
1018 Bristol Road
Selly Oak
Birmingham
B29 6HL

Contact: Richard Hallet
Tel: 021 472 0116

Chapman Hendy Associates
2 John Street
London
WC1N 2HJ

Contact: Peter Chapman
Tel: 071 831 7170

Community Education Training Unit
Trinity Royd Cottage
Blackwall
Halifax
HX1 2EX

Contact: Steve Skinner
Tel: 0422 357394

Community Projects Trust
2A Fore Street
Mount Folley
Bodmin
Cornwall
PL31 2HQ

Contact: Trevor Murden
Tel: 0208 75799

CDS Liverpool
13-15 Rodney Street
Liverpool

Contact: Sophy Krajewska
Tel: 051 707 1919

Co-operative Housing Society (CHS) London
207 Waterloo Road
London
5EL 8XW

Contact: Keith Mann
Tel: 071 401 3131

CHISEL
188a Brockley Road
London
SE4 2RN

Contact: Val Soloman
Tel: 081 694 1840

CHS Home Countries
367 Chiswick High Road
London
W4 4AG

Contact: Ginnie Worley
Tel: 081 994 2226

CHS (NW)
823a Stockport Road
Levershulme
Manchester
M19

Contact: Angela Harrington
Tel: 061 257 2636

Coin Street Co-op
99 Upper Ground
London
SE1 9PP

Contact: C. Czechowski
Tel: 071 620 1608

National Certificate in Tenant Participation
College of North East London
Dept of Environmental Health
Housing & Admin
High Road
London
N15 4RU

Contact: Neal Purvis
Tel: 081 802 3111

English Churches Housing Group
Sutherland House
70-78 West Hendon Broadway
London

Contact: Nancy Foxworthy
Tel: 081 203 9233

Federation of Hackney Tenants and Residents Associations
Old Town Hall
380 Old Street
London

Contact: Gary Spencer
Tel: 071 739 3631

HACAS
United House
North Road
London
N7 9DP

Contact: Jeff Zitron
Tel: 071 609 9491

Comment: Financial Training

Hexagon Housing Association
139-151 Sydenham Road
London
SE26

Contact: Wendy Newall
Tel: 081 778 6699

Tenant Initiative Unit
Leicester Housing Association
131 Loughborough Road
Leicester
LE3 4LO

Contact: Darrel Gough
Tel: 0533 666123

Liverpool Housing Trust
12 Hanover Street
Liverpool
L1 4AA

Contact: David Smith
Tel: 051 708 5777

National Certificate in Tenant Participation
Matthew Boulton College
Sherlock Street
Birmingham
B5 7BD

Contact: Margaret Brown
Tel: 021 446 4545

Merseyside Improved Houses
46 Wavertree Road
Liverpool
L7 1PH

Contact: Mike Hargaden
Tel: 051 709 9375

National Housing and Tenant Resource Centre
131 Avenell Road
London
N5

Contact: Margy Knutson
Tel: 071 359 4047

Neighbourhood Initiative Foundation
The Poplars
Lightmoor
Telford
TF4 3QN

Contact: Helen Foster
Tel: 0952 503628

Northern College
Wentworth Castle
Stainborough
Barnsley
S75 3ET

Contact: John Grayson
Tel: 0226 285426

Paddington Churches HA
Canterbury House
Canterbury Road
London
NW6 5SU

Contact: John Wheeldon
Tel: 071 372 5671

Partners in Change
Training for Tenant Involvement
27 Sydenham Avenue
Liverpool
L17 3AU

Contact: Paul Lusk
Tel: 051 733 3002

PEP
2 Albert Mews
Albert Road
London
L4 3RD

Contact: Roger Saunders
Tel: 071 281 3178

Offices **also** in Manchester

PIC Services
The Coach House
Kempshott Park
Dummer
Basingstoke
RG23 7LP

Contact: Jenny Gardner
Tel: 0256 397661

Peabody Advice Consultancy and Training (Pact)
45 Westminster Bridge Road
London
SE1 5HJ

Tel:　　　081 778 6699

Pieda Consultants
5 The Parsonage
Manchester
M3 2HS

Contact:　Janis Dean
Tel:　　　061 839 5107

Offices **also** in London

PPCR Associates
Swan Court
9 Tanner Street
London
SE1 3L6

Contact:　Ron Houston
Tel:　　　071 407 7452

Rodney Dykes Housing Services
The Cloisters
Halsall Lane
Formby
Liverpool
L37 3PX

Contact:　Rodney Dykes
Tel:　　　07048 31444

Safe Neighbourhood Unit
4th Floor East
Neil House
7 Whitechapel Road
London

E1 5QJ

Contact:　Tim Kendrick
Tel:　　　071 247 4227

National Certificate in Tenant Participation
School of Urban Regional Studies
Pond Street
Sheffield
S1 1WB

Contact:　Rob Furby
Tel:　　　0742 720911

South Ashton Community Project
Upper Sutton Street
Aston
Birmingham
B6 5BE

Contact:　Pauline James
Tel:　　　021 359 4133

Solon Wandsworth
49a Lavender Hill
London
E2 9QH

Contact:　Katrina O'Doherty
Tel:　　　071 223 7376

National Certificate in Tenant Participation
South Bank University
Wandsworth Road
London
SW8 2JS

Contact:　Mark Bhatti
Tel:　　　071 928 8989

South London Family HA
Rochester House
2-10 Belvedere Road
London
SE19 2HL

Contact:　Graham Baugh
Tel:　　　081 768 0890

Tenant Action Ltd
31 Oval Road
London
NW1 7EA

Contact:　Suzanne Lubran
Tel:　　　071 284 3664

Tenant Initiative Development
Services
Valmar House

8b Coldharbour Lane
London
SE5 9PR

Tel: 071 978 9249

Tenants' Resource and Information Service
(TRIS)
1 Pink Lane
Newcastle on Tyne
NE1 5DW

Contact: Tim Shotton
Tel: 091 232 1371

Tricare Neighbourhood Project
The Lodge
St Pauls Road
Ashby
Scunthorpe
DN16 3DL

Contact: Julie Briggs
Tel: 0724 864786

TPAS
48 The Crescent
Salford
Manchester
M5 4NY

Contact: Mark Lyonette
Tel: 061 745 7903

Offices **also** in London, Birmingham, Bristol & Cambridge

Yorkshire CHS
91 Spital Hill
Sheffield
South Yorkshire
S4 7LD

Contact:
Tel: 0742 787135

Appendix 4   Case study histories

Tower TMO

Tower TMO, the smallest and longest established of the case studies was a classic 'shell' co-operative. The local authority had been interested in developing a co-op for some time. In the early 1980s, the opportunity was presented in the form of a tower block undergoing refurbishment. The council wrote to all its tenants and identified 65 interested households who matched the authority's eligibility criteria for multi-storey blocks (no children under 12 and no single people under 35). Public meetings were held to explain what would be involved and when an offer of tenancy was made, it was on the clear understanding that a TMC might be developed.

There was a false start when the first agency appointed was dissolved and it was a further seven months before a new agency began work. The agency held a public meeting and invited nominations for a steering group who were to co-ordinate activities. This group was then divided into four sub-groups, with other tenants co-opted to join each group. There was no identifiable 'promotional' stage, and the sub-group immediately began discussing the adoption of a set of rules for registration as an Industrial and Provident Society. Following registration at the end of that year the co-op had its first AGM as a registered body. Attention then turned to consideration of a management agreement. This was again discussed in sub-groups and by March of that year the draft had been accepted by the membership.

Until that point everything had gone smoothly but following a dispute with the council over maintenance issues, the steering group suspended discussions for some months until these were resolved. During negotiations the tenants made it clear that they would only take over responsibility if funding was adequate. They requested that the council fund the conversion of a store to an office and equip it, pay for initial training for a worker and make adjustments to the management and maintenance allowances. Most of these conditions were agreed and following the signing of the agreement, the co-operative set about preparing for takeover. The TMO took over responsibilities just 22 months after forming a steering group.

Hilltop TMO

Hilltop TMO was located in a city with a long history of tenant organisation and with well-developed participation structures. The tenants' association had been in existence for a number of years and had been supported by a community/social work project. In 1986, the council invited the committee to join a project team to discuss modernisation. As discussions continued the 1987 White Paper on housing policy was published and the residents became concerned about private landlords and they raised the issue at a project meeting. The local housing officer who had heard of tenant management suggested that they visit a number of established TMCs. Several committee members said that these visits were crucial to their decision to proceed.

The tenants assisted in the formation of a new training agency and in mid-1988 an agency trainer started to work with the group with the remit to develop a co-operative in the area. In August 1988 the council considered the group's formal request to develop a TMO and assigned a housing officer to negotiate terms. The refurbishment of the properties which involved decanting the tenants, and the development of a TMO then moved in parallel.

Negotiations on the management agreement began in the autumn and continued for almost a year. The agreement was approved by the council in October 1989. Unfortunately, at this point, the housing officer changed post and there was a hiatus.

The tenants were decanted in 1990, while modernisation was carried out. They returned to their homes in the spring of 1991 and a new council officer was appointed to begin negotiations again, based on the new modular agreement. However, this officer also moved post and eventually the original negotiator returned to finalise the agreement. By March 1992 these new negotiations were completed, except for the management and maintenance allowances. The tenants were unhappy with the funds offered. At the time of the research, the tenants had completed training, set up their office and office systems and begun meeting as an interim TMO, but with few responsibilities and no staff. No-one was willing to predict how long it would take for the agreement to be approved and signed. The process so far had taken over four years.

Five Streets TMO

Five Streets TMO was in a 1930s estate built under slum clearance legislation. The estate appears to have been stigmatised from the outset and a series of programmes in the 1970s failed to improve the area. In 1988 the council held public meetings on the estate and suggested an application for Estate Action loan sanction to carry out improvements in the worst part of the area. Representatives from these streets volunteered to form a steering group to discuss the plans. At around the same time, the Department of the Environment funded an exercise to appraise opportunities for neighbourhood initiatives and the estate was chosen as a pilot project. The consultant worked with the steering group throughout 1988, helping them to define their aims and objectives. Following a visit to a TMC, the tenants decided to pursue interest in forming a tenant management co-operative. Although repair and maintenance issues were the major factor, a second impetus came from the discovery that the estate was being considered by the DoE for a possible Housing Action Trust (HAT). Both housing staff and the committee were concerned about this and wished to pursue an option which retained council ownership, but with tenant control.

The consultant submitted an application for funding on their behalf in December 1988 and training began in January 1989. Initially the group followed a programme devised by their consultant but for their development stage the committee decided to hire their own full-time trainer and the chair of the group was appointed as a community development worker. Discussions on the management agreement began in 1991 and this was submitted to the DoE who queried some clauses. A revised agreement was not sent to the DoE until June 1992. In the meantime the group gradually began to take over responsibilities, monitored by the council. At the time of the research the revised agreement had just been approved but further administrative obstacles hindered further progress.

Bungalow TMO

Bungalow TMO was the closest to a 'grassroots' co-operative. This small estate had an active tenants' association for many years which had campaigned against several proposals for demolition. In 1987, the tenants became concerned about the provisions of the 1988 Housing Bill and the possibility of being transferred out of council ownership. A few key activists decided that they wanted to do something which would permanently enhance their control over the future of the estate. The chair of the tenants' association had heard about tenant management and the association contacted several organisations to collect further information. They carried out a survey of the estate which found considerable support for tenant management and then wrote to the council, requesting that it consider the idea. The council meanwhile had resolved to support the formation of TMCs and had appointed a co-op development worker. Following meetings with the council and a local training agency, the association held a public meeting to form a steering group.

The first meeting was held with the training agency in mid 1988 and the steering group began a period of general training and business meetings. Consideration and negotiation of the management agreement began the following year and was completed by the autumn. However, the introduction of the new modular agreement meant that a new round of negotiations was necessary and during this period, the TMOs agency development worker left. In mid-1990 a new worker was appointed and began to work with the group toward take-over. The steering group appears to have become very frustrated during this period due to what they perceived as the council putting obstacles and barriers in their way, poor service from their agency when they were left without a worker and delays at the Department of the Environment in approving their agreement. However, during 1990 the group got an office, registered as a Friendly Society, appointed a worker, held an AGM and began to operate as a 'shadow' TMO. Formal establishment took place in April 1991 after 34 months development.

Family TMO

In this TMO, the impetus for tenant management seemed to have come from several quarters. The residents' group had been working with workers from a neighbourhood project for several years and with this support, they began to demand action to halt deterioration on the estate. In response to this, the council began to look at ways of solving the problems. A solution was suggested by a national agency, who wrote to a number of authorities inviting participation in pilot projects to develop EMBs. The agency carried out a short feasibility study on the estate which resulted in a committee report recommending a partnership between the tenants, the agency and the authority to develop an EMB. This was announced by the Secretary of State, along with approval for an Estate Action bid to modernise the houses.

Work began with a series of small group meetings to inform residents about the partnership, and the idea. Interested residents went on to form a 'residents core group' which became the focus for training and consultation. A smaller group from this 'core' became a steering group to guide the project. A large modernisation programme also ran alongside development of the TMO. In the spring of the following year, consultation was carried out with residents. Discussions then began on the management agreement which was agreed by the council a year later. There were then a series of discussions between the Council and the DoE before the agreement was approved and signed in December 1990. In the meantime a local housing office had opened on the estate, the elections were held and the committee began to operate as an interim board. The first meeting of the board took place in January 1991.

World TMO

The largest case study, World TMO also came from a council with well-developed tenant participation structures. This estate was first occupied in 1970 and there were tenants groups from the outset. In the late 1970s the council developed local tenant consultative committees and the estate residents formed an advisory management board which included residents and local councillors, along with housing, health, social services and education officers. In 1989, the Chair of Housing, several officers and tenants attended a seminar on the then new idea of EMBs. They were all interested in the idea and the management board agreed to discuss it further. Towards the end of 1989 the council appointed an officer to work with several representatives from the management board.

There were delays and frustration for the tenants during the development process. The promotional stage began well, with a series of small group meetings and the formation of a core group who began training. From this group a steering group was formed in July 1990 and the council funded the conversion of a shop unit to serve as the office and training room. Discussions on the management agreement began in 1991 and in August of that year the council held a ballot. The partly drafted agreement was sent to the council who were to provide details of stock, policies and allowances for further negotiation but months passed and no progress was made.

In November 1991 the development worker was offered a move and the group effectively stalled. They were, however, determined to carry on and in January 1992 they appointed their own agency and applied for development funding under the new S16 regime. Approval for funds was finally given in July 1992. Things were looking more hopeful. The council had a new administration and a number of new senior officers, who had been delegated the task of sorting out the management agreement and completing negotiations. The group hoped to become established by mid-1993.

Appendix 5 Examples of training programmes

'HILLTOP' TMO

<u>Promotion</u>

2 x Study visits to TMOs
1 x Housing management seminar (E)
2 x Guest speakers

<u>Feasibility</u>

5 x Co-ops training:
    Introduction to co-ops
    Committee roles
    Financial control
    Maintenance and repairs
    Allocations
2 x Study visits
1 x National conference
4 x Rules and constitutions
12 x Management agreement

<u>Development</u>

11 x Co-op training:
    Local government finance
    Co-op finance
    Budgeting
    Financial control
    Employing a worker
    Discipline and grievance
    Nuisance and harassment
    Tenancy agreements
    Management issues
    Co-op responsibilities
    Management agreement
5 x Repairs and maintenance
11 x Management agreement
6 x Co-op policies
6 x Interim Committees
10 x Practical experience learning

'BUNGALOW' TMO

Promotion

Co-op conference (E)
Publicity seminar (E)
2 x Study visits to TMOs
2 x Public meetings (Options)
Survey

Feasibility

Introduction to co-ops
Training needs
DLO repairs
Rent and arrears
Allocations policies
Rules and constitutions
Housing bill
Financial matters
Repairs and capital works
Caretaking and cleaning
Finance course (8 sessions)
2 x study visits
2 x conferences (E)
Committee skills
Housing management
Arrears and benefits
Neighbour disputes
Equal opportunities
Communications
Image of co-op

Development

Employing and managing workers (3 sessions)
9 x Management agreement
Repairs and maintenance (2 sessions)
Interviewing skills (2 days)
Worker management
Co-op seminar (E)
Rent arrears policy
9 x Management agreement
Specimen forms
Visit to local authority office
Rent accounting
Repairs
Study visit to TMO
Dealing with disputes (E)
Auditing
Introduction to computing
Introduction to budgeting
Setting the co-op budget
12 x interim committee
10 x housing practice

Appendix 6   Key task analyses of office bearers

Chairperson of Co-op/EMB - Key task analysis

Duties and responsibilities	Knowledge	Skills	Attitude
Guide TMO to achieve aims	Aims & objectives of TMO	Chairing skills	Commitment to tenant participation
Take part in decision making	What tenant participation involves	Team working	Positive view/commitment to TMOs
Chair meetings of TMO	Management agreement	Team building	Non-discriminatory
Ensure tenant participation	How the council works	Public speaking	Non-judgemental
To represent TMO at meetings with other organisations eg. council	Campaigning	Ability to articulate group feeling	Balanced/fair approach
To chair public meetings	How to negotiate	Assertiveness	Awareness of accountabilty
To speak at public meetings	How to make a presentation	Negotiation skills	Confidence
Ensure smooth & fair running of TMO	How to chair meetings	Planning skills	Calm/unflustered
Ensure equal opportunities	Rules/constitution	Ability to prioritise	Desire to increase skills/knowledge
Ensure targets are met	Accountability/democracy	Leadership skills:	Importance of value-for-money
Delegation of tasks	How to plan ahead	Clarifying	Importance of good performance
Encourage training	What makes a good leader	Summarising	
Wider community development	How to work as a team	Facilitating Discussion	
Make new contacts	Repair procedures	Supporting	
(Staff appointments)	Allocation policies	Listening	
(Staff supervision)	Caretaking	Encouraging	
(Deal with day to day business)	Tenancy agreement	Problem solving	
(Deal with correspondence)	Finance	Decision making	
(Keeping members informed)	Equal opportunities	Dealing with difficult situations	
	Monitoring performance	Self awareness	
	Decision making	Coaching skills	
	How to delegate	Interviewing skills	
	How to assess training needs	Ability to read tables/graphs/statistics	
	Employment creation		
	Crime & security		
	How to involve young people		
	(Recruitment procedures)		
	(Staff contracts & conditions)		
	(Discipline & grievance procedures)		

Committee member of Co-Op/EMB - Key task analysis

Duties and responsibilities	Knowledge	Skills	Attitude
Assist TMO to achieve aims	Aims & objectives of TMO	Team working	Commitment to tenant participation
Take part in decisions	How to work as a team	Communications	Positive view of/commitment to TMOs
Ensure tenant participation	Legal status of TMO	Listening	Non-discriminatory
Attend meetings	Management agreement	Supporting	Non-judgemental
Keep in mind aims/ objectives of Co-op	What tenant participation involves	Assertiveness	Balanced/fair approach
Listen to others/receive information	Committee structure	Decision making	Positive view of equal opportunities
Support other members/work as part of team	Committee members role	Ability to be flexible	Awareness of accountability
Represent interests of Co-op/ be accountable	How to communicate effectively	Dealing with difficult situations	Desire to increase skills/ knowledge
Ensure democratic procedures carried out	Effective meetings	Self awareness	Importance of value-for-money
Help to allocate tasks	Rules/constitution	Ability to understand tables/ graphs/drawings	Importance of good performance
Carry out the delegated tasks/take responsibility	How Council operates		
Pass on information to rest of committee/Co-op	Equal opportunities		
Monitor workings of committee/Co-op	Tenancy agreement		
Ensure confidentiality	Co-op policies on allocations		
Maintain a policy of openness	Co-op policies on repairs		
Avoid discrimination	Co-op policies on rent arrears		
Make use of/offer personal abilities	Co-op finances		
Train/ inform new members	Co-op policies on neighbourhood disputes		
	Arbitration & conciliation		
	Monitoring performance		

Secretary of Co-Op/EBM - Key task analysis

Duties and responsibilities	Knowledge	Skills	Attitude
Assist TMO to achieve aims	Aims & objectives of TMO	Team working	Commitment to tenant participation
Take part in committee meetings	How to work as a team	Literacy	Positive view/commitment to TMOs
Take part in decisions	Management agreement	Office skills	Organised
Promote tenant participation	What tenant participation involves	Keyboard skills	Non- discriminatory
Deal with day-to-day business/ correspondence	Knowledge of constitution of TMO	Communication	Non-judgemental
Keep members informed/ newsletters	Knowledge of all rules & standing orders of the co-op	Letter writing	Importance of providing information
Arrange good meeting facilities	Legal responsibilities/ requirements of TMO	Report writing	
Organise AGM	Tenancy agreements	Presentation skills	
Deal with annual returns	How the council operates	Decision making	
Initiate legal procedures	How to write letters	Interviewing skills	
(Take minutes/prepare agendas)	How to communicate effectively		
(Keep council informed)	Preparation/ presentation of reports		
(Keep records/files of membership, all minutes)	Repairs policy		
(Maintain office supplies/ equipment)	Allocations Policy		
(Liaise with solicitors)	Rent arrears policy		
(Organise recruitment of staff)	Insurance requirements of TMO		
(Maintain insurance policies)	(How to type/use a word processor)		
(Ensure health & safety in office)	(How to take minutes)		
(Registration with Industrial & Provident Society)	(How to run an office)		
	(How to keep records/ filing systems)		
	(How office equipment operates)		
	(How to complete annual returns)		
	(Recruitment procedure)		
	(Health & safety at work)		

Treasurer of Co-Op/EMB - Key task analysis

Duties and responsibilities	Knowledge	Skills	Attitude
Assist TMO to achieve aims	Aims & objectives of TMO	Team working	Commitment to tenant participation
Take part in committee meetings	How to work as a team	Numeracy	Positive view/commitment to TMOs
Take part in decisions	What tenant participation involves	Financial skills	Trustworthy
Promomte tenant participation	Management agreement	Plan effectively	Non-discriminatory
Responsible for all finances	Understand how council operates	Ability to prioritise	Non-judgemental
Submit estimates of expenditure for approval	Council finance	Communications	Importance of value-for-money
Present accounts to AGM	Finance for TMO	Letter writing	Need for financial control
Draw up budgets/forward financial planning	Accounting/book-keeping	Report writing	Conscientious
Ensure value for money	Financial monitoring/planning	Negotiation skills	
(Maintain accounting system for TMO)	How to communicate effectively	Decision making	
(Responsible for petty cash)	Know financial standing orders of Co-op	Public speaking	
(Prepare/submit financial reports)	Tendering procedures	Interviewing skills	
(Submit annual audited accounts)	How to apply for grants	Knowing when to seek assistance	
(Rent collecting & accounting)	Role of auditor		
(Rent arrears)	Preparation/presentation of annual accounts		
	(Preparation/presentation of financial reports)		
	(Petty cash/banking procedures)		
	(VAT/ Taxation)		
	(Rent collection & accounting procedures)		
	(Rent arrears procedures)		

Tenant participation worker - key task analysis

Duties and responsibilities	Knowledge	Skills	Attitude
Promote tenant participation	What tenant participation involves	Team working	Commitment to tenant participation
Ensure equal opportunities	What tenant management involves	Communications	Non-discriminatory
Promote and support tenant management organisations	Options for participation and control	Public speaking	Non-judgemental
Promote and support tenants associations	How the council works	Assertiveness	Honesty
Provide training/support to tenants	Housing legislation	Negotiation	Flexibility
Provide training support to staff	Housing finance	Motivating	Determined
Develop tenant participation policies	Tenancy agreement	Facilitating	Optimistic
Produce newsletters/reports/tenants handbooks	Repairs and maintenance	Listening	Open to criticism
Wider community development	Technical issues	Counselling	Self-motivated
Negotiate tenants demands	Allocations	Planning	Confident
Involve tenants in capital programme	Housing benefit	Time management	Desire to increase skills/knowledge
Carry out administrative work	Police	Self-awareness	
Monitor performance	Social security	Administrative skills	
	Sources of funding	Dealing with difficult situations	
	Housing Corp./DoE policies		
	LA/HA policies		
	Equal opportunities		
	Monitoring performance		
	Community work		
	Group work		
	Counselling		
	Negotiation		

Appendix 7 Bibliography

Barker, A. (1991) 'Co-ops: the issue of ownership', in *Inside Housing*, Vol. 8, No. 38, October 1991

Bell, T. (1991) *Joining Forces: A Practical Guide to EMBs*, London: PEP

Birchall, J. (1988) *Building Communities: the co-operatives way*, London: Routledge

Birchall, J. (1992) *Directory of Tenant Training Materials*, Uxbridge: Brunel University

Cairncross, L., Clapham, D. and Goodlad, R. (1989) *Tenant Participation in Housing Management*, London/Salford: IoH/TPAS

Cairncross, L., Clapham, D. and Goodlad, R. (1990) 'The Pattern of Tenant Participation in Council Housing Management', *Discussion Paper No. 31*, Glasgow: Centre for Housing Research

CATCH (undated) *Caretaking Training Plan*, (unpublished)

CATCH (undated) *Introduction to Repairs and Maintenance Training*, (unpublished)

CDS (Liverpool) (undated) *Working through Performance Expectations*, (unpublished)

Centre for Educational Research (1983) *Education, Urban Developments and Local Initiatives*, Paris: OECD

Centre for Housing Research (1989) *The Nature and Effectiveness of Housing Management in England*, London: HMSO

Chandler, H. (1991) *The Right Information: Reporting Management Information to Estate Management Boards*, London: Priority Estates Project

Clapham, D., and Kintrea, K. (1985) 'Rationing, Choice and Constraint: The Allocation of Public Housing in Glasgow', in *Journal of Social Policy*, Vol 15.1

Clapham, D., Kintrea, K., Whitefield, L., MacMillan, F. and Raitt, N. (1991) *Community Ownership in Glasgow: an evaluation*, Edinburgh: Central Research Unit, Scottish Office

Commission for Racial Equality (1991) *Achieving Racial Equality in Housing Co-ops*, London: CRE

Department of the Environment (1989) *Tenants in the Lead: the housing co-operatives review*, London: HMSO

Department of the Environment / Welsh Office (1992a) *Competing for Quality in Housing*, London: DoE

Department of the Environment (1992b) *Section 16 Newsletter (Number 1)*, London: DoE

Department of the Environment (1992c) Internal paper, London: DoE

Department of the Environment (1992d) *Notes on the Shaping Section 16 Seminar*, London: DoE

Dinan, J. (1987) *Rabbs Mill Co-operative - the story*, London: Rabbs Mill TMC

DoE/TPAS/PEP (1992) *Tenants Extra*, London: DoE (Video)

Downey, P., Matthews, A. and Mason, S. (1981) *Management Co-operatives: Tenant Responsibility in Practice*, London: HMSO

Fowler (1988) *Human Resource Management in Local Government*, Harlow, Longman

Gagné, R.M. (1977) *The Conditions of Learning* (3rd ed) London: Holt, Rinehart and Winston

Goodlad, R. (1986) *Telling the tenants: A report on written materials produced by Scottish public landlords for their tenants*, Edinburgh: Scottish Consumer Council

Harrison, R. (1988) *Training and Development*, London: Institute of Personnel Management

Honey, P. and Mumford, A. (1986) *The Manual of Learning Styles* (2nd ed), Maidenhead: Peter Honey

McCafferty, J. (1991) 'Tenants in the Lead: one year on', in *Peptalk* April 1991

McCafferty, P. and Riley, D. (1989) *A Study of Co-operative Housing*, London: HMSO

National Council for Vocational Qualifications (1988) *The NVQ Criteria and Related Guidance*, London: NCVQ

National Federation of Housing Co-operatives (1990) *Modular Management Agreement for tenant management co-operatives in local authority housing*, London: NFHC

Satsangi, M. and Clapham, D. (1990) *Management Performance in Housing Co-operatives*, London: HMSO

Scott, S. and Kintrea, K. (1992) *Rent Arrears - a problem - Tenants' attitudes*, Edinburgh: Accounts Commission

Scott, S. (1993) *Educating and Training for Change* Edinburgh: Institute of Housing in Scotland

Smith, M. (1991) *Analysing Organisational Behaviour*, London: Macmillan

Tenant Participation Advisory Service (1990) *Tenant Participation in Calderdale*, Salford: TPAS

Vroom, V. H. (1964) *Work and Motivation*, New York, Wiley

Warr, P., Bird, M. and Rackham, N. (1970) *Evaluation of Management Training*, Essex: Gower

Williams, M. and Swailes, K. (eds) (1991) *Tenant Management Co-operatives: The Development Handbook*, London: CHISEL/Hexagon HA/LB Lewislam

Yoker Resource Group (1992) *Yoker Resource Centre*, (unpublished)